CULTS AND PERSONALITY

ABOUT THE AUTHOR

Frank MacHovec is a licensed clinical psychologist whose interest in cult and ritual behavior began with publication of an article on Taoism in 1961. He has addressed state, national, and international conferences on the treatment of posttraumatic stress disorder, hypnotherapy, and applying Eastern philosophies to psychotherapy. He has ten years' experience as an expert witness in civil and criminal courts in the United States and Canada and has served on professional ethics committees in Virginia, Alaska, and Manitoba, Canada. He has authored more than fifty published books and journal articles.

In 1982 he was awarded a National Certificate of Recognition by the American Psychological Association Division of Psychologists in Public Service for his work in establishing ethical standards for the use of hypnosis. He holds two diplomates, in clinical hypnosis from the American Board of Psychological Hypnosis (ABPH), and in administrative psychology from the American Board of Administrative Psychology (ABAP). He is a member of the Society for Personality Assessment, American Board of Medical Psychotherapists, American Psychological Association, and is an Approved Supervisor with the American Association for Marriage and Family Therapy. He is listed in *Who's Who Among Human Services Professionals, Who's Who in the South and Southeast,* and two international registries, *Men of Achievement* and the *International Biographic Institute.*

In 1984, Dr. MacHovec founded the Center for the Study of the Self to research subjects not usually included in professional texts and journals, using a cross-cultural and multidisciplinary approach from all available sources, the arts and sciences, rather than only one or a select few. In this sense, his approach is a unique "Renaissance style" applying principles from a wide array of sources to explore a subject from all sides. The result has been the first book ever written on hypnosis complications (1986) and books on courtroom coping skills for expert witnesses (1987), a second grade reader series on street and home safety as a preventive to child abuse (1988–1989), a theoretical and historical study of humor (1988), and applying the scientific method to interview and interrogation skills (1989).

CULTS
AND
PERSONALITY

By

FRANK J. MACHOVEC, Ph.D.

CHARLES C THOMAS • PUBLISHER
Springfield • Illinois • U.S.A.

Published and Distributed Throughout the World by

CHARLES C THOMAS • PUBLISHER
2600 South First Street
Springfield, Illinois 62794-9265

© *1989 by* CHARLES C THOMAS • PUBLISHER

ISBN 0-398-05607-2

Library of Congress Catalog Card Number: 89-10118

With THOMAS BOOKS *careful attention is given to all details of manufacturing
and design. It is the Publisher's desire to present books that are satisfactory as to their
physical qualities and artistic possibilities and appropriate for their particular use.*
THOMAS BOOKS *will be true to those laws of quality that assure a good name
and good will.*

Printed in the United States of America
SC-R-3

Library of Congress Cataloging-in-Publication Data

MacHovec, Frank J.
    Cults and personality/by Frank J. MacHovec.
        p.   cm.
    Bibliography: p.
    Includes index.
    ISBN 0-398-05607-2
    1. Cults—Psychological aspects. 2. Personality—Religious
aspects. 3. Psychology, Religious. I. Title.
    [DNLM: 1. Mental Disorders—psychology. 2. Personality.
3. Psychology, Social. HM 281 M151c]
BP603.M26 1989
291'.01'9—dc20
DNLMDLC
for Library of Congress   89-10118
                                                                              CIP

To the world's children,
Our best hope for the future;
Fragile flowers, priceless treasures,
To be gently held, cherished,
protected, saved.

Turning and turning in the widening gyre
The falcon cannot hear the falconer;
Things fall apart;
The center cannot hold;
Mere anarchy is loosed upon the world,
The blood-dimmed tide is loosed,
And everywhere
The ceremony of innocence is drowned;
The best lack all conviction,
While the worst
Are full of passionate intensity.
    William Butler Yeats (1865–1939)
    The Second Coming

PREFACE

A book's title should describe its content, and *Cults and Personality* attempts to do so. Both *cults* and *personality* are descriptive terms but not definitive. We do not yet have good definitions of either and we need them in order to identify, classify, and cope with the increasing appeal of cults. Hopefully, this book will stimulate clinicians, theoreticians, and researchers to further exploration. They are not popular subjects among clinicians or researchers, considered more religion than science, more personal and subjective than observable or measurable. The same is true for data on cults from case law because the First Amendment of the Constitution protects beliefs and ritual practices as long as they are called religious. The result is that we are far behind in both objective analysis and reasonable legal controls of cult practices. It is hoped this book will help build a bridge between behavioral sciences and law, and between religion and the mental health professions.

There is an abundance of information on cults in TV talk shows, books, magazines, and newspapers, but little or none by mental health professionals or researchers who specialize in human behavior. Some of what is available is shocking and sensationalistic, a morbidly fascinating subject that draws attention and sells newspapers. There is much about cults that is frightening and merits great concern. Unfortunately, not all that is being reported is true. There is a great need to separate fact from fiction, reality from hysteria. This book steers a middle course between the popular and the professional, between what is known and what is unknown. It examines cults and ritual behavior in the context of personality dynamics, in the light of a wide sampling of social and behavioral scientists who observed and analyzed group behaviors since World War II.

Without such little available research data and few standard references on the subject, I have had to rely on my own twenty years of experience as a psychotherapist in two provinces of Canada, and in Washington, D.C., Alaska, Idaho, and Virginia, in treating victims of physical and sexual abuse, severe stress and exploitation. I first treated cult members in the early 1970s, an adolescent who joined a communal cult, referred by his parents to be somehow "fixed," a witch initiated in England, and many child and adult survivors of physical and sexual abuse, violent crimes, natural catastrophes and wars. I have also treated convicted abusers and murderers as staff psychologist on a medium security corrections unit and testified as an expert witness in civil and criminal cases in several states and in Canada. Ten years on four ethics committees of professional associations augment clinical experience.

My interest in comparative religions and ancient and current cults, what people believe and do about it, how they see the world and think about it, began during military service with the U. S. Marines during the Korean War (1950–1952). I became curious about "the enemy" I might face in combat, most likely Chinese or North Korean, and Buddhist. Graduate degrees, training, and experience in counseling and clinical psychology prepared me to better understand the cult experience. The result has been a series of books and articles starting in 1960 with *Tao, Voice of Nature* in *American Forests* magazine, followed by a modern English translation of the *Book of Tao*, then the *I Ching, Tibetan Book of the Dead*, and books on yoga, meditation, hypnosis, and a translation of the 1614 AD Roman Catholic exorcism rite. I have presented programs on concepts and techniques common to ancient Eastern religions and contemporary psychotherapy at state and national professional conferences.

What is "good" or "evil," like what is "normal" or "abnormal" is determined by society, influenced by its customs and traditions and majority consensus. For example, homosexuality has been a consistent sexual behavior across time but its "official" classification has changed from perversion to disorder to sexual preference in diagnostic manuals from 1955 to 1987. It didn't change, we did. Obscenity is still difficult to define legally, yet most everyone has an opinion as to when something crosses the line of propriety and good taste and becomes obscene, when it can be tolerated and when it is unacceptable. In like manner, all cults are not evil but they all have a potential for evil when they divide families, socially and emotionally isolate people, interfere with education, career, or home life, and shape personality according to cult values and principles and not by individual free choice. Cults that engage in unlawful acts, in mental, physical, or sexual abuse of animals or people are a danger to society and evil by those acts alone.

The object of this book is not to shock but to awaken, to provide light not heat, a deeper, clearer understanding of what cults are and why they continue. It is hoped it will be of help as a teaching tool for general use, a convenient reference for therapists and teachers, courts and police, parents and prospective or current cult members to identify and explain the risks involved. To be helpful to readers, there are appendices listing organizations concerned about cults which can provide further information on this subject, a model animal protection ordinance, and an alphabetical listing of cult organizations. The index was constructed to provide quick access to specific subjects in the text.

If one child can be saved from pain, one survivor's search for self assisted, a family reunited, a former cult member helped to fulfil career, educational, or life goals, it will be worth the time and effort in its writing.

FRANK J. MACHOVEC

ACKNOWLEDGMENTS

My grateful thanks to the following organizations and individuals which provided valuable background information, much of which is included in this book or cited in the references: American Family Foundation; Believe the Children; the Cult Awareness Network and their WATCH Network; Dr. Catherine Gould; the Humane Society of the United States; Ken Lanning of the Federal Bureau of Investigation; the National Center for Prosecution of Child Abuse; the National Children's Advocacy Center; Gerald F. Ragland, Jr.; and Rex Springston of the *Richmond News Leader*.

CONTENTS

Cult Classification Inventory; effective interviewing; cults and mental disorders: dissociative, anxiety, and personality disorders; therapies and treatment variables: actualization therapy, self-therapy, syzygy, family therapy, hypnosis; prevention; conclusions.

Appendices:

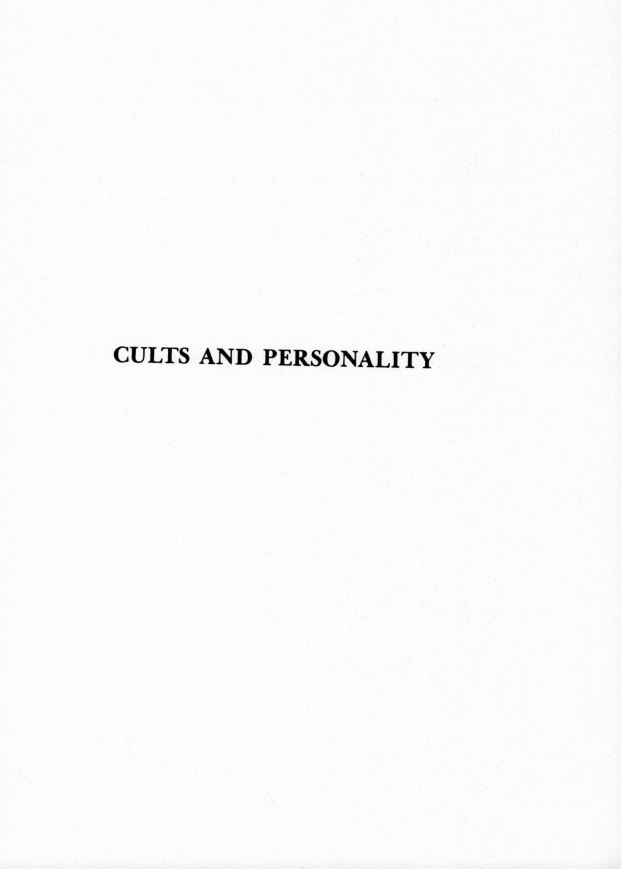

CULTS AND PERSONALITY

Chapter One

CULTS: WHAT ARE THEY?

*Flight from the self almost invariably
turns into a rush for a compact group*
Eric Hoffer
The Passionate Mind (1955)

CULTS TODAY

It is estimated that there may be as many as 5000 cults in the United States, with a total membership of 3,000,000 and some with more than a million members (Allen & Metoyer, 1987). If this is so, about one in 100 Americans are cult members. A number of them are active in extremist criminal cults. Cult crime and ritual are increasingly reported in the news media. In San Francisco, a "street person" was sexually abused and killed, a pentagram (5-pointed star) carved on his chest. On Long Island, a teenager was stabbed repeatedly and his eyes gouged out during a 4-hour Satanic ritual. Evidence at crime scenes suggest that animals and humans *are* being abused and killed as part of cult rituals. Older police officers have reported seeing cult materials at crime scenes years ago but were not then aware of their significance. There is a striking similarity to these crimes, across time and across the nation, beyond chance or coincidence (Allen & Metoyer, 1987).

Exposes of cult crime and ritual abuse include organized religious groups such as The People's Church of Jim Jones, alleged Satanic cult practices in day care centers, among high school students, and ritualistic abuse and murders by isolated individuals. It is difficult to determine how much of these are connected, but some law enforcement officers suspect there may be organized hard-core criminal cults operating nationwide involved in drug dealing, prostitution, child pornography, kidnapping, and ritual murder. Other law enforcement experts report that they have expended a great deal of time and effort to search for criminal cults and have discovered no convincing evidence. Other crimes have been attributed to cults such as fraud, extortion, desecrating public and religious places, and grave robbing. The "white collar" crimes, fraud and extortion, have involved large, nationwide cult organizations. Desecration and grave robbing have involved small, extremist Satan cults or acting-out teenage "dabblers" usually on drugs and with very little in-depth knowledge of Satanism. Some suspect that hardcore criminal Satanic cults develop their own sources for animal and human sacrifice and are careful not to leave evidence.

Some fear that children reported missing are kidnapped victims of extremist cults. Some of these children are victims of kidnappers with mental problems or murderers not related to cults. Many missing children are kidnapped by a parent denied legal custody in divorce proceedings. There have been charges of extremist Satanic ritual abuse by one parent against the other in the battle for child custody (Hopkins, 1988). Very few have been found to involve cult or ritual practice. If the charged parent is eccentric, does not belong to a traditional church or temple, is socially withdrawn with few friends, the unscrupulous can conduct a modern-day witch hunt.

Adult survivors of alleged ritual abuse, most of whom are in active psychotherapy, have been the major source of information about child ritual abuse and murder. The reported crimes occurred years before and there has been little or no hard evidence. There is, however, some evidence that some children *are* victims of cult crime and ritual abuse. Regrettably, we cannot yet reliably estimate their numbers. News media and TV talk shows have caused a great deal of hysteria based on personal accounts of alleged victims, in unprosecuted cases, with little or no factual research statistics or case law data. There are two million cases of child abuse reported annually but only half prove founded. On the other hand, it is possible that organized criminal cults have a network similar to that of gay male pedophiles discovered in 1973. One mailing list numbered 50,000. Before 1973 there was no evidence of such a network, just as today we have no hard evidence of extremist criminal Satanic cults operating across state and national borders. For years so-called "chickenhawks" have befriended runaway children at bus and train stations to lure them into pornography and prostitution. Extremist criminal cults can very easily use these same methods.

What is the truth? Many people have had more than casual interest in the occult, the supernatural, and what lies beyond life and thought as we know it. Science fiction, horror, and monster movies, and children's nursery rhymes are examples of this preoccupation. Monsters and devils have been movie box office hits: *Dracula, Frankenstein,* the *Wolf Man, The Exorcist,* and *Amityville Horror.* The "wicked witch of the West" played a major part in the popular film classic *Wizard of Oz.* Devils and witches appear at the door every Halloween, which is also "the witches' sabbath." The opera versions of *Hansel and Gretel* and *Faust* have played to packed houses for a hundred years.

Superstitions from the Middle Ages continue, such as the "God bless you" response to a sneeze. It was believed the life force or soul was expelled in a sneeze and the devil might capture it. Spontaneous figures of speech suggest at least a preoccupation, perhaps an unconscious belief in devils and hell: "Go to hell (or to the devil), hell of a mess, get the hell out of here, beat or scare the hell out of, play the devil's advocate." Common sense and technology are often left behind when *Tarot* cards or the *I Ching* are consulted, or tea leaves, palmistry, astrology, or channelling, today's "pop" spiritualism. Proctor and Gamble received up to 15,000 phone calls a month expressing concern that their trademark was Satanic (Lyons, 1988, p. 140). The stars on the U.S. flag and in Chrysler and Texaco logos, are pentagrams, artistic not demonic, though some see what they want to see and suspect Satanic involvement.

All these are evidence of preoccupation with phenomena beyond normal human experience, avoided by most researchers because to them it is almost entirely subjective, less subject to scientific and statistical analysis. Because his research showed other cultures widely separated by time and distance shared this interest, the psychiatrist, Carl G. Jung (1968), theorized it reflected a *collective unconscious* of the human race, a shared cultural heritage of *archetypes.* "It has contents," Jung wrote, "that are more or less the same everywhere and in all individuals" (p. 4). Lyons (1988) saw cult crime and ritual abuse as "disguised forms of myth, centuries old, of a body-snatching, orgiastic, cannibalistic, secret society that preys on humanity from subterranean cellars" (p. 15). Freud saw it as the *id,* the "beast" in everyone, seeking expression, or a regression to childhood fears and fantasies (Ehrenwald, 1956). Humanistic theorists see it as an imaginative projection of basic insecurity.

Well staged multisensory rituals can have powerful impact. Being "live," the cult member is an active participant. Ancient Greek morality plays were quite moving and had a powerful cathartic effect on the audience, portraying humans caught in gripping conflict, the chorus chanting advice and caution. Still the model for drama, their continued popularity for 2500 years testifies to their effectiveness. Cult rituals with costuming, music or chanting, candles and incense, strong unconscious imagery and emotional involvement, can be as effective. Even without such elaborate ritual, a susceptible delusional individual can be receptive to strange and mystical ideas and act on them. As police gather conclusive evidence and courts convict, cult crime and ritual abuse will become part of a database for further research. We are in desperate need of such "hard evidence." Without it we are subject to misinformation, exaggeration, confusion, and hysteria.

Sutcliffe (1961) described a *credulous* and a *skeptical* attitude toward paranormal experiences. While his observation applied only to hypnosic phenomena, it is especially relevant to the cult experience and the perception of evil. A credulous person consciously or subconsciously agrees with the existence of an evil force or devil and is more likely to project bias, preconceived notions, and generalizations which are not valid. The skeptical person overdoes being objective, is consciously or subconsciously dubious, resistant, can ignore and be less attentive to important, relevant information. In simpler terms, we tend to see what we want to see, what we have been conditioned to see. Search long enough and you will find information to support any conclusion. With respect to cults, we must see truth in total context, across history and culture, beyond the seeming reality of the moment. That, in essence, is the *scientific method.*

It is very important to define and differentiate cults since they range from loose, informal groups of individuals who do not meet regularly and do not live together communally, family groups of fellow believers, to residential communities international in scope. It is important, too, to differentiate between *criminal cults,* those that regularly violate the law by violence and committing crimes, such as extremist Satanic cults, *harmful* or *destructive cults,* which by deception, fraud, and manipulation have high-risk potential for psychological harm, and *constructive* cults, with little or no risk. In addition, the cult experience can be further categorized into three basic target populations: children, teenagers, and adults over 18 years of age.

There is a wide range of reported cult crime and ritual abuse. It varies with ideology or belief of the cult and their practices and intent, from the unusual to the disgusting. As for ritual child abuse, there have been shocking descriptions of the deliberate degradation and demoralization of young children, defiled with smeared blood, feces, and urine, repeatedly abused physically and sexually, forced to participate in mutilation of animals, even murder, placed inside dissected animals or humans to symbolize rebirth, and to drink blood and eat flesh, feces, and urine. Evidence of such revolting behaviors is scanty but increasing in police and court records across the country.

Public and family concern about possible psychological harm from the cult experience has introduced some new problems and controversies. "Exit counselors" or "deprogrammers" are available for the systematic rehabilitation of cult members, sometimes against their will, usually financed by concerned families. This raises the question of the cult member's right or freedom of choice to be used, abused, misled, and deluded and a family's right to rescue a loved one enmeshed in a cult, to question whether there was fully informed consent. Cults are considered by law to be religious organizations and this gives them First Amendment protection, freedom of religion. Just as patients in a mental institution have the right to refuse medication, religious cult members have a legal right to remain there. In the case of mental patients, physicians can override refusal for medications if they can justify the need. Many parents of cult members of legal age want that same right.

There are reports of positive effects from the cult experience. Membership of young adults in a large, nationwide cult organization may be preferable to living on the street, in a severely disrupted home, or dependency on street drugs. Some claim cults provide a stable social situation, empathic support, and can resolve conflict and even serious psychopathology (Galanter, 1983). Religious conversion in a cult setting has been described as having a therapeutic and integrative effect, together with other mental, emotional, spiritual, and physical benefits (Robbins & Anthony, 1982). One writer confirmed cult use of indirect, deceptive manipulation, peer pressure, and hypnosis or meditation rituals on recruits in crisis or transition but denied there was evidence of "brainwashing" or coercion in recruitment or maintenance (Thomas, 1979).

Certainly, the cult experience is more complex than it is simple. There are many variables, in the person and in the cult. These diverse factors and forces act at varying intensity and interact in varying degrees, with varying effect (Maleson, 1981). It will take this entire book just to describe the scope and depth of the cult experience. The logical first step is to arrive at working definitions. To demonstrate the need to define and differentiate cults, consider these two descriptions of groups and decide whether or not they are cult behaviors:

CASE 1. A group of people meet privately in the outdoors around a fire where they chant, dance ritualistically, and beat drums. All are attentive to the ritual, actively involved in the process, some trancelike, quite emotionally involved in it.

CASE 2. A small group of men regularly meet in secret to discuss current societal problems, traditional values of religion and government, and ways to improve them.

Many consider both cult rituals. *Case 1* could apply to Haitian Voodoo, Santeria (pronounced Santa-Ria), African tribal rituals, and also those of North American Indians and some religious services in most communities. *Case 2* could apply to groups such as those led by Socrates, Buddha, Jesus, Ben Franklin, or Adolph Hitler. There is a *valence* or perceived value, positive or negative, in every cult, based on many variables of belief, values, practices, group norms, and their effects.

A cult or religion (some cults claim to be religions) is somewhere between 100 percent "good" and 100 percent "evil." There are negative aspects in the most orthodox traditional religions, and positive aspects in the most radically unorthodox. Some devout Christians bomb and burn abortion clinics, a clearly illegal act. Others shoot each other in northern Ireland. Sikhs kill Hindus in India and Moslems kill Hindus in Sri Lanka. Arabs kill Jews and Jews kill Arabs along the Mediterranean. In the 1800s, an African or North American Indian tribe was considered hostile or "heathen" to explorers, their beliefs and rituals perceived as negative or "evil." Today, voodoo and Santeria are generally seen negatively, but North American Indian rituals are viewed as positive.

This book's central focus is on cults with high-risk potential of significant negative psychosocial effect, mental, physical, or sexual abuse, of animal or human injury or death, so-called *destructive cults*. Good or evil, cults have existed throughout history in every culture and will very likely continue. They vary in size, type, and ritual practices. Viewing and evaluating cults only in the context of current case law, police records, or media reports of crime or mind control ignores history and increases the risk of overgeneralizing, scapegoating cult groups which function peacefully and in good faith. This book is not intended to discredit them. Racism, sexism, and other extremist *isms* have grown from ignorance, half-truth and oversimplification, when only one side of an issue was considered, and that subjectively.

The Pilgrims who sailed for America and religious freedom were considered a cult by the Christian majorities of Europe. Satanism can be part of an organized "religion" protected under the First Amendment or one or more "dabblers," or part of a delusional system of a mentally ill person, or a convenient defense for a psychopathic criminal. There are many variations in scope, depth, and practice among cults. When they violate human rights or the law, individually or in a group, they should be prosecuted. We are faced with the paradox of high principle in one cult and crass depravity in another. To differentiate "good" from "evil" it is necessary to carefully examine cult and ritual behaviors, define and understand them.

DEFINITIONS

Three standard reference dictionaries give the preferred definition of *cult* as "formal religious veneration or worship" (*Webster's Ninth New Collegiate*, 1983), "a system or community of religious worship and ritual" (*American Heritage*, 1985), or "a system of religious worship; devotion or homage to person or thing" (*Little Oxford*, 1986). Negative aspects are introduced in alternate definitions: "a religion regarded as unorthodox or spurious . . . great devotion to a person, idea, or thing, a literary or intellectual fad" (*Webster's Ninth New Collegiate*, 1983), and "a religion or religious sect generally considered to be extremist or bogus . . . obsessive devotion or veneration for a person, principle, or ideal especially when regarded as a fad . . . an exclusive group of persons sharing an esoteric interest" (*American Heritage*, 1985).

"Terrorists" from Middle East countries who hijack or bomb airliners and kidnap, keep or kill hostages are perceived as *cultists* in the West but are heroes or martyrs at home where the "cult" is the majority. If only "obsessive devotion" to a person, idea, or thing is a major criterion of a cult, then smokers and nonsmokers, chocolate freaks, car nuts, retirees, feminists and male chauvinists, Alcoholics Anonymous, aerobic and diet groups, and avid hobbyists are all cultists. These are not cults but formal or informal groups of people who share a special interest in a common idea. Some have cult characteristics but not enough to warrant use of the term. As a general rule, if the members run the group with rotating leadership it is not a cult. Most cults run the group and control the lives of members and potentially the personalities of its members. Cult involvement is a matter of degree and a question of definition. We are in desperate need of more clarity and understanding of all the factors of cult practice.

Current dictionary definitions do not adequately describe current cult and ritual practice. There is a critical need to sharpen awareness of what cults are and to better understand what they are doing so that reasonable limits can be set by societal and legal standards. The following definition is suggested:

> A *cult* is a group of persons who share in a special interest differing from the established majority or current religious, social, or cultural values, who meet regularly to continue and extend their purpose or mission independent of previous relationships with family, friends, religion, school or career, with beliefs, practices and rituals which reinforce cult values and norms.

This definition applies to all cults, constructive and destructive, those with predominantly positive and negative valence. Those with high-risk potential to the individual usually recruit members deceptively, manipulate and exploit them, replace individual with deviant group norms and values, and interrupt and interfere with normal baseline personal growth and personality development. These high-risk cults require further definition because of their nature and the following is offered, based on a review of literature from former cult members and therapists who have worked with them:

> A *destructive cult* is a rigidly structured absolutist group usually under an authoritarian, charismatic leader which isolates itself from established societal traditions, values, and norms, recruits members deceptively without informed consent, and retains them by continually reinforced direct and indirect manipulative techniques which cause personality and behavior change, deny freedom of choice, and interrupt and obstruct optimal personality development.

TYPES OF CULTS

Cults can be described by their major focus or function: *religious, psychotherapy* or *personal growth, political,* or *popular* or *faddist. Religious, psychotherapy,* or *personal growth cults* deviate from traditional approaches in theory or practice. Examples: Unification Church, Hare Krishna. *Political cults* are composed of militant political activists who seek to change or overthrow the current government. Examples: Extremist groups of political assassins, or terrorist groups who hijack or bomb airliners, or take hostages. The word *assassin* is derived from the Arabic *hashshishin,* a Moslem cult during the Middle Ages described later in this chapter.

Popular, personality, or faddist cults are groups of people who share an exaggerated enthusiasm for and obsessive loyalty to a person, product, object, idea, or place, out of reasonable or realistic proportion. Obvious excess differentiates shared enthusiastic interest from cults, a fan from a fanatic, such as fad dieters, martial arts, heavy metal music, Elvis Presley fans, Beatlemania, UFO zealots, *Star Trek* "trekkies," and computer "addicts." Cults are perceived negatively because they most frequently get TV news and press coverage for antisocial or illegal acts such as mental, physical, or sexual abuse, animal mutilation, murder, kidnappings, fraud, or because of strange beliefs and rituals. Cults that are seen as secretive and private and outside mainstream society increase the perception they are "different, strange," and are viewed with suspicion, distrust, even fear.

Cult and *culture* have the same Latin root, *cultus,* meaning care or adoration, the past participle of *colere,* to cultivate. According to *Webster's Ninth New Collegiate Dictionary* (1983), the best guess for the first significant use of these words dates *culture* to the 15th century, *cultivate* at about 1620 AD, and *cult* at about 1679 AD. The word's history is a very good reflection of the problem of definition. Think about it yourself, and check with others in a simple word association test: Classify as *positive, neutral,* or *negative* the words *culture, cultivate, cult.* Chances are *cult* will be considered *negative* and *culture* and *cultivate* positive or neutral.

Socrates and Jesus were nonconformists who led small groups which differed from and opposed the views and values of the majority. Both were considered dangerous, tried, convicted, and executed by legal due process of the time. The cults of Christianity, and Buddhism and Islam, grew to become majorities in certain parts of the world and major world religions by the millions who affiliated with them. Each of them contains minority groups with special interests that satisfy the current dictionary definition as cults, such as Hassidic Jews and the Kabbala, Gnostic Christians and the Nag Hammadi or Dead Sea Scrolls, charismatic Christians, Sufi Moslems and Zen Buddhists.

In the context of world history, today's cult can become tomorrow's culture. The Hippocratic Oath still taken by physicians originated in the Cult of Asklipios in ancient Greece. Mithraism was a popular secret society or cult group among soldiers of ancient Rome. The Isis-Osiris cult in ancient Egypt, of Hammurabi in Babylonia, of Dionysus and Eleusis in Greece, have all contributed to what has become world *culture*

(Frazer, 1940). Many of these cults were described as "devil worship" by early Christian authorities.

CULTS IN HISTORY

To illustrate their variety and historical and cultural roots, three cults are described here: Mithraism, classical witchcraft, and the hashishin.

Mithraism

Mithraism originated about 6000 years ago in Persia (now Iran) and spread to Babylon, India, Greece, and Rome. Mithraism flourished for 2000 years, was popular among soldiers of the Roman legions, and a major competitor of early Christianity until the Edict of 391 AD which forbade "pagan worship." Hittite tablets unearthed in 1907 and dated to the 14th century BC refer to Mithraism (Vermaseran, 1963). It is *Mitra* in The *Vedas*, the most ancient scriptures of Hinduism (c. 1000 BC), and *Mithra* in the *Zend Avesta* (c. 1000 BC), Persian scriptures that describe Zoroaster or Zarathustra (661 BC), "a wonder-child born of an immaculate conception . . . to bring forth a highly enlightened religion" (Berry, 1956, p. 37). According to Zoroaster, Mithras was born from a rock between the Earth Mother and Heavenly Father, holding a globe (fiery light) in one hand, a dagger (action) in the other. He is one of three deities to judge the dead, the god of light, helper of Ahura Mazda, god of wisdom, enemy of Ahriman, god of darkness. The Jews "translated Ahriman into Satan" and Christians followed but with Satan as a fallen angel and not a god and without reference to Mithras (p. 38).

Mithras was most frequently portrayed in bas relief or statuary kneeling on one leg on the back of a bull, holding its head up with his left hand and a dagger in his right, its point on the bull's neck. Other pictographs show him wearing a red pointed hat (Phrygian cap), a ring on his right hand, and holding the *caduceus,* the magic staff of Hermes, or with a large snake around his body which signified wisdom and immortality. Three major ceremonial objects were used in Mithraic ritual: a *gold crown* with many-pointed tips, symbolizing the sun, its rays, and supernatural power; a *hammer* or *club* signifying man's creativity (a tool or weapon); *the bull* representing animal passion, the force of nature, elemental power to be overcome, managed, and controlled, also the Moon (as opposed to sun), elemental water, or Venus, the female or passive principle (Daraul, 1971; Vermaseran, 1963). Membership was by invitation and considered an honor and distinction.

Degrees, grades, or orders were conferred in natural caves or cellars made to resemble caves which symbolized "the celestial vault" (Vermaseran, 1963, p. 37) These have been found in England, France, Germany, Yugoslavia, Rumania, Italy, most of them defaced by early Christians at about 400 AD who considered Mithras to be the anti-Christ. There were three basic degrees conferred, the first called *Sacramentum* (oath) or the *Order of the Crow.* The crow symbolized death and rebirth, the death of ignorance in the initiate, the rebirth of enlightenment in him, and was also the messenger of the gods, symbol of Mercury and elemental air. The initiate fasted three days, was blindfolded, bound, and naked, pursued by wild animals and demons (ritual team in skins and costumes), was sworn to secrecy, tattooed on both hands, and lectured on the meaning, signs, handgrip, and password of the degree. A statue of Mithras was then unveiled as drums and cymbals sounded. Wine was drunk from a cymbal signifying contact with a higher power. Members knelt at low stone tables as the initiate ate a piece of sun-dried bread symbolizing the union of man (bread) with the supernatural (the sun). He was then given the password of the first degree.

The second degree was called *The Secret,* the *Order of the Soldier.* In the ritual, the statue of Mithras was considered to be alive and the initiate offered bread and water to symbolize his submission and service to him. The gold crown was offered to the initiate but refused with the statement: "Mithras is my crown." Mock combat then followed between the initiate and animals and soldiers. The third and last of the basic degrees was *The Lion,* the *Order of the Lion of Mithras,* a special high or priestly degree to which all members were not eligible, according to Daraul (1971). The lion signified elemental fire, the fire of action, and light or enlightenment. The ritual was held only when the sun was in the zodiacal position of Leo, the lion (July 21 and August 20). The initiate was "purified" with honey on his hands, tongue, and head. Honey was considered a purifying agent more fitting for this degree and of a higher quality than water. This anointing symbolized good deeds (hands), good words (tongue), and good thoughts (head, soul, or spirit).

There were four additional degrees, making a total of seven, but Daraul (1971) and Vermaseran (1963) differ in their name, content, and sequence. Daraul's formulation seems more likely and logical in sequence: the *Persian,* based on the cult's origins, using a grey tunic, honey, a sickle or scythe, and symbols of crescent moon and Saturn; *Runner of the Sun* or *Heliodromus,* with Oriental costume (sun rises in East) with yellow belt (sun), blue globe (heavens), horses and whip (sun's course), halo and torch; *Father* or teacher, using a throne (power), red robe and cap (status), ring and staff (wisdom); *Father of Fathers* or Patriarch. Daraul adds another: *King of Kings,* an exclusive degree reserved for the Shah or national leader).

Competition between large numbers of adherents sharing in common ideas and values result in time in a mixing or diffusion where each picks up certain characteristics of the other. In this way, some Mithraic practices were adopted by Christianity. For example, the "birthday of the sun" was celebrated every year on December 25th and some historians suggest early Christians chose this date as "birthday of Christ" to first compete with, then to replace the "pagan feast." Current consensus among Biblical scholars is that Jesus was probably born in April. Another vestige of Mithraic belief is the bullfight in Spain and Mexico, well attended and popular, portraying man against bull, or the dignity and beauty of humanity (elegantly dressed matador) against the power and passion of elemental nature (enraged bull). The matador's uniquely human intelligence and skill overcome the beast, within himself, for spectators, and in the cold reality of the ring). It is very meaningful to afficionados—and it's 100 percent Mithraic!

Ancient cults provided its members with a code of conduct learned under the stress of initiation rites. In the 20th century, we thought we discovered that multisensory impact increases the effectiveness of learning. We proved it with teaching machines, soundfilm, and the "discovery method" and "learning by doing." With today's technology we can do more to our senses with banks of high fidelity "surround sound" speakers, large screen cinerama and omnimax and 3-D movies, even holography. The cultists of Mithras, Isis-Osiris, Pythagoras, Asklipios, Cybele, Delphi, Dionysus, and Eleusis, knew the value of multisensory impact and about learning and stress conditioning as any reasonable review will substantiate (MacHovec, 1984, 1980, 1978, 1976, 1975). Ancient cults used preparatory purification rites of washing or massage, rhythmic chants, repetition, controlled fear and stress by fasting, augmented by alcohol or herbs, special diets, sleep and sensory deprivation by isolation and insecurity with graduated emotional support, and selective sensory overload in a superbly designed sequential development of symbols and meaning integrated with basic drives and personality dynamics.

The popularity of cults, their spread to other lands, languages, and cultures, and their longevity suggest they satisfied basic and universal needs. The cult of Mithras was one of the best known and most popular in ancient times. It was perceived as a positive, character-building, male fraternal order not so different than Freemasonry today. We will next examine an ancient cult which continues today, predominantly female, perceived negatively and condemned in the past by churches and secular courts: witchcraft.

Classical Witchcraft

"There have always been witches." This frank statement is from *The Malleus Maleficarum* or "witch's hammer," once the official manual of the Catholic Church and considered by Montague Summers, authority on witchcraft who translated the book, as "the most important work in this whole vast library of witchcraft" (1971). In his introduction, Summers commented: "Throughout the centuries, witchcraft was universally held to be a dark and horrible reality, an ever-present, fearfully ominous menace, a thing most active, most perilous, most powerful, and true . . . derived from secret and sombre sources, ancient gods or rather demons" (pp. vii, xi). In his 1974 book *Witchcraft and Black Magic*, Summers divided "students of witchcraft" into three groups: "believers who admit the evidence and in part at least its diabolical explanation; sceptics who deny both and regard the whole business of witchcraft as the product of hysteria and gross credulity; rationalists who accept the evidence but deny the supernatural explanation" (p. 112). The term *classical witchcraft* differentiates the original, authentic form from earliest history from the many mostly superficial current adaptations.

Malleus Maleficarum was written late in the 15th century by two Dominican priests and professors of theology, Heinrich Kramer and James Sprenger to satisfy the need for a manual for detecting witches in response to a papal bull issued by Pope Innocent VIII in 1484 condemning "the heretical depravity" of those who "abandoned themselves to devils, incubi and succubi . . . incantations, spells, conjurations, and other accursed charms and crafts . . . " (p. xliii). Religious "inquisitors" would determine whether a person was a witch, then "the secular arm" of public magistrates and judges would try them for this capital offense. From 1487 to 1500 fourteen editions were published, sixteen editions from 1574 to 1669, in German, French, and Italian. It was on the desk of every magistrate and judge, according to Summers, "the ultimate, irrefutable, unarguable authority" on witchcraft.

Politics and witchcraft were intertwined in the Middle Ages and in medieval times. The "black arts" (magic, overlooking (evil eye), casting spells, poison potions) were punishable by death since ancient Rome, yet witches were always available for these services, mostly to the nobility, despite this severe penalty. In 578 AD the English queen's son died allegedly due to witchcraft and several witches were tried, convicted, and executed. In 583, the French King Chilperie's son died and a court official was charged with administering potions he obtained from witches. In 829 witchcraft in France was punishable by death. In England in 1232, a judge accused a bishop of ingratiating himself to King Henry III "by charms and incantations." In 1324 town burghers paid a "necromancer" to kill King Edward II "by black arts." The mistress of Edward III was charged with using love potions on the old king. In 1419, Henry V charged his stepmother Joan of Navarre with his attempted murder by witchcraft. In 1431 Joan of Arc was tried and convicted of "heresy and sorcery" and burned at the stake. Shakespeare (1564–1616), keen observer of behavior, referred to the occult and witchcraft in *Macbeth* (1605), to *Hecate,* queen of Hades, and the three witches in *Macbeth* (1605), "so withered and so wild in their attire . . . weird sisters . . . secret, black, and midnight hags . . . that keep the word of promise in our ear, and break it to our hope." Engelbert Humperdinck's "fairy opera" *Hansel and Gretel* (1893) portrayed a witch who lured children and baked them into gingerbread.

Prosecution of suspected witches peaked in the 16th and 17th century. Estimates range from 4000 hangings in England to millions in Russia (Sargant, 1957). In his book *A History of the Inquisition* (1888), Henry Charles Lea reported 133 alleged witches burned at the stake in one day in Saxony in 1589. Matthew Hopkins, a "witch finder" in Essex County, England convicted and hanged 60 women in one year. He specialized in "special marks" such as moles, liver spots, and warts which he analyzed as supplemental teats to suckle imps (*succubi*). Arthur Lyons (1988) reported worldwide estimates of total executions for witchcraft from several hundred thousand to nine million. Witchhunting spread to the American colonies where in 1691 nineteen alleged witches were executed in Salem (now Danvers), Massachusetts. William Sargant, a British psychiatrist, reported in his book *Battle for the Mind* (1957) "of the many thousands of suspected witches burned in Europe, only a small proportion seem to have been actually connected to the cult" (p. 198). Some suspects gave detailed accounts of "infanticides and overlookings (evil eye) and other abominable practices."

The *Malleus Maleficarum* considered witchcraft "high treason against God's majesty" from "carnal lust which is in women insatiable" (p. 47). Male witches were called *wizards* in the *Malleus,* not *warlocks* and were seldom mentioned in the book. The devil was seen as "infinitely more apt to do harm through the agency of witches . . . a greater offense to God by usurping to Himself a creature dedicated to Him" (p. 123). Witches were agents of devils, heretics "to be put to the torture in order to make them confess" (p. 89). Torture was justified because "it is as difficult, or more difficult, to compel a witch to tell the truth as it is to exorcise a person possessed of the devil" (p. 224). According to the *Malleus,* anyone can be bewitched, "even the blameless and innocent and just," though three types of person were thought to be immune: those who prosecute witches; those who make lawful use of the power and virtue of the Church; those "blessed by Holy Angels" (p. 89). Later in the text: "The devil can in no way enter into the mind or body of any man, nor has the power to penetrate into the thoughts of anybody unless such a person has first become destitute of all holy thoughts and is quite bereft and denuded of spiritual contemplation . . . lacking in the gift of divine grace" (p. 120).

Three "degrees of witches" were listed: those who harm and cannot heal; those who heal and cannot harm; those who heal and harm. The first is "the most powerful class of witch" (p. 99) but all witches are agents of the devil and "copulate with devils" in the form of *incubi* (devils in human form, usually visible only to the witch). They contract with devils alone or in a group in a "solemn ceremony like a solemn vow" where they "abjure the Faith, forsake holy Christianity and the worship of the Anomalous Woman" (the Virgin Mary), vow never to venerate the sacraments and subvert worship, homage forever to devils, bring others into witchcraft, "make certain unguents from the bones and limbs of children, especially those who have been baptized" (pp. 99–100).

According to the *Malleus,* witches "subvert the innocent" with help from devils. Typically, this was done in three ways: when the victim was weary such as from "grievous loss of temporal possessions"; through "bodily lusts and pleasures . . . carnal desires and the pleasures of the flesh"; at times of sadness or feeling vengeful, such as when "scorned by lovers." Six ways witches "injure humanity" were listed: induce evil love; plant hate or jealousy; bewitched sexual dysfunction (usually impotence due to perceived loss of penis or premature ejaculation); diseases; deprived reason; death. Devils, by their very nature, were described as keenly and quickly aware of weakness. The *Malleus* described the strengths of devils according to St. Augustine: superior knowledge (to humans) though faulty reasoning; understanding of human nature: alert, aware, quick thinking, quick-witted; able to predict famine, disease, and death.

"Witches Who Harm But Cannot Heal"

The following are the distinguishing characteristics of witches who, according to the *Malleus Maleficarum* "can harm but cannot heal," who can *do* but not *undo* evil acts. They are edited from the text, enumeration mine (p. 99).

1. Human sacrifice, "in the habit of eating and devouring the children of their own species"
2. "Raise hailstorms, hurtful tempests and lightnings" that kill
3. "Sterility in man and beasts"
4. "Make horses go mad under their riders"
5. "Transport themselves from place to place through the air, in body or imagination" (*transvection*)
6. "Affect judges and magistrates so they cannot hurt them" (usually by *overlooking*, "the evil eye")
7. Bewitch animals and people "with a mere look"
8. "Keep silence under torture"
9. Cause trembling and terror in those who come to arrest them
10. "Show to others occult things and foretell the future naturally or from devils"
11. "See absent things as if they were present"
12. "Turn minds to inordinate love or hatred"
13. "Render men impotent"
14. Cause abortions in animals and humans and "kill infants in the mother's womb by exterior touch"
15. Cause plagues and death
16. Exorcism of the bewitched

EXORCISING THE BEWITCHED

Besides the need to be aware of the characteristics of witches, the *Malleus* (p. 184) gave recommendations for the detection of bewitching and its removal (enumeration mine):

1. A "good confession" (sacramental confession preferred) by the bewitched and others as a preventive.
2. "Diligent search" of the room "in all corners" and "under the threshold of the door," the house and grounds, especially bed-clothes and mattress, for bewitching objects and burn or destroy them.
3. "All bedclothes and garments should be renewed."
4. Move—change houses if necessary to escape the evil.
5. The bewitched should go to church, especially on Holy Days, preferably in the morning, and be with clergy "the better if the priest also has confessed and is in a state of grace."
6. The bewitched sits or kneels, holding a candle as others who are present pray for his or her deliverance.
7. The bewitched should recite a litany starting with "Our help is in the name of the Lord," with one "appointed to make the response."
8. Sprinkle holy water on the bewitched.
9. Place a stole around the neck of the bewitched.
10. The bewitched should read the psalm "Haste Thee, O Lord, to deliver me."
11. The bewitched should continue the Litany for the Sick, saying at the Invocation of the Saints: "Pray for him and be favorable; deliver him, O Lord," continuing thus to the end.

The *Malleus* recommended "this sort of exorcism" be continued "at least three times a week . . . where the prayers are to be said, then in the place of the prayers let him begin the exorcism, and continue in the way we have declared, or in any other better way as seems good to him" (p. 184). This procedure need not be followed step by step. "That which cures one person," the *Malleus* cautioned, "does not necessarily cure another" (p. 179). There are other safeguards recommended: holy communion; recite the Lord's Prayer or Apostles' Creed; visit shrines; prayers of holy men; belief in and acceptance of God's will which allows it; inspirational music; sprinkling holy water on yourself; and attaining grace "which is in the righteous than the grace of the sacraments."

LAWFUL ENSURING EFFECTIVE EXORCISM

To ensure incantations, benedictions, and exorcisms are "lawful" as well as effective, the *Malleus* (p. 180) pointed out they are best delivered by "enchanters whose art and skill lie in the use of words" and according to seven requirements taken from St. Thomas Aquinas (enumeration mine):

1. No expressed or tacit invocations of devils.
2. No unknown names lest they conceal superstition.
3. Nothing untrue or irrelevant.
4. No vanities or charms.
5. No faith in the method of writing or reading about a person "which has nothing to do with the reverence of God."
6. Attention only to sacred words and their meaning.
7. "The looked-for effect must be left to the Divine Will."

Not prescribed in the *Malleus* but used widely in witchcraft trials was the *ordeal of the stool* (Sargant, 1957). The suspect was forced to sit 24 hours cross-legged on a hard stool in the center of an empty room, without sleep, food, or water. It was believed that her imp would come within 24 hours to be suckled and the suspect was observed continually. A hole was fashioned in the door for the imp to enter. The room was swept regularly to prevent an imp in the form of a fly or spider. Any insect discovered which could not be killed was considered to be an imp. Sargant quotes Hutchinson: " . . . imagine a poor old creature under all the weakness and infirmities of old age, set like a fool in the middle of a room," seated on the hard stool all day and night such that "circulation of the blood would be much stopped, her sitting would be as painful as the wooden horse . . . they confessed any tales that would please them and many times they knew not what" (p. 200).

In many jurisdictions, all body hair was shaved off and the suspected witch body searched "so as not to hide some superstitious object" (p. 227). Suspects were walked backwards into the court and forbidden to touch anyone, to prevent their casting a spell or using "the evil eye." They had no legal counsel, informants need not be named or known at trial, and there was no appeal. The history of witchcraft is one of extremism by both practitioners and prosecutors and a hysteria that resulted in fear and suspicion in the innocent and terror and death to the hundreds of thousands of women tortured and killed, most of whom were probably not witches. Current usage of the term "witch hunt" for a useless, fool-hardy investigation is a reminder of one of history's darker chapters.

SATANISM

Witchcraft is a form of Satanism but currently there is a wide range of Satanic "worship," from an individual's solitary obsession, temporary experimentation of small groups of "dabblers," to formal religious ser-vices of an organized "church" or "temple" of Satan. There have been teenage suicides and murders of teenagers by peers or persons obsessed or deluded with Satanism, so-called *stoners.* "Heavy metal" rock music, with its lyrics and garish record jackets of strong Satanic content has been found at ritual sites and Banner (1989) reported its use during Satanic rituals. It would seem to have the character and quality of a reinforcer to someone already obsessing on Satanism. Many years ago the popular song *That Old Black Magic* also had Satanic content. The idea is not at all new. In a 1970 San Francisco rock concert, one person was stabbed to death during the song *Sympathy for the Devil,* two more died and a hundred were injured in the ensuing panic (Lyons, 1988). The multisensory overload of *shock rock* with its loud volume, incessant rhythm, and droned repetitious lyrics resemble the chanting and sing-ing of rituals such as voodoo and Santeria.

These behaviors suggest that Satanic or similar cult or ritual practices can add stress to an already sensitive or vulnerable weak ego with limited emotional controls, common in adolescent years. Preoccupation can lead to obsession, eroding reality testing and weakening critical judgment. This, in turn, increases the potential for impulsive acting out in cruelty, violence, or murder, toward the self, animals, or others. Extremist cults validate abnormal thought processes, even crime and violence, for its members. Widely publicized "churches" or "temples" of Satan are often fronts for exhibitionists, narcissists, or entrepreneurs to indulge their grandiosity, and nonconformist rebellion against traditional religion, family, or society. Some, the most dangerous, firmly believe in Satanism and actively take part in all the ancient practices, including mental, physical, and sexual abuse, mutilation, and murder. In so doing, they meet the criteria for "witches that harm and cannot heal" in the *Malleus Maleficarum.* It is hoped they are a very small minority of so-called Satanists. Since what they do is not only illegal but "shocks the conscience," punishable by severe sentences, they operate in secret, difficult to apprehend, their numbers unknown. There is such a variety of Satanic cults it is not possible to categorize or catalog them here.

We will now examine a third cult, one which was both political and religious, composed of men and women, deeply rooted in history, with a long shadow into today's troubled Middle East: the *hashishin* or "order of assassins."

THE HASHISHIN

In 1092 AD, Hasan, Sheikh of the Mountain, leader of the Hashishin, stood on the ramparts of a castle high in the Persian mountains talking with an emissary of Emperor Malik Shan, who was asking for Hasan's surrender and allegiance. Hasan pointed to a sentry high in a turret, gave a signal, and the sentry saluted then jumped to his death. Hasan told the emissary he had 70,000 men and women who would do the same: "You ask me to surrender. This is my answer. Go!" (Daraul, 1971). Hashishin were so named because they used hashish in their rituals. They were Ishmaelis, later also called Khojes or Malwas, Moslems of the Shiite sect who believe in a direct link from God (Allah) to Mohammed (Muhammad) and to their current Imam (Hasan in 1092). The hashishin established the *Abode of Learning* in Cairo, "a training ground for fanatics who were conditioned by the most cunning methods to believe in a special divine mission . . . a complete transformation of the mind of the student" (pp. 2–3). Typical candidates were gullible, impressionable teenagers but it was reported Hasan would "buy unwanted children . . . and train them in implicit obedience and with the sole desire to die in his service" (p. 22).

Hasan required the initiate to pass through seven degrees, then allowed to wear the white tunic and red sash of the Hashishin, signifying innocence and blood. Details of these degrees came from study of manuals by Jawani, a Mongol official after the Mongols invaded and occupied the Hashishin stronghold. It was based on "false analogy and every other device of argument" to discredit previous teachings and values. The two final degrees stressed that "all religion, philosophy, and the like were fraudulent" and there is "no such thing as belief; all that mattered was action and the only possessor of the reasons for carrying out any action was the chief of the sect" (pp. 5–6). The initiate became dependent on cult leaders for truth and wisdom, since all other sources were refuted.

Over time and in practice, dependence became blind loyalty not unlike the 913 in the People's Church of Guyana ordered by Jim Jones to die.

The Hashishin also impose seven *Rules of the Order:* cast no seed upon rocks (select good candidates); flatter prospective candidates; knowledge (to raise doubt and uncertainty); oath never to betray secrets or secret teachings; importance of the organization (many powerful leaders belonged); intensive oral examination of previous degree work, allegorical meanings, and supervised meditation on an alleged saying of Mohammed: "Paradise lies in the shadow of swords." Since the time of the Crusades, probably before, the Hashishin would take hostages and either hold them for ransom or use their services. Daraul reported "one was a physician, another a famous astronomer, a third the greatest painter in Persia" (p. 30). "To the shores of Tripoli," the second line of the Marine Corps Hymn, refers to the Tripoli pirates who followed the hashishin practice of hostage taking and who may, in fact, have been members of that cult.

After the Crusades, the Mongols invaded Persia and occupied the land. Mamluk, Sultan of Egypt and a Sunni Moslem, drove out the Mongols in 1260 AD and then used the Hashishin for his own purposes. Daraul suspected that the Thugg cult of India had connections with the Hashishin. A Thuggi password is "Ali bhai Salam," definitely not a Hindu expression. The words *assassin* and *thug* are in current use today, rooted in the Crusades of the Middle Ages. Daraul suggested that all European secret societies, religious and secular, borrowed titles such as Grand Master and sequential, experiential degree work, from the Hashishin. Iranian followers of the Ayotollah Khomeini, Imam of the Shiite sect, share in that religious and cultural heritage. Khomeni's $6 million bounty for the murder of the author of *Satanic Verses* continues the Hashishin tradition. To us they are cultists. To them, we are the cultists which Khomeini called "the Great Satan." The "wise men of the East" in the Christmas story were *Magi,* royal astrologers from Persia who would have been familiar with the legend of Mithras.

CHARACTERISTICS OF HARMFUL CULTS

The foregoing sampling of cults in history was to acquaint you with how cults originate and function. We can now more closely examine how cults can be harmful. Regardless of type, cults with high-risk potential

for physical and psychological harm share most or all of these distinguishing features:

Charismatic leader	Intrusive group activities
Monopoly on truth	Ideological commitment
Exclusivity and isolation	Emotional desensitization
Deception or fraud	Debilitation
Strange beliefs or practices	Degradation
Loss of autonomy	

Charismatic Leader. There is usually a dominant charismatic leader
with excellent communications skills especially in the group setting and
strong ego needs to lead and control others as sole authority, frequently
claiming divine revelation or viewed by followers to be directly linked to
God. Most are persuasive, verbal compulsives with a great need to assert
themselves and manipulate others. They are perceived to be deeply
caring and committed to the cult's values and purposes. They usually
lack formal education, training, and experience in religion or philosophy, and as a result their teachings are theoretically weak, superficial,
incomplete, inconsistent, seldom original, and frequently borrowed from
other sources. Usually there is a metaphysical "gimmick" or "hook" to
get attention and just enough information, usually in measured doses, to
maintain interest. The psychodynamics of cult leadership are described
further in the next chapter.

Monopoly on Truth. The cult leader and therefore the cult itself, are
the sole source of absolute truth and that all else is error or evil. Some
cults consider parents to be devils or agents of Satan. It follows, then, that
other religions, family and societal values, customs and traditions, are all
deficient since they do not reflect the absolute truth which has been
made known exclusively to the cult leader and therefore available only
to the cult members. Most cults see their sacred mission to be to convert
the world. It has arrived at a level of enlightenment or understanding
superior to that of others. Most cult philosophies offer nothing new or
original. Dramatic, forceful delivery, often repeated, surrounded by
committed leaders and peers gives new members the impression there is
more truth and stability than is actually so.

Exclusivity and Isolation. The cult deliberately isolates itself, separated
from and in basic disagreement with commonly held beliefs and standards.
Being sole possessors of absolute truth, the world is viewed in distinct
"us-they," right-wrong, good-evil dichotomy. There is no middle ground,
no gray area. Members feel "special" and enriched because of this exclu-

sivity. The isolation of the cult makes it impossible for external reality to penetrate. As far-fetched as the "exclusive" message may seem to those outside the cult, within the cult it is a unifying force in closely shared identity, an organized whole, providing more order and structure than many members realized before or would have tolerated outside the cult. The illusion of exclusivity provides cult members feelings of satisfaction, security, and well-being. Unusual costuming, symbols, rituals, ceremonies, and daily routine add to and reinforce the illusion.

Deception or Fraud. Some cults deliberately deceive prospective members by misrepresenting themselves and the cult's identity. They "hook" converts any way possible, by deception in the form of evasion, misrepresentation, denial, manipulation, or deliberate lying. "Love bombing," is the manipulative technique of giving rapt attention to potential recruits to impress them with the supposed caring attitude of the cult. In transactional analysis terms, this is called a "plastic fuzzy" rather than a genuine "warm fuzzy." In his 1980 book *The Third Wave,* futurist Alvin Toffler commented that cults "peddle" friendship and acceptance, like a car, insurance, or time share salesperson. Another technique is "heavenly deception," such as when wary potential recruits, who ask if they are getting involved with a cult, are assured they are not. Some cults use attention-getting and trust building popular causes such as world peace, a charity, or personal growth. Some have used names of well-known organizations in these areas with no cult connection. Deception is justified because it is felt recruits would not be receptive if they knew the identity of the cult. This mental shell game continues until the cult recruit is at an optimal level of readiness to remain in the cult. Monetary gifts are encouraged to "impress" or "gain the favor" of God. Use of deception has been the basis for the charge of fraud in court cases brought against cults by former members and upheld in a 1989 case before the California Supreme Court. It is one of the most common complaints of former cult members.

Strange Beliefs and Practices. There are special rules, routine procedures, lectures, and rituals unique to the cult, regularly repeated. They provide a rigid structure and carefully controlled environment with measured doses of regularly repeated multisensory input. These reinforce feelings of exclusivity and the belief that the cult has a monopoly on truth. Repeated ritual such as chanting or meditation with a mantra add to security feelings and may also exert a hypnotic effect. Multisensory impact, just as in theatre productions, adds to the effectiveness of cult indoctrination. The use of abstract symbols, vague mystic or occult concepts, or speaking in tongues circumvent ego defenses and minimize cognition and critical judgment. Some cults use drugs to further enhance these effects.

Intrusive Group Activities. In most cults, nothing is done in private. Daily routine, meals, even sleep are shared. There is little or no leisure time. Continually shared group activities constitute enforced physical conformity which in turn reinforces emotional and ideological conformity. They also make the individual's dependency on the cult complete. Leader and peer pressure discourage independent thought, withdrawal or inactivity in cult practices, ensure maximal effect of the 24-hour treadmill of cult conditioning, and prevent escape.

Ideological Commitment (cognitive narrowing). Members first adapt to, then adopt the cult's mission or purpose, regardless of how illogical or erroneous. Abstract, vague ideas replace the usual cognitions attached to daily routine and decisionmaking outside the cult—school, work, sports, home life—and constitute thought stopping. Diversity of opinion is discouraged, not tolerated, which further narrowly shapes mental processes. Cognitive input is transmitted from the cult to the individual on but one frequency and incessantly. Continued participation in the cult entrenches and deepens conviction, defies reason and logic, and becomes in effect an encapsulated psychosis, a severe thought disorder. Example: Nazi commitment to an Aryan "perfect race" and detailed plans to kill Jews; followers of Jim Jones who refused to leave Guyana when it was evident he was deteriorating and there was no future living isolated in the jungle.

Emotional Desensitization (flattening). Since room and board and structured daily activities occupy the cult member, there is initially a feeling of safety and security. Emotions are insulated from the stressors and stimuli of everyday life outside the cult, replaced by the endless repetition of unchanging cult life, a protected vegetative state. Deceptive practices used for recruitment lead to an idealization of emotion, an artificial acting out of what unconditional caring should or could be like rather than truly experiencing and spontaneously applying it. The cult becomes the surrogate family and religion and life, a total life experience, all needs met in one place, without the need for decisionmaking or free choice. It is an existential, static world, neither rooted in the past nor future-oriented. Previously held family, social, or religious values fade. Feeling level communication is no longer needed and erodes to shallow, flat, blunted affect, reflected in a dull, dazed, or glazed eye look. Homer described this effect in his *Odyssey* 3000 years ago when Odysseus (Ulysses) visited "the land of the lotus eaters." Anyone who "ate of the lotus . . . had no more wish to bring tidings nor to come back" and was "forgetful of his homeward way" (Eliot, 1909, p. 122). It is quite possible this state of mind is a form of hypnosis (MacHovec, 1975).

Debilitation. Fatigue and malnutrition have been reported by former cult members. In most cases, this has involved heavy work schedules such as from 7 AM to midnight, designed to provide the cult member with the opportunity to serve God or the cult or to sacrifice for the cult. The strict vegetarian diet imposed by some cults is low in amino acids and continued use can result in a nutritional deficiency.

Degradation. For members in large, nationwide religious cult organizations, it is degrading to be recruited by deception, manipulated into mindless subservience, conforming to a regimented schedule day and night, without privacy, denied individuality where everyone looks, thinks, feels, and behaves alike, severing all ties to the past. For small children in extremist criminal cults, the degradation of physical, sexual, and mental abuse, deprivation and isolation combine into terrifying multidimensional trauma that has caused dissociation into multiple personality or psychotic decompensation.

Loss of Autonomy. All of the foregoing combine to relieve the individual of responsibility for continuing personal growth and personality development. It is a regressive, soporific effect, returning the individual to childhood dependency under an idealized parent figure, where life is predictable and protected, without competition or the need to think, create, and plan ahead, a packaged, perfect world, the land of Oz. It is for the personality a state of discontinuity, interrupting the individual's progress toward self realization. As the world becomes packaged, so also the self. Cult members give more than they get psychologically and emotionally. The tight structure of a cult, especially where members live together, is a powerful force to maintain and reinforce conformity. Sherwin Harris, a Jonestown survivor, observed that "this is an example of what some Americans will subject themselves to in order to bring some structure into their lives" (Toffler, 1980, p. 355).

SECRET SOCIETIES

"Secret society" is another term frequently misused. It came into use about 1829 and is currently defined as "any of various oath-bound societies often devoted to brotherhood, moral discipline, and mutual assistance" (*Webster's Ninth New Collegiate Dictionary*, 1983). Interestingly, the *American Heritage Dictionary* (1985) does not list the term. If secret societies were really secret, little or nothing would be known about them. Freemasonry is considered a secret society by some of its critics, yet its members openly wear Masonic lapel pins and rings, their meeting places are known and Shriners, a branch of Masonry, enjoy high public visibility. Books describing Masonic ritual are available and easily accessible at most larger public libraries. In the early days of the church, Christians met in secret and used passwords for recognition and security and was by dictionary definition a secret society. Hitler propagandized Jews as participating in a secret society to dominate the world. The *Secret Service* is a branch of the U. S. Treasury Department which guards the President and other high government officials and investigates counterfeiting. Classifying these private or religious organizations and federal agency as secret societies is not correct, though some satisfy current dictionary definition.

There are cults which operate as secret societies but which do not meet the dictionary definition. We need a better definition and the following is offered: A select group of persons who join together to share in a system of beliefs or values using oaths, rituals, signs, or passwords not made known publicly and who do not publicly describe, promote, or represent themselves as members of the secret society. Examples: Certain witches covens, extremist Satanic cults, and other similar organized groups. Secret groups can be loosely organized, such as one that does not meet regularly, only as needed, and in different places, or well organized such as a larger group which uses mailings, phone or computer nets, regularly scheduled meetings and activities.

Dictionaries list words based on rising usage to the point there is a need to catalog and describe them. We can trace society's interest in an idea through the history of the words used to describe that idea. Cults have been known for centuries and many major historical and religious movements began as cults. Technically, secret societies are by their nature cults, but not all cults are secret societies. If a cult operates openly at announced meetings in places known to the public (Masonic Hall), it isn't secret, though its activities may be attended by members only. Most business and religious board meetings are not open to the public and are not secret societies.

THE OCCULT

The word *occult* is closely related to *secret* as in *secret society*. The root word is from the Latin *occultus* which came into widespread use about 1500 AD to mean to conceal from view, applied to *occulting* or intermittently flashing beacons or signals and in astronomy when the sun is *occulted by* the moon. But the preferred or most frequent usage, which rose about 1567 AD, is pertaining to "supernatural influences, agencies or phenomena" and next, "beyond the realm of human comprehension; inscrutable" (*Webster's Ninth New Collegiate Dictionary*, 1983; *American Heritage Dictionary*, 1985). In terms of the history of word usage, it is an older word than *cult* or *secret society*. The *Columbia Viking Desk Encyclopedia* (1968) defines *occultism* as "belief in supernatural sciences or powers such as magic, astrology, alchemy, theosophy, and spiritism" (p. 785). Since the purpose of occult study was to expand power, guard against evil, and predict the future, it was the forerunner of experimental research. Seligmann (1948) observed that "magic gave a stimulus to experimentation and, in a broader sense, to thinking" (p. 322).

People who feel lost or inadequate, who see little or no purpose to life, who are depressed and insecure, are susceptible to a cult or secret society which claims to know the secret of the life or some special truth. If these secrets and truths are not readily obvious, hidden and requiring a special search or unique approach, available to and practiced only by those chosen and initiated, the group can be further described as *occult*.

MYSTICISM

Mysticism is "the practice of uniting one's self with the Deity or other unifying principle of life," usually in a religious setting, or "any sort of nonrational belief" (*Columbia Viking Desk Encyclopedia*, 1968, p. 735). Mysticism has deep historical roots, from the Greek *mystos* and the Latin *Mysticus*, and is closely related to occult. The word rose to widespread use about the 14th century. About 1736 AD, the preferred usage was "the experience of mystical union that is neither apparent to the senses nor obvious to the intelligence" and secondly "direct knowledge of God, spiritual truth, or ultimate reality" can be achieved subjectively by intuition or insight (*Webster's Ninth New Collegiate Dictionary*, 1983, p. 785). The *American Heritage Dictionary* (1985) defines it as a "spiritual discipline" toward "direct union or communion with ultimate reality or God through deep meditation or trancelike contemplation." It also includes "vague and groundless speculation" (p. 827).

The mystic tradition has made a valuable contribution to world culture. Every major world religion has a mystic component, such as the Gnostic Christians, Hassidic Jews, Sufi Moslems, and Zen Buddhists. The Saints Theresa Avila, Catherine of the Cross, John of the Cross, Augustine, and Aquinas were mystics. The Society of Friends (Quakers), and the late Carl G. Jung and Thomas Merton typify modern mystic thought and ideas. Not all cults, secret societies, occult or mystic groups are evil. Only a detailed study of each can differentiate a cult or cult-like organization along the continuum of "good" or "evil" according to societal and subjective values.

RELIGIONS

Some cult organizations claim to be religions and some organized religions function much like cults. There is a gray area of overlap and it is difficult to differentiate one from the other based on current word usage and dictionary definitions. *Webster's Ninth New Collegiate Dictionary* (1983) defines religion as "the service and worship of God or the supernatural . . . commitment or devotion to religious faith or observance . . . a personal set or institutional system of religious attitudes, beliefs, and practices, scrupulous conformity, or a cause, principle, or system of beliefs held to with ardor and faith" (p. 995). The *American Heritage Dictionary* (1985) defines it as "belief in and reverence for a supernatural power recognized as the creator and governor of the universe" or "a particular integrated system of this expression" (p. 1045). The *Little Oxford Dictionary* (1986) defines religion as "belief in superhuman controlling power, especially in a personal God or gods entitled to obedience" (p. 460). The composite term *religious cult* seems more appropriate than *cult* or *religion* to describe the organizations and practices in this book.

The following comparison of traditional with cult religion is adapted from Schwartz and Kaslow (1982):

	Traditional Religions	Contemporary Cults
Charismatic leader		X
Submission to authority	X	X
Communal lifestyle		X
Isolation from family		X
Deceptive recruiting		X
Fear or hate outsiders		X
Strange beliefs	?	X
Outside mainstream society		X

SECTS

A *sect* is an organized, identified, distinctive subgroup within a larger organization or which has separated from it, based on certain deviations or refinements of belief or practice. Examples: Baptists, Presbyterians, Lutherans, and Methodists as Protestant sects. Islam has Sunni and Shiite sects, Buddhism has two major branches, Mahayana and Hinayana, and Judaism has Orthodox, Conservative and Reform branches. Cults that endure over many years and grow into nationwide or international organizations will very likely experience the same schisms as the major religions, reflecting a greater variety of beliefs and practices.

CONCLUSIONS

Cults offer a neatly packaged, self-contained *ideology* to believe in, indoctrinated systematically into cult members by a continual process of frequently repeated lectures, rituals, and group behavior and norms. Use of myth or superstition, magic or mysticism, abstract ideas and symbols, difficult to objectively prove or disprove, weaken critical judgment and increase suggestibility. "Hero worship" of a charismatic leader, coupled with submission to rigid discipline stifles free expression and personal autonomy and responsibility, increases dependency, and docile acceptance of the cult's strange and unorthodox beliefs and practices. A relatively flat drone-like cult personality gradually replaces previous identity, interrupting career or education, and interfering with normal personality development. Ties are broken with family, friends, and previous norms and values. In this "new world" it is more difficult for the individual to differentiate normal from abnormal, right from wrong, legal from illegal.

Constructive or "good" cults can be identified by their effect on the individual. They tend to emancipate and activate the person, enhance personality development, and help the individual realize the true self and strengthen it. "Hero worship" is role modelling, an effort at equalization, to emulate and not worship the leader. The personality becomes more active, not more passive. Constructive cults do not disrupt home, work, or school life or isolate the cult member from family but tend to improve these relationships. Cult values complement and do not conflict with accepted, established norms and standards of the community and nation. When isolated from mainstream society, they are more private than secret, not defensive, and openly share ideas with anyone interested in learning more about them with full informed consent.

Cults have existed throughout history and continue today. By their beliefs and practices they deviate from societal and majority values and norms. They vary widely in type, scope, and depth. Some maintain high ethical and moral standards and do nothing unlawful or harmful to their members or others. They present no threat to mental or physical health and are normal variants of traditional religions. Some are restrictive and subject their members to rigid discipline which stifles personal growth and optimal personality development. Extremist criminal Satanic cults continue primitive, pagan practices which can involve antisocial or violent unlawful illegal acts such as animal or human sacrifice, mutilation, and mental, physical, or sexual abuse.

It is difficult to differentiate some cults from religions, sects, secret societies, occult or mystic special interest groups. Only a detailed study of cult organization, beliefs, values, and practices can do so. Cults with high risk of harm share most of these characteristics: charismatic leader; monopoly on truth; exclusivity and isolation; deception or fraud; strange beliefs and practices; intrusive group activities; ideological commitment; emotional desensitization; debilitation; degradation; and loss of autonomy.

Chapter Two

CULTISTS: WHY ARE THEY?

> ...*acuter minds perceive how easy it is to*
> *dupe their weaker brother and to play on his*
> *superstition for their own advantage.*
> Sir James G. Frazer
> *The Golden Bough* (1940)

Who are these cultists with such strange beliefs? Why do they do such strange things? As police reports and court cases show, they can be your neighbors or coworkers, relatives or friends, perhaps in your own home. For reasons we will now examine, they "dupe their weaker brother and play on his superstition for their own advantage" (Frazer, 1940). To understand this exploitive need we must evaluate cult and ritual behavior in the context of the psychodynamics of personality, for that is where it functions.

SOCIOCULTURAL FACTORS

As we saw in the previous chapter, *cult* and *culture* were both derived from the same Latin root *cultus*. The study of cultural similarities and differences is the subject matter of cultural anthropology, and the following key concepts apply to cult and ritual behavior, taken from the 1978 textbook *Cultural Anthropology* by Joseph Aceves and H. Gill King:

Culture	Ideal culture
Enculturation	Real culture
Ideology	Personality
Western tradition	Deviant

Culture as an anthropological concept is defined as "the source of all the learned behavior of any human being" (Aceves & King, 1978, p. 24). *Enculturation* is the process of becoming "completed" or "socialized" within a given society and culture and includes both instinctive and learned behavior (p. 48). *Ideology* is a "set of ideas about the nature of

33

reality," sometimes biased by an individual's subjective philosophy (p. 25–26). *Western tradition* is an "interrelated set of ideas about human-kind" rooted in Greek, Roman, and Western European ideas "with some input from Arabic sources" (p. 16). *Ideal culture* "embodies ideals and values" of "what ought to go on in a society" and *real culture* is "what actually goes on" (p. 55). *Personality* is viewed by anthropologists as influenced by "the social and cultural reality in which we grow up, although each of us experiences our culture in a unique way" (p. 58). Individuals or groups which differ significantly and consistently from societal norms are *deviant.*

Applied to cult and ritual behavior, we can see that where and when you were born and what happens to you as a result are powerful forma-tive factors in shaping personality, the learnings, yearnings, and earn-ings of the self. Born into an extremist Satanic cult shapes and influences personality and behavior accordingly. Such a cult is a deviant subculture whose ideology not only differs from societal norms but is in conflict with them and attempts to subvert and reverse them. This type of cult functions more like a nomadic tribe than a subculture within the larger society. It has never accepted Western tradition or values. It is primitive, simplistic, and unsocialized in its philosophy and practices, and animistic and pagan in its religion and ritual, evidenced by animal and human sacrifice, mutilation, and physical and sexual abuse.

NAZISM: FROM CULT TO CHAOS

Three behavioral scientists, all skilled observers of human nature, reported on Hitlerism's rise from cult to national party and an interna-tional threat: Erich Fromm (1941), a Berlin psychologist, Joost Meerloo (1949; 1956), Dutch psychiatrist who escaped from a Nazi prison, and Victor Frankl (1963), Austrian psychiatrist and inmate at Auschwitz more than three years. These mental health experts provide us with valuable insights into negative aspects and the potential danger in the cult experience.

Erich Fromm described the mental state of the German people during World War II in his 1941 book *Escape from Freedom:* "Millions in Germany were as eager to surrender their freedom as their fathers were to fight for it" (p. 5). Freedom, he wrote, is ambiguous: *to be* free or to *escape from* freedom. He described a longing or wish for submission, overt or internalized, which complements and feeds into the leader's lust for power and "arouse and mobilize diabolical forces . . . we had believed to be nonexistent or at least to have died out long ago" (p. 7). These are products of the social process, learned, not instinctive, because "man's nature, his passions, and anxieties are a cultural product . . . new habits of adaptation" (pp. 12–15). Individual personality differences are due to "elasticity and malleability" which are "reactions to certain life conditions" (pp. 16–17).

Basic survival needs such as hunger, thirst, and sleep have a "certain threshold beyond which lack of satisfaction is unbearable" (p. 17). Also unbearable is the "horror of aloneness," personal or moral: "the basest kind of pattern is immensely preferable to being alone." Fromm wrote that "moral aloneness is the most terrible" and "religion and nationalism, as well as any custom and any belief however absurd and degrading, if it only connects the individual with others, are refuges from what man most dreads: isolation" (p. 20). People escape from freedom "to acquire the strength which the individual self is lacking . . . a more or less complete surrender of individuality and the integrity of the self . . . to fuse one's self with somebody or something outside of oneself" (pp. 140–141). The self is surrendered by the follower who "tries frantically to get rid of it and to feel security again by the elimination of this burden" (p. 152).

Fromm describes several factors which facilitate self surrender: feeling insignificant and helpless; mental or physical pain and suffering; feeling part of a larger whole; blind admiration for the leader; busyness or fatigue. "One gains a new pride in participation in the power in which one submerges" which is security against the "torture of doubt," of making decisions and personal responsibility, since "the meaning of life and identity of self are determined by the greater whole into which the self has submerged" (p. 156). Many followers are not consciously aware of their dependence. Some insulate themselves by withdrawing into automaton conformity, others into grandiose euphoria shrinking the outside world (p. 185). Both are steps toward mental illness, thought or mood disorders.

Fromm saw in the followers "masochistic strivings" of inferiority, powerlessness, and individual insignificance with marked dependence on "powers outside themselves, on other people, institutions, or nature" usually reframed by the leader as love or loyalty (pp. 142–143). The leader is plagued with the same needs and drives channelled into pursuing more power and driven by three "sadistic tendencies":

1. *Power,* absolute and unrestricted power over those who are kept totally dependent
2. *Exploit* followers, to use and defraud them in a consuming way, mentally and materially
3. *Abuse* followers or others, to see them suffer mentally and physically

Fromm contended the reason for sadistic drives is not to inflict pain but complete mastery and dominance since there is "no greater power over another person than that of inflicting pain" (p. 157). The leader needs followers "very badly since his own feeling of strength is rooted in the fact he is master over someone." Leader and follower have a "symbiotic relationship," a mutual dependence to get what they want using each other, neither able to stand alone. This give-to-get interdependence can be exciting. Freud theorized that this is because dominance-submission amalgamates the sexual (eros libido) with the death-wish (thanatos libido).

Fromm claimed there are sadomasochistic tendencies in everyone. We are all vulnerable to "authoritarian characters," those with a basic psychopathic pattern who cannot adapt to and defy higher authority. They are opportunists and manipulators. The end always justifies the means and "love, duty, conscience, patriotism have been used as disguises to destroy others or oneself" (p. 180). Enemies are charged with what the leader himself seeks (projection). People are seen as either powerful or powerless, to be used or abused (narcissism, sadism). There is no higher power except that the leader strives to achieve and so "it leads to nihilism, to the denial of life . . . and always succeed in finding some object" (p. 173, 180). There is always a threat to power from the outside (paranoia). To suffer without complaining is of high value as is not trying to lessen or eliminate it (masochism). Destructiveness is a "kill or be killed" attempt to prevent being destroyed by society (psychopathy, sociopathy). This is, of course, a reality for extremist cults that injure, kill and commit other crimes.

Fromm speculated that followership may involve a form of hypnosis. This may occur when there are "thoughts, feelings, wishes, and even sensual sensations we subjectively feel to be ours . . . put into us from the outside, but are basically alien" (p. 189). This hypnotic-like process can begin with some agreement of conviction or sharing similar feelings such as frustration, envy, fear, guilt, or hate. This initial fellow feeling opens the follower to the leader's increasing manipulation, indirectly through cult members or directly by the leader. In time, the deceptively distorted material is swallowed, integrated into behavior and ultimately the personality as a "pseudo character" which differs from the real or genuine self. This results in feelings of intense insecurity, relieved by increased conformity to the leader and cult, a tragic vicious circle that spirals downward into personality disintegration. This is the basic underlying mechanism of the so-called Stockholm syndrome (Harnischnacker & Muther, 1987). Pseudo characters give canned answers and believe them to be original and personal. Responses may seem rational and logical but are copies, not genuine. The mind has been raped. In cults, it is a repeated attack.

Joost Meerloo was a psychiatrist who escaped from a Nazi prison, became Chief of Psychological services for Free Netherlands, and later joined the faculty of Columbia University. A victim of a mass cult and a trained, experienced mental health professional, his observations and insights are especially useful. His book, *Delusion and Mass Delusion* (1949), begins with Meerloo's own poem, which aptly describes criminal cult and ritual behavior:

> To be a part of human tragedy,
> To know all things so very well,
> But still to act against all intellect.

In his book, Meerloo described deception as the first step in the process of deluding by "politically inspired fictions. . . . mental tricks easily substituted for logic and . . . most compatible with our own desires" (p. 6). These become a "self-satisfying pseudo-philosophy" to us which we then "hide behind." To "move the masses" the leader uses "such vague terms whose real significance defies definition," This "word magic" is ambiguous to vent a broad cross section of hearers and has "great cathartic value" (p. 31). Ancient Greek morality plays are an example of how the audience can be emotionally stirred. Hollywood's movie romanticization of gangsters is an example of reframing opinion, most notably those with Humphrey Bogart, James Cagney, George Raft, and John Garfield.

The most sinister aspect of creating delusion is by use of "primitive thought" which Meerloo defines as "false figurative language that dims our thinking" (p. 26) and is "bent to the dictatorship of sensual impulses; it does not think but acts in shortcuts" (p. 44). It can "overcome or narcoticize by a flood of suggestive pictures and allegories" (p. 24). In the Middle Ages, this technique resulted in uncontrolled emotionality . . .

mourners were paralyzed by sorrow for weeks . . . collective hallucinations . . . not subject to debate or correction and generally insensitive to experience" (p. 23). This can become *autistic* thinking, where "escape into fantasy and dream life violates all contact with reality," a lack of personal identity and identification with others, inwardly directed, full of impulses and fictions (p. 44). "Fantasy," Meerloo commented, "is the greatest enemy of the intellect" (p. 37).

Many prefer the "childish dreamland of ignorance" to avoid the responsibility for wrong knowledge and actions. "We learn to select from superfluous wisdom" (p. 36). Like cult practices today, the Nazis used "diabolic dialectic and ceaseless rationalization" and "imagination and myth" which are "often stronger than truth . . . archaic images are forever regaining possession of reality." Gradually, people lose themselves to avoid facing problems of their own and become "pseudo philosophers." Mental imagery can have a "dictatorial role" and "create such chaos of impression that logic can no longer find its way." Meerloo warned we have become hypersensitive to suggestion, "grateful to anyone who takes us in hand and clears our path through the chaos of our thoughts and images" (p. 87).

He suspected that deluding people may involve a form of hypnosis. "Some gruesome tale" gets the attention and begins with a basis of truth, then elicits regressive feelings of unfairness or injustice, isolates critical judgment, involves archaic instinctual forms of thinking, error gradually replaces reality "to such an extent it is impervious . . . incorrigible ideas for which many normal men are willing to die" (p. 18). Fascinating catchwords, penetrating formulas, unconscious longings, rhythmic sound and motion, fixation on a symbol, are "seductive and fascinating and deeply moving" (p. 85). "Repeat again and again your simple motto and the many half-sleeping beings follow you passively" (p. 83). Once established, the delusion "perseveres as an impenetrable mental armor" (p. 4), with a selective stupidity, regressing to the "innocence of childhood" (p. 38).

Meerloo concluded that we are "constantly swayed" and that "it is impossible to evade the suggestive pressures of the world around us" (p. 3). He recommended two preventive practices: first, we must confront, criticize, and correct our thinking continually (p. 28); second, we have to "give up the dogma of identical thinking in all human minds" (p. 21).

Psychiatrist Robert Lifton (1983) studied Chinese communist "thought reform" used in the 1940s through the Korean War, a system he described as "totalism." He credited journalist Edward Hunton with introducing the now widely used term "brainwashing" from the Chinese *hsi nao* which translates "washed brain." He found "isolation" to be the central feature of Chinese thought reform. Prospective converts were isolated emotionally, culturally, and ideologically, as well as being separated physically from the community. Denied freedom of choice in daily activities, unable to express their individuality, group living and the group process became a powerful force acting on the individual day and night, shaping a collective consciousness, the agent of thought reform and "conveyor of its message" (p. 152). He described contributing factors which facilitated thought reform, such as a relative lack of firm commitment to a philosophy of government or life, feelings of purposelessness, confusion, or dissatisfaction. Many students and younger converts initially had an attitude of "social nihilism... iconoclastic criticism of existing cultural forms, and an urge for direct and absolute experience" (p. 470).

Lifton discovered that educated people such as missionaries and scholars were converted in time to Chinese communist philosophy and principles. He reported that this process is reversible through reliving the experience, sharing it with others individually and in groups, and by writing about it, which he described as "disengagement" and "declaring the identity shift." The dynamics are similar to Freud's *anamnesis*, going back to traumatic experiences, and *abreaction*, reliving them. He reported separation anxiety after repatriation, a sense of loss despite the realization that the experience was negative, similar to the *survival guilt* of combat veterans and war refugees. Anxiety and stress was experienced from decisionmaking and exercising personal responsibility after the structure and controls of "totalism." Rehabilitation becomes a renewed struggle of identity over ideology (p. 223).

He contended that there is a universal "craving" or "search" for "new modes of existence" is "part of the broad human consciousness" and can "blind the scientific, political, artistic, and spiritual." It can swing positively or negatively and can be "a viable alternative to totalism" (p. 471). He was optimistic and positive about the future despite attempts at totalism and thought reform. He based this conviction on the similar needs of youth throughout the world, for privacy, personal freedom, and self-expression, readily observed in their individualism and nonconformity in art, music, literature, and "patterns of nihilism." He believed future "alternate visions" would "in part depend upon a more accurate perception of current human transformations . . . all aspects of human life" and "continuity with one's personal past." This confident optimism was not shared by other observers of harmful group process such as Freud, Fromm, Meerloo, Frankl, Hoffer, Riesman, Goffman, Packard and Shostrom. He concluded we should expend "more conscious effort to preserve specific elements within our heritage" even when they are in "a process of being altered." He urged us to "learn to live with a good deal of conflict, confusion, and ferment" (p. 471). He saw "danger" in our "tendency to symbolize the universe within a suffocating circle of hatred" but that we have the ability, imagination, ingenuity, and "physical and emotional resiliency" to break out of that circle, especially when we perceive our existence as most threatened (p. 472).

In his 1963 book, *Man's Search for Meaning*, Victor Frankl described his observations and impressions as an inmate at Auschwitz concentration camp for more than three years. Despite his own near-death experience there, and the loss of his entire family except for his sister, he arrived at a nonviolent philosophic overview: "We have come to know man as he really is . . . that being who invented the gas chambers . . . also that being who entered the gas chambers upright, with the Lord's Prayer or the Shema Yisrael on his lips" (p. 214). He saw the same duality among inmates, some "behaved like swine . . . others behaved like saints." Which is realized "depends on decisions not on conditions" (p. 213). He disagreed with both Freudian instinct and behavioristic learning and conditioning as the basis for human nature: "Man is not fully conditioned and determined," Frankl wrote, "he determines himself, whether to give in to conditions or stand up to them . . . is ultimately self determining . . . does not simply exist but always decides what existence will be, what he will become in the next moment . . . free to change at any instant" (p. 207). Despite severe restrictions and deprivation, "the last of human freedoms is to choose one's attitude in any given set of circumstances, to choose one's way" (p. 104).

Frankl's description of personality change in the camps is similar to that described in cults: "No instinct tells him what he has to do, no tradition what he ought to do; soon he will not know what he wants to do. More and more he will be governed by what others want him to do thus increasingly falling prey to conformism" (p. 168). Also true of long-term or severely stressed cult victims: "Only slowly could these men be guided back to the commonplace truth that no one has the right to do wrong, not even if wrong has been done to him" (p. 144). Even undergoing senseless suffering, Frankl felt "what matters above all . . . is the attitude we take on suffering upon ourselves" (p. 178). He quoted Nietzsche: "He who has a why to live for can bear almost any how." In Auschwitz, Frankl wrote, "we fancied ourselves to be something but were treated like complete nonentities." What sustained them was "inner value anchored in higher, more spiritual things" and a sense of humor which "more than anything else . . . can afford an aloofness and an ability to rise above any situation even if only for a few seconds" (p. 68).

Logotherapy is Frankl's contribution to psychotherapy. It is a future-oriented existential analysis of will-to-meaning, the search for the hidden *logos* or meaning of one's existence, and to fulfill that meaning. The basic motivation is actualizing values and not "mere gratification and satisfaction of drives and instincts . . . or mere adaptation and adjustment to society and environment" (p. 163). Mental health is based on a balance with a "certain degree of tension" between what has been achieved and that to be achieved, "the gap between what we are and what we should become" (p. 166). We therefore don't need "a tensionless state" but striving toward "some worthy goal." The despair we sometimes feel over the meaninglessness of life is "spiritual distress" and not a mental disease (p. 163).

After World War II there was considerable media coverage of "the Nazi mind," a search for some explanation for the cruel excesses of Hitler and his followers. Personality testing was done on eight Nazi war criminals at Spandau prison. Early grouped data suggested Nazis were different. In 1946, Kelley reviewed the data and concluded Nazi personalities were "not unique and not insane and could be duplicated in any country of the world today" (p. 47). Thirty years later, in 1978, Ritzler agreed but suggested they may have been opportunistic "successful psychopaths." In 1989, Zillmer, Archer, and Castino reevaluated the original test data using current more sophisticated scoring criteria and two separate computer programs. They found evidence of a variety of significant personality problems in seven of the eight Nazi leaders, possible thought disorders in four, and poor impulse control in two. "Although Nuremberg revealed to the world the terrible crimes committed by Hitler's followers, the use of any overall descriptors to attempt to summarize the personality functioning of this group appears unjustified" (p. 98). Was there a Nazi mind? No, just a variety of largely negative and destructive personalities sharing in a common cause. Every society has its share of such personalities, and while Nazism occurred in Germany, no nation is immune to such extremist movements.

THE LONELY CROWD

David Riesman's book, *The Lonely Crowd,* was published in 1950. In it, he defined *social character* as "patterned uniformities of learned responses" which were "deployed in work, play, politics, and childbearing activities" (p. v) "more or less permanent, socially and historically conditioned organizations of drives and satisfactions" (p. 14). Riesman's social character is less inclusive than personality which is the total self, biological and physical, and which we will explore further later in this chapter. His central theme is the *inner-directed* and the *other-directed* person. Earlier generations lived in the same home, neighborhood, or city, worked at similar occupations and for the same firm, attended the same church and married an ethnic peer, just as their parents before them. Most of these activities were internal to the family unit and fostered a basically introverted, *inner-directed* character. These character types had a strong, deep, clear stay-put, rock-solid self concept.

After World War II, the middle class population became more mobile, moving wherever opportunity called. Young people intermarried racially, ethnically, and religiously and chose careers not even available to the previous generations, such as computers, television, and airlines. This required more contact with and approval of others, a more extroverted *other-directed* character. The result has a greater need to feel acceptance and belonging to substitute for the close, small-town feeling of childhood. Other-directed people are generally less certain of political, religious, or moral convictions, friendlier on the surface but actually more shallow socially, are less grounded in themselves and so less stable. They have "no clear core of self to escape from" (p. 169).

Cult leaders are skilled at seeming to fill the empty core of other-directed people. Doing so is more emotional than cognitive, more into feelings than thoughts. They are what Riesman described as "mood leaders, in the position of an actor, looking for response from an audience." They have taken us "from morality to morale" (p. 265). He attributed this to the effect of group dynamics, personal growth, and encounter groups. If Riesman were here today, he might observe that cults have taken us another step, from showman to shaman. Placed in the context of society, culture, and Western tradition, it is a step backward, to primitivism, ignorance, and violence. Since Riesman's 1950 book there have been two wars (Korea, Vietnam), jet airliners replaced propeller planes and fly higher and faster, the interstate highway system for faster more direct road travel, fast food restaurants so we can eat more quickly, computers to help us think faster, and TV to see news as it happens worldwide. In this great rush we do most things with less depth and care. We are too hurried (and harried) to stop to ask questions with insufficient time to reflect and construct incisive questions. Critical judgment is relaxed, suggestibility increases along with susceptibility to a leader who matches St. Augustine's description of a devil's strengths, listed in Chapter 1. These are also the ingredients for susceptibility to hypnosis (MacHovec 1975).

Riesman observed that "utopian political thinking may be hidden and constantly changing, constantly disguising themselves" (p. 372). He felt that "the crisis mood of the press" lessened public interest in politics, but hoped this would nurture "newly critical and creative standards." Riesman could not know the impact of TV, street drugs, the disillusionment of two wars without decisive victories which cost many lives, scandals in government and religion, and great changes in world trade and the job market. These developments do not appear to have raised critical and creative standards and in fact may have weakened them. He ended his book with the conclusion that the idea people are created free and equal is "both true and misleading." They are "created different" and lose "social freedom and their individual autonomy in seeking to become like each other" (p. 373). Like Fromm, Riesman also acknowledged the deep and powerful need to conform, to fit, to belong somewhere to someone. The cult is a ready-made quick fix, instant spiritual food, a mental Band Aid® that relieves pain temporarily but then continues to stick on—hard.

THE PASSIONATE MIND

Eric Hoffer contended in his 1955 book *The Passionate State of Mind* that "self deception, credulity, and charlatanism are related" (p. 52). He saw pride as a powerful motivator that weakens critical judgment. "Give people pride," he wrote, "and they'll live on bread and water, bless their exploiters, and even die for them" (p. 29). Hoffer described the exploitive process as largely verbal word magic by a clever, skillful, communicator who "turns thin air into absolute truths . . . self-contempt into pride, lack of confidence into faith . . . guilt into self-righteousness" (p. 34). Being subjected to such persuasion is "to attach people to words . . . detach them from life and possessions and ready them for reckless acts of metaphysical doubletalk" (p. 44).

Hoffer observed that when people believe they are the sole possessors of truth they are "likely to be indifferent to common everyday truths" (p. 52). For this reason cult members see no need to continue the everyday pursuits of career or education, family relations, or contacts with friends. It is a "flight from self which invariably turns into a rush for a compact group" (p. 34). This indoctrination process "insulates the deviant against reality and against their own selves" by words wedged between consciousness and self (p. 46). The cult becomes the total world in a quest to transform the world into the cult just as the cult became their world. As for the potential for harm in such gross distortion of reality, Hoffer cautioned that "there is no telling how deeply a mind may be affected by the deliberate staging of gestures, acts, and symbols" (p. 112).

CULTS AS ASYLUM

In his 1961 book, *Asylums*, Canadian sociologist Erwin Goffman described the effect of living in a *total institution* which he defined as "a place of residence and work where a large number of like-situated individuals, cut off from the wider society for an appreciable period of time, together lead an enclosed, formally administered round of life" (p. xiii). Goffman listed five types of total institutions: residential treatment facilities such as hospitals; special settings such as for the blind, aged, or orphaned; protective environments such as prisons and POW camps; worklike task settings such as schools and work camps; and "retreats from the world . . . often serving as training stations for the religious" (p. 5). This latter type most closely resembles cult organizations.

Goffman pointed out that none of the elements or characteristics he described are "peculiar to total institutions" nor are they present in all of them, but each "exhibits to an intense degree" many of the same features (ibid). By sharing time and common interests, total institutions provide "something of a world . . . with encompassing tendencies." *Encompassing* is a function of the "barrier to social intercourse with the outside" (p. 4). There are four characteristics of total institutions:

1. Same setting and authority for work, play, and sleep.
2. Shared daily activities

3. Tight schedule, highly structured
4. "Enforced activities: in a "single rational plan" to fulfill "official aims.""

If there is too little structure and therefore more available free time, boredom results. If there is too much activity with little or no free time, the result is demoralization and "mortification." There is always some degree of disparity between total institutions and societal values such as work-for-pay and career development, family loyalty, formal education, and the individual's own personal development. Total institutions "disrupt or defile" by denying a person's "command over his world, adult self-determination, autonomy and freedom of action, and failure to retain adult executive competency" (p. 43). Expressive behavior which is further evidence of autonomy is discouraged and weakened. *Looping* is a method of social and behavioral control in which defensive reactions are targeted, isolated, and inhibited to establish and reinforce conformity. Examples of defensive reactions: humor, individual thinking, verbal and nonverbal behaviors. Similar place, peers, diet, or costume, sharing the same rituals, "institutional lingo," and other group norms, with little privacy or individual decisionmaking, all reinforce conformity, "an enveloping tissue of constraint," what Goffman termed *regimentation* (p. 36).

In time, total institutions effect cultural change on the individual, a process Goffman called *disculturation,* defined as "untraining" which renders one "temporarily incapable of managing certain features of daily life on the outside" (p. 13). It also can produce "shifts in moral career," progressive changes in basic beliefs about the self and others (p. 14). Anyone who voluntarily joins an institution has "already partially withdrawn from his home world" (p. 15). Some roles can in time be reestablished but "other losses are irrevocable and may be painfully experienced as such." Some losses "may not be possible to make up, at a later phase of the lifecycle, the time not now spent in educational or job advancement, in courting, or in rearing children" (ibid). Individuals "sick with his world or guilt-ridden" may be relieved by joining the institution (p. 48). Some experience *colonization,* what I term *nesting,* where they enjoy or delude themselves into enjoying the security and satisfaction of the institution (p. 62). Some experience *conversion,* assuming a role and identity according to the institution's ideals (p. 63).

SOCIAL PSYCHOLOGY

Social psychologists have contributed several useful models to explain an individual's behavior in groups directly relevant to cults. *Stimulus response theory* (Kimble, 1961; Skinner & Bem, 1970) described how rewarded behavior continues and becomes conditioned in the individual. Dollard and Miller (1950) saw *imitation* and imitative behaviors as reinforcing, in time integrated into the personality. Bandura and Walters (1963) considered individual conformity to group norms as a function of *social learning.* Kurt Lewin's *Field theory* (1951) views present behaviors in the context of current situations, the immediately operative "field." Freud's *psychoanalysis,* on the other hand, is largely historical, tracing current behaviors back to antecedent events and the effect of instinct. *Behaviorism* (Skinner, 1953) focusses on contingencies and consequences of behavior as reinforcers for subsequent behaviors.

Gestalt theory (Asch, 1946) sees perception as a complex of previous conditioning and the brain interpreting what is happening, the result often exceeding the sum of factors and stimuli. *Attribution theory* (Kelley, 1967) describes how negative information from sources considered negative is rejected, such as cult members dismissing parents' expressed concern about them. *Balance theory* (Heider, 1958) sees social interaction as the individual's attempt to achieve balance and stability. *Cognitive dissonance theory* (Festinger, 1957) contends that holding two opposing beliefs or cognitions motivates the person to relieve the conflict (dissonance), usually by choosing and defending what is seen as more positive, regardless of evidence to the contrary. Thus, many cult members hold tenaciously to unfounded beliefs and strange practices. *Social exchange theory* (Kelley, 1961) sees social interaction as positive reinforcement from a mutual exchange of rewards.

MANIPULATORS AND ACTUALIZORS

Everett Shostrom commented in his 1967 book *Man, the Manipulator* that "modern man is a used car salesman talking us into an automobile we wouldn't otherwise buy" (p. 13). That description matches cult recruiters as described by former cult members. Fritz Perls, founder of Gestalt therapy, wrote in his introduction to Shostrom's book that life, for many of us is "boring, empty, and meaningless . . . caught in the web of our own manipulations." He described it as a "continuum of deadness to aliveness . . . from self-defeating to self-fulfilling potentials" (pp. 7–9).

Using Perls' polarity principle, a concept taken from ancient Chinese Taoism, Shostrom postulated two contrasting behavioral styles: *manipulators* and *actualizors*. Manipulators are those who exploit, use, and strive to control themselves and others as things or objects in self-defeating ways. Actualizors are the opposite, "expressors of the actual self" and "a rare bird in pure form," who appreciates self and others as persons with "unique potential." We are all part manipulator and part actualizor somewhere along a continuum between these two poles, another Zen concept. As manipulators, we use "phoney tricks" learned "from cradle to grave to conceal the actual vital nature of ourselves" and in doing so reduce ourselves into things or objects to be controlled (p. 14).

According to Shostrom, a manipulator "habitually conceals and camouflages" thoughts and feelings behind a "repertoire of behavior . . . from arrogant hostility to servile flattery in his continuous campaign to serve his own wishes . . . an anxious automaton refusing to take responsibility for failures and constantly blaming someone or something else" (p. 14–16). He saw *power* as the major motivation for *active manipulators*, complete and total power which transforms people into things by "capitalizing on their powerlessness . . . gaining gratification by exercising gratuitous control over them." They usually have some "top dog" status or rank which facilitates control. Victims are *passive manipulators* by allowing themselves to be transformed into things or objects. Manipulation, he concluded, is a "style of life," a recurrent pattern, much like Eric Berne's TA concept of a *life script* (pp. 41–42).

Shostrom attributed his concept of *actualizors* to the self-actualizing person described by Abraham Maslow, who estimated that only 1 percent of people had a life "enriched" by using all their potential. Manipulators use an "ocean of words," live in a busy word world which does not allow them to experience or enjoy life. Here is a table adapted from Shostrom's comparison of major factors of this polar principle (pp. 50–51) which he saw as a continuum from "deadness and deliberateness to aliveness and spontaneity."

Manipulators	*Actualizors*
DECEPTION (phoniness)	HONESTY (authenticity)
Tricks, techniques, an act or role play, to fit the situation, to get attention and impress	To be and to become, to express and articulate the authentic, real, genuine self

UNAWARE (irrelevant)
"Not with it," not aware of the "big picture," of what's really important; sees what they want to see

AWARE (relevant)
"With it," aware, tuned in, to nature, art, music, and full di— mension of life and self

CONTROL (overcontrol)
People chess, to control, use and abuse

FREEDOM (spontaneous)
Open to new experiences and learnings to grow

CYNICISM (distrust)
Basic distrust of self and others

TRUST (faith and hope)
Basic trust of self and others

Shostrom agreed with the view of Carl Jung that the first half of life is involved with achievement, in school, work, personal and social relation-ships, marriage and family, the second half "when the inner self develops." If it doesn't, "the individual will slowly get sick, for the rules of the afternoon of life are not those for the morning of life" (p. 52). He saw *manipulative religion* as that which fosters distrust of our own nature, an impediment to achievement and self-actualization since it keeps its mem-bers "more like a helpless child who constantly needs the external help of ministers and priests." *Actualized religion* is more internal and fosters "self-direction and self-growth" (p. 112).

There are four key concepts in Shostrom's formulation which serve to protect the self against manipulation: *awareness, uniqueness, contact,* and *freedom:*

Awareness. Shostrom considered his most important idea to be that we need not be manipulators or hopeless victims of manipulators (p. 101). Awareness decreases manipulation and increases actualization. He agreed with the Gestalt therapy concept of "the continuum of awareness," a focus on the obvious, what is experienced moment to moment in three dimensions: here vs. there; now vs. then or the future; feelings vs. sensing-thinking. Shostrom's awareness is "a form or nonstriving," being who and what you are at the moment, even in a temporary phoney manipulative behavior. It is possible to "critically experience" manipula-tive roles because of their obvious self-defeating quality. From them you can see more clearly "complimentary actualizing behaviors." This is an ancient Taoist teaching, to know beauty one must know ugliness (MacHovec, 1962). He concluded that awareness of the "futility of manipu-lative strivings leads naturally to the centered power of self esteem" (p. 103). He recommended patients be asked to role play "the wise therapist" to facilitate awareness.

Uniqueness. Shostrom credited Martin Buber (1951) with inspiring the actualizor aspect of personality. In his 1951 book *The Way of Man*, Buber wrote: "Every person born into this world represents something new, something that never existed before, something original and unique." Everyone is "a new thing in the world," he wrote, "and is called upon to fulfill his particularity . . . actualization of his unique, unprecedented and ever recurring potentialities and not the repetition of something . . . already achieved" (p. 16). Shostrom saw self-actualization as an "exciting pursuit of perfection . . . joy that comes from interpretation of both strength and weakness, to freely skate between all potentials" (p. 58).

Contact. When two or more people share in the actualization process, it is "core to core," on the "inner range of potentials . . . one's real, authentic, actualizing self." This requires "sufficient security and openness to contact one another deeply . . . liking plus openness plus contact." Shostrom commented that such intimate sharing is "rare and difficult to establish" but that without one or two "meaningful contact relationships," self actualization is not possible. Manipulators cannot do so because core-to-core contact risks exposure. They choose control over contact, evaluating over receptive listening, persuasion over appreciation (pp. 61–65).

Freedom. Shostrom emphasizes the need for freedom, to think and to grow, which he sees as "the capacity to make a choice, to choose between alternatives." Doing so ensures the person is "a subject and not a puppet or an object." Actualizors may "play the game of life" but are aware of it and play it "tongue in cheek." They know life is more a dance than a win-lose game, and they dance with all their "complimentary potentials . . . enjoying the process." He agreed with Karen Horney's description of *Appolonian tendencies* toward "mastery and molding of life" with freedom, and *Dionysian tendencies* toward "surrender and drift" without freedom (pp. 97–98).

Shostrom expanded Perls' *top dog—underdog* polarity concept (pp. 37 and 55). He defined top dog as "the active, energetic, authoritative part of the self and underdog as the passive, compliant, submissive side." The quality of leadership and followership are important variables and are positive or negative factors and influences in cult organizations.

Shostrom's Top Dog—Underdog Polarities

Valence	Top dog	TO	Underdog
+	DICTATOR (strength)		WEAKLING (sensitivity)
−	LEADER (Winston Churchill)		EMPATHIZER (Eleanor Roosevelt)
+	CALCULATOR (control)		CLINGING VINE (dependency)
−	RESPECTOR (Gandhi)		APPRECIATOR (Pope John 23rd)
+	BULLY (aggression)		NICE GUY (warmth)
−	ASSERTOR (Lincoln)		CARER (Albert Schweitzer)
+	JUDGE (critical)		PROTECTOR (supportive)
−	EXPRESSOR (Jefferson)		GUIDE (Buddha)

MEDIA MANIPULATION

In his 1957 bestseller *Hidden Persuaders,* Vance Packard detailed the growth of *motivational research* or MR, a "depth approach" to market research which began after World War II. What he observed in media manipulation has occurred also in the deceptive practices of many cults. He reported a 1950 article in the *Journal of Marketing* in which James Vicary suggested applying "psychiatric methods" to market research since human behavior is not always logical or rational. He described how Ernest Dichter, "Mr. Mass Motivation," urged ad agencies to realize they were "one of the most advanced laboratories in psychology" which can manipulate "motivations and desires" (pp. 27 and 31). Packard credited the definition of motivational research or MR to Louis Cheskin, a Chicago market research executive: "What motivates people in making choices" using "techniques to reach the unconscious or subconscious mind" since most people make choices by "factors of which they are unaware" (p. 7).

Packard observed that advertising and promotion involve probing for "points of vulnerability in subsurface desires, needs, and drives" such as the "drive to conformity" and "yearning for security." Once these are identified "psychological hooks" are "fashioned and baited and placed deep in the merchandising sea for unwary prospective customers" (p. 37). He listed *eight hidden needs* targeted by market researchers: emotional security, reassurance of self-worth, ego gratification, power, love, roots, creative outlet, and immortality (pp. 72–83). There are other aspects which help access these needs, such as symbolization, status or image, and pursuing pleasure and avoiding pain. The effect is *in* and *back*, into sensual or sexual experiencing and infantile needs satisfaction (regression).

In the thirty years since his book was published, media manipulation has evolved into attention-getting quick, deep thrusts, because attention span is diminishing and senses are increasingly overloaded. Politicians and televangelists have joined major corporations in using TV time and clever ads and direct mail, implemented by expert consultants. Elections have become media events and verbal combat between media manipulators. War and crime scenes are seen nightly on TV in living rooms nationwide. Videotape movie rentals bring theatre into homes. We are surrounded by, immersed in, an audiovisual sea of stimuli loaded with manipulation and suggestion. Planned obsolescence is a loss of "proportion in living" because we are "so quickly dissatisfied with last year's models," according to Packard. Do today's cults seek to replace old model religion with a new import? Close scrutiny shows cults are old wine in new bottles, but deceptive recruiting clouds critical judgment. Are cults "fast food religion," a philosophical quick fix of shallow, oversimplified ideals, like the promise of TV commercials?

Packard questioned the morality of "playing upon hidden weaknesses and frailties . . . on secret desires for self-enhancement . . . manipulating small children" (p. 288). He quoted Kleber Miller in the June, 1954 *Public Relations Journal* who asked "what degree of intensity is proper in seeking to arouse desire, hatred, envy, cupidity, hope, or any of the great human emotions . . . the right to manipulate human personality." Packard concluded that these practices show "disrespect for the individual personality" (p. 259). He ended his book with optimism: "We still have a strong defense . . . we can choose not to be persuaded" (p. 265). We can't be manipulated if we are aware of the process. We need a *recognition reflex* to prevent the "petty trickery of small-time persuaders" or "powerful leaders." We must also understand ourselves and see that some of our thoughts and feelings are not rational. "It's easier to be nonlogical," Packard wrote, "but I prefer being nonlogical by my own free will and impulse." His final advice to us: "Depth manipulators invade the privacy of our minds . . . which we must strive to protect" (p. 266).

PSYCHOSOCIAL DEVELOPMENT

Life Stages

In his 1950 book *Childhood and Society*, psychoanalyst Erik Erikson described eight *life stages* which everyone passes through sequentially. At each stage the individual proceeds with one of two kinds of coping strategies, each influencing psychosocial development. Vulnerability to cult recruitment is increased if there has been significant problems in psychosocial development. Cult leaders and avid cult members are likely to have had more negative than positive life experiences across these life stages.

STAGE 1: Basic trust or mistrust
> Babies are totally dependent on others to feed and clothe them and to keep them warm, dry, and safe. If these needs are not optimally satisfied, the baby develops a basic mistrust of others.

STAGE 2: Autonomy or shame and doubt
> Toilet training and other forms of self-control mark this stage. We learn when to "let it go" and when to "hold it in." Failure results in shame and self-doubt. Mastery leads to increased self-confidence and a sense of autonomy.

STAGE 3: Initiate or guilt
> This is the stage of exploration and experimenting, of curiosity and experiencing. Critical, punitive, overcontrolling or overprotective parents can cause guilt in the child.

STAGE 4: Industry or inferiority
> Erector or Mechano sets, doll houses, and endless scrawly sketches and coloring books reflect industry and feelings of adequacy and competence. Frustration at this stage engenders feelings of inferiority.

STAGE 5: Identity or role confusion
> If all goes relatively well during the previous stages, a clear perception of self or self-identity is formed. If on balance, life experience has been negative, there is likely to be confused identity and role, an unclear self-concept.

STAGE 6: Intimacy or isolation
> Feeling good about one's self opens the personality to a sharing emotional relationship, intimacy. Thwarted, the individual is likely to withdraw, isolated and alienated from others.

STAGE 7: Generativity or stagnation
> Doing something positive with yourself and others is the major feature of this stage, reflected in school, sports, church, clubs, hobbies,

or making a home and raising children. The reverse is to give up, drop out or burn out, and stagnate.

STAGE 8: Ego integrity or despair
This final stage is one of self-realization and self-actualization, fulfillment, becoming a whole person, being real, genuine, accepting self and others. This stage is learned and earned. You can't get here without insight, wisdom, balance, and usually some humor. The reverse: depression, despair or unresolved anger, resentment, shame or guilt.

Need Levels

The psychologist Abraham H. Maslow described psychosocial development in terms of *need satisfaction,* in an ascending hierarchy from basic survival to self-actualization. For our purposes they are arranged as follows:

NEED LEVEL 1: Physiological needs
These are basic survival needs such as food, water, air, warmth, shelter, clothing.

NEED LEVEL 2: Security
This is the need to be reasonably safe and cared for, free from external danger, sudden shock (or noise), falling, bumps, and scrapes. The child psychiatrist, Leo M. Kanner, taught his students the biggest task of parents the first five years is simply to keep the child alive.

NEED LEVEL 3: Emotional support
This is the "apronstrings" dependency stage, where there's someone to be with, to give permission to "do your thing," tuck you in at night or wipe your nose.

NEED LEVEL 4: Approval
Very strong in teen years, this is the need for acceptance and belonging, approval and fellow feeling, satisfied by career, clubs, church, participative sports, or hobbies, and negatively by fads, cliques, gangs, or cults. Erich Fromm considered this a very powerful need.

NEED LEVEL 5: Self-actualization
Fulfillment, realizing one's potential and real self, to become, reflected in completing education or training, successful job search or promotion, or buying clothes, a new car, home, or furniture that's "the real you," simply rearranging furniture or redecorating rooms, or being awarded the Nobel Prize!

Neurotic Needs

Karen Horney, psychiatrist-psychoanalyst, described ten *neurotic needs* which relate to the cult experience:

1. *Excess affection or approval.* Never satisfied or content.
2. *Someone to take over.* Escaping personal responsibility.
3. *Narrow limits.* Structure with low standards.
4. *Power.* Anything goes, the end justifies means.
5. *Prestige.* Status is indirect power over others.
6. *Exploit others.* Use and abuse everyone and everything.
7. *Personal admiration.* Narcissistic, ego trip, waiting to be discovered, for fame and fortune.
8. *Achievement.* Workaholic overachieving.
9. *Self-sufficiency.* Unable to settle down, frequent moves and job changes, no deep emotional ties.
10. *Perfection.* To be perfect is to be invulnerable.

Four Faces of Self

Horney also described individual psychosocial development in terms of four concurrent or coexisting selves:

> REPUTATIONAL SELF, the self others see in you;
> IDEALIZED SELF, the self you aspire to be;
> PERSONAL SELF, the self you think you are;
> REAL SELF, the actual reality of who you are.

Major Psychosocial Factors

Cult participation can satisfy needs for safety and security in an organization bigger than self, the emotional support and approval of others who share in the fellow feeling of the cult, and the prepackaged pseudocharacter or pseudo-identity described by Fromm and Meerloo earlier in this chapter. They meet most neurotic needs as well. Social, cultural, psychological, genetic, and environmental factors are all combined in the body and mind, the total personality or self. If these are predominantly negative, the individual is more likely to be vulnerable to cult involvement. Here is a summary of major psychosocial factors which provide an instant cross-section or physical-mental snapshot of personality and an initial impression of overall character strength:

Birth (DNA and gene pool; birth complications)
Age (generation, credibility, communications gaps)

Race (minority or majority; problems)
Sex and *appearance* (hypersensitivity; inferiority)
Infancy and *early childhood* (accidents; abuse; illnesses)
National, regional, ethnic, cultural differences
Parental relationships (harsh, permissive, inconsistent, critical, over-
    protective)
Sibling relations (birth order; role models; problems)
Peer relations (childhood or imaginary playmates; problems)
Home setting (safe; rich or poor; rural or urban)
Alcohol or *drug abuse* (yours, significant others)
Economic or *social status* (parents vs your own)
Intelligence (with naive idealism)
Education (school phobia; grades; sports; problems)
Physical health (disease history; accidents)
Mental health (family incidence; genetic predispositions)
Sexual (experience; orientation; preference)
Occupation (fits education, training, abilities, interests)
Marriage or *living with* (choice, compatibility of partner; problems)
Child management (harsh, permissive, inconsistent, critical, overprotective)
Religion (active, inactive, preferred values, extremist)
Politics (overinvolved; indifferent)
Hobbies (none, some, obsessive, changed)
Habits (excess smoking, drugs, drinking, eating)
Finances (money management problems)
Military/war (stressful; combat; authority problems)
Loss and *stress* (crises; catastrophes; crime; trauma)

The majority of people with problems, medical, mental, and criminal, can be understood by a careful analysis of these factors. Some, who have had deviant behaviors, cannot be wholly explained in this way. In their youth, Hitler aspired to be an artist, Stalin a priest, and Jim Jones was an ordained minister. Howard Becker commented in his 1963 book, *Outsiders*, that "instead of asking why deviants want to do things that are disapproved of we might better ask why conventional people do not follow through on deviant impulses they have. We all have inner demons" (p. 102). Eric Hoffer (1955) described the soul of the autonomous person as a "volcanic landscape" with a "seismic line running through it, the line of separation from the self." He saw motivation, impulses, and wishes as originating "along this line of cleavage" (p. 21).

PERSONALITY DYNAMICS

Psychoanalytic Theory

Sigmund Freud, founder of *psychoanalysis,* saw personality as formed by three *ego states:* the *id,* the beast within, primitive, instinctual, impulsive, pleasure-seeking, irrational, and fantasy-dominated; the *superego,* repository of values, conscience or morality, restrictions, inhibitions, and controls; the *ego,* reality-oriented manager or executive, rational and moderate, the compromiser-negotiator between id and superego. Ego decides to go on a diet, superego helps you follow it, and id is always ready for a hot fudge sundae. Ego decides to marry, superego gives its blessing, and id anticipates at regular sex. All three ego states coexist within you though their relative influence varies among people and within you from time to time.

Freud described five sequential stages of personality development:

ORAL, from birth, sucking and swallowing and mouth-centered activities such as thumbsucking, nailbiting, chewing gum or tobacco, smoking, drinking from bottles, or oral sex.

ANAL, at about age 2 or toilet training, when you "let go" or "hold it in," continued with compulsive talkers (verbal diarrhea), or scrooge-like tightwads (anal retentive). Our everyday expressions prove a preoccupation with anal activity: "Oh shit . . . don't give a shit . . . pain in, or my achin' ass . . . shove it . . . asshole" etc.

PHALLIC, when boys attach more to mother and resent father (*Oedipus complex*), but fear reprisal (*castration fear*) and girls attach more to father and resent mother (*Electra complex*) and are frustrated because they can't have what daddy's got (*penis envy*).

LATENCY, prepuberty from about age 7 through 12, when the sex drive is not significant, what Freud termed *infantile amnesia.*

GENITAL: Puberty, then onward and upward! Hormones awaken the sleeping id into starry-eyed romance, awkward dating to maturity, marriage and a new family unit.

Freud compared the mind to an iceberg, only a small part above the surface (conscious), most of its content below the surface, inaccessible (the *unconscious*), *repressed* thoughts, feelings, and painful memories beyond reach except by systematic psychotherapy or dreams, "the royal road to the unconscious." To better understand Freudian theory, watch the movie classic *Spellbound* with Humphrey Bogart, Ingrid Bergman, and Oscar Homolka. For a more lighthearted, humorous approach see *Lovesick* with Dudley Moore, Elizabeth McGovern, and Alec Guinness as the ghost of Freud.

Directly related to cult behavior is Freud's analysis of the individual in a group setting (1921). He observed that group members seek to merge with the leader (transference), "to introject the object into the ego-ideal." This member-to-leader interaction is a regressive idealization. Jung, as we will soon see, would very likely have described it as an archetypal symbolization. Libidinal involvement is similar to that in hypnosis (Kriegman and Solomon, 1985, p. 241). It is a relationship of master and pupil, performer and interested spectator, a "much frequented pathway to sexual object choice . . . an affectionate devotee, even a friend or an admirer, desires the physical proximity and the sight of the power who is now loved only in the 'Pauline' sense" (Freud, 1921, pp. 135–139).

Analytic Theory

Carl Jung was a Swiss psychiatrist and colleague of Freud who later broke from Freud to found Analytic Theory. Jungian concepts most relevant to cults are the *collective unconscious* and *archetypes.* The collective unconscious is a direct link to the cultural heritage of the human race from "ancestors right back to the earliest beginnings" (1969, p. 112). In it are the *archetypes,* primitive images from the darkest, most distant recesses of the mind, such as god, hero, wise old man, magician, trickster, devil or evil god, father, mother (madonna) or earth mother, witch, virgin, child, death, or life. The *persona* is a public mask one wears performing certain roles and function unlike the real self. *Anima* is the female essence in men, *animus* the male in females. The *shadow* is the id-like dark, primitive "other side" of the personality. The *self* is the total personality, above and beyond ego, which synthesizes and integrates conscious and unconscious material.

Behaviorist Theory

John Watson, an American psychologist, is credited with founding *behaviorism* in 1913, in militant opposition to Freud's theory of the unconscious. Based on learning and conditioning, it denied the existence of any behavior which cannot be objectively seen and therefore measured. Insight, intuition, and unconscious material were not empirically measurable, subjective, unscientific. It sought to identify and measure behavior by type, frequency, duration, and intensity under carefully controlled conditions. All behavior, even psychosis, is learned according to orthodox behaviorists. Life is a series of experiments and the world is the laboratory.

Everything said and done are *cues,* opportunities for pleasure or pain, *reinforcers* to reward and continue the behavior or to ignore and extinguish behavior. "Bad" habits, such as smoking, overeating, drinking, or nailbiting, are reinforced by the relief from tension they bring. B. F. Skinner, Watson's successor as leading proponent of behaviorism, added the concepts of *operant conditioning* and *successive approximation.* Where behaviors occur without specific stimulus and can be changed or *shaped* by a systematic schedule of planned tiny steps (*operant conditioning*).

Humanistic Theory

Carl Rogers and Abraham Maslow made major contributions to *humanistic psychology,* called "the third force" of personality theories in contrast to Freudian psychoanalysis and behaviorism. Rogers' *self theory* and *client-centered therapy* emphasize freedom of choice as an ongoing process of personal growth, measured in the "here and now" (*existential*) rather than the "there and then" of psychoanalysis (*historical*). It is based on what is happening within the individual (*experiential*) rather than strictly what is observed, as in behaviorism. The goal is *self-actualization* in an atmosphere of *unconditional positive regard.*

Abraham Maslow described 15 "ego transcending" *B-level characteristics* which he observed in self-actualized people, such as independent judgment, values, and lifestyle, originality and creativity, and a sense of humor, and being comfortable alone or with others. He found that self-actualized people share *B-values* such as spontaneity, simplicity, honesty, unity with destiny or fate, childlike playfulness, uniqueness and autonomy, a sense or feel for beauty and elegance, and a readiness to change, to let go of previously held ideas and opinions. They have *peak* or *oceanic experiences* with a sense of awe, wonder, reverence, humility, or self-surrender. More sophisticated cultists plan their rituals to include peak experiences.

Transactional Analysis

Eric Berne was a psychiatrist who founded *transactional analysis* or TA, a way of analyzing human interaction (Stewart & Joines, 1987). It is my opinion that Berne simply popularized basic Freudian theory. He described three coexistent *ego states* in everyone: the *Parent,* either critical or caring, full of values and standards mostly from real-life parents;

the *Adult,* moderator and data processor between overbearing Parent and overindulgent Child; the *Child* is where all our feelings are, happy and loving in the *Natural* or *OK Kid* and fearful and sadistic in the *Adapted* or *Not OK Kid.* These are very similar to Freud's superego, ego, and id. In the cult experience, the Not OK Kid is mainly involved, the Adult confused with half-truth and misleading generalizations, and the Parent gradually replaced with the cult's conscience or lack of it.

Berne's unique contribution is the concept of *transactions.* One of my Parent, Adult, or Child ego states transacts with one of your ego states with every word and action exchanged. A *game* is a transaction with a win-lose payoff, pleasure for the winner, pain for the loser. Cult involvement is a TA game with a win for the cult leader as Big Daddy or Big Momma and loss by the cult member Dumb Kid who remains subservient, dependent, always growing up but never coming of age. Berne called this type of game *kick me.* People stay in games because *negative strokes are better than no strokes at all,* according to Berne. The ideal relationship in TA theory is *intimacy,* a game-free interaction between two emancipated, responsible Adults. In cults, leaders and followers are rarely if ever equal and cult members are in a submissive and subservient one-down position. In TA terms it is a variation of a *kick me* game.

Self Therapy

Heinz Kohut is a psychoanalyst described by some as theoretically midway between Rogerian humanism and Freudian psychoanalysis (Kahn, 1985). He saw personality as developing by strengthening the *self,* a term used both by Rogers and Kohut, not by Freud. Kohut's self differs somewhat from Rogers and is in three *sectors:*

1. *Exhibitionism and grandiosity,* the boastful self of childhood, like the song lyrics "I can do anything better'n you, yes, I can" to modest self-confidence;
2. *Twinship,* fellow feeling or the need to share and "merge" with siblings, close friends, parents, or significant others (called *selfobjects*) from which is gained a "basic sense that one's life has purpose and meaning," moral imperatives of right and wrong, ideals, and "heroic imagos" (Kriegman & Solomon, 1985, p. 246). From twinship energy is acquired to pursue goals. Without it, goals seem uninspiring and there is often depression and meaninglessness overcome by fixing on "strong admired figures" which erodes reality testing and regresses into infantile dependency and primitization of mental processes ("psychological incest").

Kohut considered twinship as an "idealized selfobject" or "alter ego" and an alternative to Freud's Oedipus complex.

3. *Idealization* or *role modelling,* immature hero worship to personal self-realization (Kohut, 1984). Personal growth and personality development is a gradual process from *archaic selfobjects* like figures of omnipotence to *empathic selfobjects* with whom we can share a mature, mutual love in which each person feels greater than either alone, $1 + 1 = 3$.

Cults undermine these three sectors by maintaining dependence, denying individuality, and interrupting further personal development. Kriegman and Solomon (1985) applied Kohut's self theory to the cult experience. They see it as an idealization transference or "revival of an early phase of development . . . fixation on the omnipotent object" (p. 241). Typical cult recruits are likely to have had real or imagined "early traumatic disappointments" with one or both parents which were not fully internalized as selfobjects and cause "structural defects in their personalities." Such individuals are in a need state, susceptible to new idealized selfobjects to fill the emptiness, offset depression, and complete their self structure. "Normal" personalities merge with selfobjects, mirror and role model from them consistent with the "true self." In time permanent, internal personality structures are built and gradually strengthened into the autonomous, authentic self. If this process is obstructed the personality remains "fixated on an archaic selfobject" and there is likely to be "intense object hunger" (p. 244).

Cult leaders who knowingly or inadvertently become an idealized selfobject or idealization transference in susceptible individuals interrupt and obstruct optimal personality development. Charismatic, intrusive, aggressive, challenging, or confrontive cult leaders have high-risk potential for psychological harm as has been demonstrated in encounter groups (Yalom & Lieberman, 1971). Many cult leaders have a narcissistic, grandiose personality with little or no interest in helping members attain self-sufficiency and autonomy. The converse is true because leaders need followers and do not wish to share or dilute their exalted position. They deceptively offer twinship but at the price of conformity and surrender of self.

Initially, recruits feel "filled," satisfied, secure, at peace with self, with the cult's ready-made artificial, plastic self, an off-the-shelf pseudo-personality. With incomplete idealization of real-life parents they search for and find in the cult leader an external selfobject with which to merge, a regression moving the clock back to relive childhood with the ideal parent. It is a narcissistic infantile transference to a magical, omnipotent parent-authority which, like the fantasies of childhood, can be intensified if threatened. It becomes a symbiotic mutual dependency between active and passive narcissists lacking "a clearcut sense of personal morality as well as a sense of direction or purpose in life" (p. 246).

The following is a graphic comparison of cult and narcissistic personality interaction adapted from Kriegman and Solomon (1985, page 243):

Cult offers	*Narcissist needs*
1. Strong charismatic leader	Merger with idealized selfobject; repair member's self deficit
2. Group support and cohesion	Twinship merger and mirroring; pseudo-intimacy erodes personal autonomy
3. Relief of emotional pain (anxiety, depression, loneliness, withdrawal)	Relieve fluctuating self-esteem, emotional pain, and fragmentation of self
4. Membership in elite group	Validate grandiosity, compensate for insecurity and depression
5. Total equality under a caring idealized leader	Relief from stress of intense emotion (envy, jealousy, rage)
6. New belief/values system and purpose to fill an empty	Curative fantasy to restore self and relieve emptiness at cost of "normal" life goals and values

Kohut's major contribution to greater understanding of personality and also to the cult experience is his basic view that narcissism is a large part of the self, "half of the contents of the mind," the other half being objects of narcissism, the selfobjects (1971, p. xiii). When there is "narcissistic personality disturbance" such as in the cult experience the "narcissistic libido" cathects (connects) to "archaic objects" of "the archaic self" at an "early portion of the time axis of psychic development" (p. 3). Kohut saw this as "analogous to instinctual investment of unconscious incestuous objects in the classical transference neurosis" (p. 4). A strong charismatic leader can become a grandiose, magical fantasy image in a repressed, infantile, and immature personality which cannot accept the leader merely as a person or as an equal but rather as a needed part of the follower's infantile, immature, or incomplete self. This has been referred to as the "Wizard of Oz" effect common at the initial phase of therapy, changing to an acceptance of the "wizard therapist" negatively as a person, finally as a friend. Harmful cults interrupt personality development and can regress it to an early, formative, impressionable stage most like that of childhood, probably the latency period of ages 7–13.

Syzygy

Syzygy theory views human experience as a function of the relative dynamics of three basic forces, continually interacting like force fields: *stasis* (ST), *action-reaction* (AR), and *transcendence* (T). Stasis is the basic state of repose, of stability and depth, a constant warm bath or reassuring hug. Similar to conservatism in politics and orthodoxy and fundamentalism in religion, ST personalities and organizations resist change and seek to save and preserve tradition, the status quo. It is an "if it ain't broke don't fix it" and "good enough for father good enough for me" attitude. It is the world's oldest model of behavior. "Mother Nature" and the universe demonstrate ST in their order, overall stability, predictability, and esthetically in their restful beauty, in earth and sky, cloud and mountain, recurring day and night, seasons, climate, and moon cycle, and laws of physics such as gravity, sound, light, and electricity. Ancient temples, medieval cathedrals, and esthetically pleasing modern churches and temples, and anything that projects "heritage" is strong ST imagery. Patriotism, religious faith, ethics and morals, standards and values are ST traits and "law, law and order, peace, love, government, home, family, and church or temple" are ST words. Smiling at a baby not yours is a universal, warmly human ST behavior. ST can be seen in the basic stability that emerges from Erikson's life stages and Maslow's need levels.

Action-reaction (AR) is the basic state of change, of acting to or reacting from a force or factor intruding on a static or stable object, situation, or person. In nature, a storm is an AR force against an otherwise stable climatic pattern. War is an AR force on a nation and its people and peace is ST. By their nature, cults are AR and traditional religions are ST. Cults are "new," different, intrude upon and compete with traditional religion. Orthodox, fundamentalist, traditional religions are "old," established, relatively unchanging, and seek to preserve their heritage. ST and AR are in constant interaction, illustrated in the Taoist *yin-yang* symbol of polarity, paradox, conflict, and change. Traditional religions tend to defend the *yin* of repose and stability. Most cults offer the *yang* of change and impulse.

ST and AR intersect in conflict situations. "Phone your mother" or "what would your mother say" are sparks of friction from AR to ST. In nature an earthquake, volcanic eruption, or hurricane are AR intrusions which offset ST balance. Cults are AR intrusions into ST society. The Jamestown colony in 1607 Virginia was constructive ST; the Jonestown commune in 1978 in Guyana was destructive AR. The law, slow to change, careful and deliberate, is predominantly ST. Established personality theories and systems of psychotherapy are ST, new theories and therapies are AR because they are *reactive* to previous theories and therapies. Scientific journals are ST when they screen what is and is not "scientific." This book is ST with its references and documentation but what you are now reading is AR if it introduces a "new" and "different" view of cult and human behavior which may *change* your attitude or opinion.

	Cosmology	In history	Major Dynamic	Quality
ST	Steady state	Evolution	Conformity	Tranquil
AR	Big bang	Revolution	Change	Turbulent
T	Regeneration	Realization	Innovation	Transcendent

ST is Newtonian linear order in all phenomena, physical and mental, the ancient Chinese Taoist *yin* dark field. AR is Poincare's "science of chaos," seemingly random and disordered, change and nonconformity, the Taoist *yang* light field. T is the wholistic totality of yin-yang interaction of nature, the universe, and personality. Syzygy theory joins the individual to the universe, internally and externally, to facilitate exploration of outer and inner space. To do so it is open to all sources of information, science and religion, art and science, the subjective and the objective, ideographic and nomothetic. As we have seen thus far in this book, the cult experience touches on religion and the behavioral sciences. It can be full understood only with an open, eclectic approach.

Syzygy theory cautions that psychotherapy as it is currently practiced may not be effective in helping former cult members to achieve autonomy and self-realization. Most personality theories and systems of psychotherapy seek to help *adjust* to the realities of life and better understand and strengthen the self. For former cult members, this risks a return to a similar mental state which rendered them vulnerable to a cult-dependent experience. To do nothing more is to restore the AR conflict and confusion in a futile search for the old, basic ST which caused or contributed to the problem originally. This is a major shortcoming of many current therapies. In the complexity of the space age, adjustment and adaptive coping are not enough.

Syzygy differs from most theories and therapies with the addition of the third basic life force, *transcendence* (T). It is the state of *becoming* (Allport) by transcending both positive and negative aspects of the past. It is to realize Maslow's *B-values* and one's true nature which may be like or unlike the past. Therapies that help individuals to *be* are limited to self-understanding. Syzygy helps them *become* in a Zen-like "mystic leap" into a new, different, better self from the ping-pong push-pull of ST–AR polarities. The postcult authentic self may not be at all like the precult or cult self but a third person. To attain T is to understand and accept, to work through the past, own it and digest it, then realize the unique, natural *transcendent self,* one's own yin-yang interaction, where the "whole" exceeds the sum of its parts. This is far more than adjustment. It is *actualization, fulfillment, self-realization,* all that Maslow and Shostrom described. It is B. F. Skinner's *Walden II,* also a Shangrila experience, strongly and totally integrated into the personality.

ST, AR, and T can be understood as three distinctively different force fields of equal intensity, like three stars in close position which appear congruent but which retain their integrity. They are a triangulation of basic natural life forces. A line drawn between them forms a triangle, which is the personality. Ideally, it is equilateral, ST, AR, and T of equal proportion. For most people the triangle of personality is broader at the base (ST and AR) than at the top (T). The push-pull of conformity vs conflict and change can occupy one's life force almost totally, with little time or opportunity for upreach and outreach into the "mountaintop experience" aspirational, inspirational, spiritual, creative, transcendence. For many, aging brings wisdom, another way of describing increasing T-awareness from years of repetitive ST–AR interaction. T can occur in a sudden flash of insight or "Ah hah!" experience, the *satori* of Zen, a momentary glimpse of T in an otherwise ST–AR existence. The syzygy process is START, to resolve ST and AR conflict, attenuate their "noise," see through them and into and through all previous experiencing, integrate them, own them, let them "be," then use them as a springboard to T, the Tao of life, its ultimate meaning for the individual. Both old and new factors and antagonistic forces are used as tools to fashion a new, better, more real and natural self. T is for most a moving (peak) experience, an "Ah hah" flash of insight, a feeling of relief, reverie, and deep satisfaction. It is like the legend of the Phoenix, the mystical bird that died, then recreated *itself* from its own ashes, more beautiful than before. This goal of syzygy theory is called *the Phoenix phenomenon.*

CULT LEADERS

While there are exceptions, most cults are led by strongly charismatic leaders who alone interpret the mission of the organization usually by the authority of an alleged direct connection with God, often through personal and unwitnessed visions. The size and type of cult are two variables that affect leadership style. Leaders of large nationwide organizations have been predominantly male Caucasians of average or above intelligence and with highly developed interpersonal and group communications skills. Most observers would concede that they are "personable" or "charming." They are skilled at finding and using a "gimmick," an attention-getting "psychological hook" to arouse curiosity, then fascination, drawing prospective members into the organization with the anticipation of gradually learning more and deeper truths. Successful cults are a closed system which initially provides close support and fellow feeling and a sense of safety and security. The "warm hug" at intake becomes a "bear hug" stifling individuality, free expression, and optimal personality development. Cult leaders usually do not mingle freely with the membership but appear regularly and ceremoniously in programs and rituals.

Larger multistate or nationwide cult organizations closely resemble traditional religions in size, scope, and by their established practices and relatively fixed beliefs. Often, they are led by narcissistic leaders with a "Messiah complex" requiring adulation by others, a disguised need for power and control. Jim Jones and the People's Temple in Guyana is an example of such a cult. Smaller cults usually operate locally in one city or state and tend to be more extremist and criminal, since they have no external controls and their smaller numbers enable them to function without as much public notice. Those that engage in antisocial behaviors and ritual abuse and murder are likely to be led by a psychopath. The Symbionese Liberation Front that kidnapped Patty Hearst and the Manson "family" are examples of smaller criminal cults. A third type of leader is found in an isolated local cult, frequently an obsessed, misguided person who overdoes a the cult experience, or naive youth fascinated or obsessed with occult role plays or rituals with a peer leader.

Silverman (1975) described "victimizers" as persuasive and charismatic leaders who have "correctly gauged the frustrations, hopes, and aspirations" of others and are able to effectively articulate them (p. 17). Their conversation is more manipulative than communicative, their techniques provocative, dramatic, and attention getting. Deep inside, they feel "basically helpless" because they can achieve only through others, and have a deep sense of alienation, loss, or deprivation "which must somehow be made up and this can only be done by and through others" (p. 17). There is a seemingly insatiable need for control, to justify actions and conduct, and blame others for problems (p. 24).

To these leaders, "all the world's a stage" and life is enacted like a play in which "all the bodies on the floor at the end of the last act will take bows at curtain time." Many cult leaders exhibit stage presence and a flair for the dramatic, much like actors and actresses. Clinically, it's a narcissistic trait with histrionic features. Since life for them is unreal and "staged" there is "no sense of wrongdoing," no real sense of owned responsibility (p. 18). This leads to stereotyping and oversimplification such as a sharply differentiating "us-them, good-evil, right wrong" and childish exaggeration and externalization ("The devil made me do it . . . you are either with us or against us . . . God is with us . . . convert or perish"). Silverman traced this leadership style to early childhood and suspected it to be shaped by parents and others, according to their needs and wishes (p. 22). If parents are arbitrary, capricious, or unpredictable, the neophyte leader develops "mind reading" to survive, "the first prerequisite of a charismatic leader" (p. 23).

There are nine characteristics of victimizer-type leaders, according to Silverman (pp. 15–17):

1. A deep sense of *alienation* from others and from society compensated for by the cult's enforced conformity and sharing and projected into goals such as universal brotherhood, world peace, cosmic unity, etc. Example: Most large cult organizations.

2. Severe *deprivation or loss* and an inability to accept them and striving to retrieve what is lost and rigid, refusing to give up anything. Example: Hitler, Stalin.

3. Need for *total domination*, to take over with absolute and total

control, and to eliminate all opposition, real or imagined. Example: Hitler, Stalin.

4. *Super-idealism,* constantly justifying actions on moral grounds, such as past injustices, present deficiencies, and simplistic, unrealistic future plans. Example: Stalinist Russia's foreign policy.

5. *Attribution-externalization.* Deprivation and loss are *always* due to external forces and causes. Example: Nazi propaganda that pre-World War II German economy was Jewish conspiracy.

6. *Provocation techniques,* to set up a situation then use it to advantage, "people chess," such as pushing to crisis or orchestrating an emotional peak then criticizing the loss of control or poor coping skills. Example: Hitler's self-provoked invasion of the Sudetenland early in World War II.

7. *Insatiable needs.* Whenever goals and needs are satisfied, they are replaced by new ones, into infinity. Ex. Che Guevara moving to Bolivia when Cuba revolution ended.

8. *Language manipulation,* word magic, skillful use of mass, small group and interpersonal communications. Example: Goebbels, Hitler's propaganda minister, who was also a Ph.D. in political science.

9. *Hero worship.* The cult leader usually has a rich fantasy life, of heroes or heroines past and present. Example: Hitler and Wagner, Nietszche, Teutons, and the Aryan race.

PSYCHOPATHS AND SOCIOPATHS

Leading an extremist, criminal cult would be consistent with two deep-seated behavior and personality patterns, the *psychopath* and the *sociopath.* Glueck and Glueck (1950) suggest they are formed by age 6, Cleckley (1941) considered them to be forms of psychosis, and Guttmacher (1953) saw their cause as a combination of child abuse and emotional deprivation. Brain damage or dysfunction has also been suggested since parts of the brain and midbrain are involved in pleasure-seeking and rage. Not listed in the DSM, the standard psychiatric diagnostic manual, the closest official diagnosis is *antisocial personality disorder.* Psychopaths and sociopaths can and often do have traits of other listed personality disorders such as borderline, narcissistic, avoidant, paranoid, passive-aggressive, and obsessive-compulsive. They differ markedly from them by their repetitive behavior, lifestyle out of mainstream society and social norms and in extremist criminal cults, violence and crime.

Psychopaths are, directly or indirectly, impulsive thrillseekers who ignore or violate societal and legal standards. They are uncivilized, undersocialized, and have somehow never learned to care about others. They seem to have a predatory instinct, totally selfish and without conscience. Their ruthlessness is vented through ambition and avarice or violence and crime, in a cult, business, politics, even religion. Some have above average intelligence and achieve power through clever self-promotion and strong hypnotic-like charisma, faking genuine feelings. Usually, they have a deep resentment or hate for authority figures. They demonstrate their superiority by outwitting the police and exploiting victims. Violence and crime are especially exciting to the psychopath, to have an innocent person under total control with power over life and death. Frequently insensitive to pain themselves, ritual abuse can be an obsessive preoccupation, even humorous to them in a sordid, gruesome way, a vehicle for imaginative and macabre "fun."

These characteristics of the psychopath are paraphrased from Cleckley (1941): superficial charm or intelligence; no delusions or irrational thoughts (formal diagnostic definitions, not the same as Meerloo's described previously); little or no anxiety and no shame or remorse; unreliable, insincere and untruthful; selfish, unable to love; superficial, mechanical sex life; emotionally impoverished, lacks caring or feeling, not really friendly; poor judgment, crimes hardly worth the payoff or risk; lacks insight and really meaningful life goals; may talk suicide but rarely acts on it; alcohol and drug abuse common and lower self-control increasing danger of antisocial acting out. They are a close match of St. Augustine's description of devils. Hitler, Stalin, Jim Jones at Jonestown, and convicted serial killers had many psychopathic traits. A psychopath can build a thriving business in illicit street drugs, wholesaling to sociopathic dealers.

Sociopaths also disregard or violate social norms or laws, but they do so less directly than the psychopath, such as prostitutes, substance abusers, repeat drunk drivers and gamblers, and credit card fraud or forgery. Usually, they are what many call "losers" and "loners" who live and work in the shadows, indirectly, passively self-destructive by the pain, discomfort, and poor health and the cost in money, time, and energy of others. *Spongers* are sociopaths who "milk" what they want from *suckers*, well meaning, naive rescuers. Those who don't "give" are called *bastards* by sociopaths.

CULT MEMBERS

It is not possible to describe one typical cult member since they vary widely in age and personal needs. At Jonestown, People's Temple members were mixed racially and ranged in age from newborn babies to grandparents. Generally, in large nonethnic communal cults, 18–25 year-olds predominate and are mostly intelligent, middle class Caucasians usually with some college education or are college graduates. Seemingly stable, many have overcontrolled hostility, are passive-aggressive or frustrated, lonely, and depressed, alone for the first time, with few close friends and without a meaningful support system. Their naive idealism and tendency to believe in simplistic solutions to complex problems and unmet dependency needs contribute to their vulnerability to a cult or religious conversion experience (Ungerleider & Wellisch, 1978). Susceptible individuals will affiliate with almost any cult and do not "shop" for the most appropriate to their needs. Many are recruited on campus in class, in dorms, at meetings on politics, peace, or personal growth, or at sports events and concerts, at resorts, in cafeterias, fast food restaurants, parties, libraries, post offices, shopping malls and supermarkets, bus or train stations or airports, hospitals and clinics, or on the street, wherever students meet, study, shop, eat, or spend leisure time. MacCollam (1979) quoted a parent who described cult recruiting as based on the "six I's" of innocence, idealism, inquisitiveness, independence, identity crisis, and insecurity. Other cult recruits are "strays," frequently with family problems, lonely and depressed, socially inept or isolated, dissatisfied with traditional religion or societal values. Some are substance abusers or homeless street persons.

In 1980, a survey of 1000 northern California high school students found differences between those likely and not likely to join cults "rather subtle," more a matter of degree than kind (Zimbardo and Hartley, 1985). These susceptible teenagers did, however, view cults more positively than their resistant peers, their fathers had higher status occupations, they watched TV less, read newspapers more, and were "reasonably accurate in identifying groups as cults" (p. 120). Less significant variables were reading magazines less, eagerness to consider opposing views, positive acceptance of prototypical cult members, average grades, more experience with religious practices, and fewer brothers. Media and interpersonal communications about cults were positive or negative influences.

This study found that most cult recruiters were perceived neutrally by students and "friendly" or "unfriendly" by an equal number of the others. "Decided interest" in a cult was reported by 12 percent but offset by a like number who reported feeling "afraid" of cults. The top ten negative aspects of cults were costume, jewelry or badges, slogans and mottos, selling food, showing pictures, selling flowers, handing out literature, describing cult programs, eye contact, and showing affection (love bombing). Prime contact sites were on the street, airports, at home, bus stops, parking lots, school grounds, on vacation, a friend's home, at work, park benches, restaurants, theatre, church meetings, summer camp, or public auditoriums. Purposes of contact were soliciting funds, providing information, selling products or services, or recruiting new members.

Zimbardo and Hartley "reject the notion of a random process" of contact by a cult recruiter "by which a decision is made" and they point out that this differs from "journalistic and clinical case portraits of the cult seeker" or "innocents deceptively manipulated" (pp. 141–142). They isolated *contact variables* of "approached" and "not approached" cult prospects, and *affiliative variables* of "would reject" and "would consider/ accept" joining a cult. Some variables apply to both contact and affiliative variables such as seeing the cult's purposes and the prototypical cult member positively. Media exposure, grades, religious practices, and father's occupational status influence contact but not affiliative variables which are a "complex interaction" of precontact knowledge and values, recruiter impact, contact setting, and "especially the student's cognitive transformation of those inputs into affective ties, perceived congruence, and empathetic associations."

They suggest that their results may differ from other clinical, research, and media reports because of the younger age sampling and the focus on the initial stage of what may be a longer shaping or tracking process. They agree that some recruiters may "artfully guide and shape the responses of the target person," misrepresent, falsify, and manipulate to "test the waters for a promising catch" (p. 143). They conclude that a "surprisingly sizable" number of the 1000 students reported "personal contact with a cult member," many more than once. More than half were "receptive to the possibility of attending a cult function if invited" and most of those who had never been approached "expressed an interest in having some contact with a cult activity" (p. 139).

Only a very small fraction of teenagers involved in cults are referred to mental health professionals and fewer are seen by researchers. One source of information on the mental state of today's teenagers is to randomly sample cross-sections of adults who daily observe them. Rabiner (1988) described a nationwide phone survey of 1001 adults to assess the current problem areas experienced by teenagers and their severity. The question "Do you personally know a teenager or child that experienced any of the following problems?" yielded these results: conflict with parents (72%); alcohol abuse (58%); drug abuse (56%); depression (56%); unwanted pregnancy (48%); crime (42%); runaways (37%); child abuse (32%); attempted suicide (27%); committed suicide (17%). Eighty-six percent agreed that "families find it difficult to admit their children need professional help," 73 percent agreed that "parents don't seek professional help for children because they don't want anybody to find out about their child's behavior," 65 percent agreed that "people are afraid of those who have been treated for mental illness," and 57 percent agreed that "mental illness in children is an embarrassment to families." This recent study demonstrates that the need for mental health services continues to be a stigma to families and suggests the likelihood problems will be avoided or denied until of crisis proportion.

Most mental health professionals specializing in the treatment of children and adolescents agree that adolescence involves testing limits, exploring and experimenting in a search for self and identity, meaning and reality. Uncertain of the future, with career and life goals neither clearly seen nor firmly established, cults provide a packaged personality and the illusion of security in a comfortable, orderly structure and safe, nonthreatening, noncompetitive, predictable, repeated routine. Acceptance, approval, and affection from self-assured, enthusiastic, persuasive "new friends" with answers and commitment seem to fill the void and give life new meaning. Adolescence is also a major life phase between childhood and adulthood, where fantasy fades and reality and responsibility emerge. Fantasy role play games, Satanic or occult groups, interrupt that process to indulge or obsess in fantasy or naive idealism, to regress and linger or escape freedom in a castle in the mind. To young "rebels without a cause," cults are an outlet for hostile acting out in nihilistic groups such as *stoners* and *skinheads.* To those fascinated with mystic and occult ideas, cults and fantasy role play games satisfy curiosity. They interrupt optimal personality development, put it on hold, and beckon toward an inward, downward spiral to obsessive preoccupation, experimentation with progressively violent rituals, physical and sexual abuse, ultimately animal and human sacrifice. "Is Satanism a hard reality,"

Norris and Potter asked, "or a psychiatric metaphor for a society going mad? Perhaps both" (1985, p. 180).

CONCLUSIONS

Cults have existed throughout history. Those that survive influence and are influenced by society. Social, religious, and behavioral observers over the past fifty years, and former cult members, their families and friends, are consistent in their descriptions of the cult experience, what it is and what it does. Loneliness and isolation, insecurity and inadequacy, are powerful motivators. To overcome what Fromm called "the horror of loneliness" people will escape from freedom. Manipulation is preferred to actualization it it offers the individual structure, stability, security, and close support. Pride in the group becomes a powerful reinforcer, along with continued, repeated routine and rituals (Hoffer). Leader and follower join in a tacit mutually dependent sadomasochistic symbiotic relationship. Sadistic leaders seek unlimited power over followers who are abused and exploited (Fromm). Cults can be asylums of escape and refuge from painful realities and the discomfort of personal responsibility. The uncertain self yields to the absolute certainty of the cult.

Strongly charismatic leaders with highly developed communications skills (word magic) deceive and manipulate to maintain control (Meerloo, Shostrom). This process is essentially retrograde, more regressive than progressive, interrupting and obstructing optimal personality development (Rogers, Maslow, Kohut). It involves unconscious processes such as regressive parent-child imagery (Freud), archetypal symbolization (Jung), and childhood fantasy. Unchecked, this process can lead to primitive thinking, pagan ritual, and uncontrolled emotionality (Hoffer). In addition to these social factors and leadership variables, psychological factors can add to the predisposition to the cult experience (psychosocial factors). These factors involve learning and conditioning from infancy to the present (Skinner), adjustment at key life stages (Erikson), relative needs satisfaction, healthy (Maslow) and neurotic (Horney), reward-reinforcement (Kimble) or exchange of rewards (Kelley), imitation (Dollard and Miller), and a search for balance and stability (Heider). A ready-made, packaged cult personality replaces the previous, weak self (Kohut), and further reinforced in time, defends the cult with weak and illogical arguments when confronted with "dissonant" facts (Festinger), attributing negative connotations to any criticism from outside the cult (Kelley).

Multimedia advertising dulls critical judgment (Packard), rapidly changing technology and economic and political unrest have forced us out of our inner-directed shells (Riesman), and work layoffs and mergers, terrorism and war, rising substance abuse and crime, threaten security and increase self-doubt. Human nature, consistent with the history of civilization and the laws of nature and the universe, share a triad of force fields which converge with varying intensity (syzygy): stasis, a basic stability, reflected in law, government, and traditional religion; action-reaction, the force of change and reactivity, of the "new" and "different," presently reflected in popular cult movements; and transcendence, intuitive insight, a seemingly mystic leap into a holistic or holographic synthesis of all three forces. When they converge the self is in syzygy, what other theorists have called self-realization, selfhood, personhood, fulfillment, or actualization.

Chapter Three

THE CULT EXPERIENCE: BELIEFS, PRACTICES, RITUALS

*There is no telling how deeply
a mind may be affected by the
deliberate staging of gestures,
acts, and symbols*
Eric Hoffer
The Passionate Mind (1955)

THE QUESTION OF EVIL

Mental health professionals speak of disorders and treatment for them, or problems and helping clients explore solutions for them. Psychology split from philosophy in the Middle Ages to avoid making value judgments such as what is right or wrong, good or evil. That is still its posture. The emergence of cults and the realities of cult crime and ritual abuse make it necessary for the behavioral sciences and mental health professions to become involved. Otherwise, little help can be provided to victims and their families, or to society to most appropriately reduce risk and prevent excess. We need more accurate information about short and long-term effects of the cult experience from clinicians and researchers. That can't be done from a distance. There have been too few articles in professional journals of detailed case histories describing treatment variables, outcome, and conclusions. If media coverage is any indication, public concern is high, confirming the need for more data— and help. But behavioral sciences and mental health professionals have not yet fully awakened to the need and view this as a remote fringe area, more religion than science.

Psychotherapists and researchers must come to grips with the question of evil. There have been references to it throughout history, in every society and culture, of evil as a force or negative influence. In Judeo-Christian scriptures, the first evil was temptation, when Adam and Eve ate the forbidden fruit. Lucifer was an angel who became the devil, a fallen angel. Cain and Abel were brothers, one good and one evil. The ancient Chinese and Persians saw life as a dynamic balance of two forces, good as light, evil as darkness. The ancient Egyptians symbolized good in Horus, evil in Set. The New testament described how Judas betrayed Christ, an evil act. There are similar themes in the world's poetry, prose, and drama. Shakespeare's *MacBeth* and *Hamlet* portray ruthless ambition and murder. Robert Louis Stevenson's *Dr. Jekyll and Mr. Hyde* is a classic tale of evil within a person and also a good, early account of multiple personality disorder. *Faust* was a 16th century doctor who sold his soul to the devil for youth and power. That legend inspired the music of Berlioz, Gounod, and Liszt, and the writers Goethe and Thomas Mann.

There is a common thread through all these sources, that evil or the idea of evil is a universal force with deep historical roots. Further, it is as Nazi cult victim Victor Frankl observed after more than three years in Auschwitz, within each of us. We are daily surrounded by evidence of it, in the newspaper, TV newscasts, cruelty, crime, unethical practices, war. In law, there is *malum in se*, what is inherently wrong always and forever, and *malum prohibitum*, what the law (and present society) says is wrong. With malum in se, the law is ahead of the mental health professions, which remain in a malum prohibitum awareness of mental disorders. Some researchers have reported abnormal brain waves in convicted criminals. Are their brains wired wrong? Is criminality involved somehow with body chemistry? A simple vitamin deficiency can masquerade as schizophrenia. Is there a "bad seed," a genetic predisposition toward conscienceless evil? Current consensus suggests a combination of factors, both hereditary and environmental.

In 1963, psychologist Stanley Milgram conducted research at Yale University on individual decisionmaking, specifically the interface between orders by an external authority and individual conscience (Tavris, 1974). Volunteers were told they were participating in an experiment on memory and learning. They were seated at a shock generator with 30 switches labelled from 15 to 450 volts and told they were in the role of a "teacher." The "student" was strapped into a chair and electrodes were attached to their bodies. Every time a student made a mistake, greater electric shock was to be applied. Milgram found that most people were very uncomfortable applying the shock, but two-thirds of them threw the 450 volt switch even after being told it might injure or kill. The experiment was replicated off campus in a commercial building without public university connection and half the "teachers" gave maximum shock. In no case was electrical shock anywhere near the force marked on the switch labels, so no one was hurt, but they could have been.

These experiments raised considerable controversy about informed consent, use of deception, and risks to the mental health of experimental subjects. Some researchers felt the volunteers really knew nothing adverse would happen and trusted the researchers and scientific ethics (Adair, 1973). Similar experiments have been conducted in Germany, Italy, Australia, and South Africa and with similar results. In his book *Obedience to Authority,* Milgram described situations where authority overrode conscience, such as when an authority figure is physically present, in a group of conformists to authority, or when the victim is not actually seen or touched. More than 1000 people, men and women, skilled and unskilled, with varying education, went all the way. Based on his research, Milgram concluded "ordinary people . . . without any particular hostility on their part, can become agents in a terrible, destructive process" (Tavris, 1974, p. 77). These ordinary people behaved much like psychopaths or sociopaths. He explained obedience as the result of hierarchical authority. The volunteer promised to help, feels obligated to do so, and as time passes finds it difficult to exit, more and more involved in the mechanics and minutia of what is happening, and misses the big picture or total context along with a loss of personal responsibility. Some volunteers even criticized the victim as deserving to be punished, for being stupid and missing questions.

Applied to cult behavior, Milgram's research explains social and psychological pressures to remain in a cult, and the use of such common cult practices as frequent peer group activities, seldom being alone or out of effective range of a cult leader or activist, and how society (intangible) and the family of origin (absent) are scapegoated. It is consistent with the observations and conclusions of social and behavioral scientists quoted throughout this book. While the word magic of cult leaders have great power and influence, no Hitler, Stalin, or Jim Jones could have taken power not given by the "ordinary people" who were their followers. As we have seen, there was no Nazi mind just as there is no Cult mind. There is only mind, behavior and personality, and we have learned since World War II they are sensitive and vulnerable, changing and elastic, and can be used either creatively or destructively.

MAGIC AND MEANING

Hippocrates (460–377 BC), physician in the cult of Asklipios, author of 87 medical treatises and the Hippocratic Oath still used today, and regarded as "the father of medicine," was an authority whose works stood the test of time and a marked contrast to the cults described in previous chapters. Twenty-five centuries ago he approached medical and mental disorders objectively and with what we now call the scientific method. He was the first to differentiate acute from chronic disorders, to emphasize the need to take a careful history, and to "do no harm" when providing treatment. Attributing a divine or evil cause to illness was quite common in ancient Greece, just as in Afro-Caribbean and Satanic cults today. In his essay *On the Sacred Disease*, the disorder we call epilepsy, Hippocrates observed: "It appears to me to be nowise more divine nor more sacred than other diseases but has a natural cause" (Ehrenwald, 1956, p. 200). He understood human nature and perceived the motivation of those who sought to mystify illness: "They give themselves out for being excessively religious and as knowing more than other people ... using divinity as a pretext ... to institute a mode of treatment which is safe for themselves, namely, applying purifications and incantations" (p. 201).

Albert Schweitzer, medical missionary to Lambarene, West Africa, personally observed the decline then the renewal of primitive bush religion and described it in his essay *Black Magic Reborn*. In it he reported that the first European missionaries arrived in Lambarene in 1874 and by 1890 were "solidly entrenched." When he arrived in 1913, "all magical beliefs had practically disappeared." In 1924 "native nationalism" arose and the "core of this nationalism was magical belief ... primitive faith." He saw it as a way "to oppose the invasion of occidental ideas." Salvation, dependency on God, "in a word, the notion of religion remained unknown or at best secondary ... primitive beliefs show no sign of real spiritualization." The real motivation behind primitive religions is power, according to Schweitzer. He differentiated them from secret societies which practiced "the cult of ecstasy." Primitive "fetishists," he wrote, are "a much lower category" because they practice "power to chase away evil spirits ... rites which go back to very ancient times" (Ehrenwald, 1956, pp. 78–79).

A scientifically trained observer, Schweitzer witnessed the power of taboos and reported two cases of death due to violating them. The first case was a student at a missionary school was told never to eat bananas nor any food from pots where bananas had been cooked. One day his schoolmates told him the fish he was eating came from a pot that still contained leftover bananas. He was "immediately overcome with convulsions and died in a few hours." The second case was a man whose father told him "to have numerous progeny." He had three children when his father visited him and forcefully reminded him of the taboo. The man fainted, fell into convulsions which persisted several days until he died. Anticonvulsant medications had no effect. Schweitzer concluded: "Natives stand in so great an awe of taboos that they are subject to psychological shocks the violence of which we cannot imagine" (pp. 79–80).

In his monograph *Totem and Taboo,* Freud considered magic to be a form of wish: "At bottom, everything accomplished through magic means must have been done solely because we wanted it" (Ehrenwald, 1956, p. 81). The underlying principle of magic, "the technique of the animistic method," Freud claimed, is "omnipotence of thought." This kind of thinking is primitive because "the animistic phase is succeeded by the religious and this in turn by the scientific." In the animistic phase we ascribe omnipotence to ourselves. In the religious phase which follows it we submit to the gods "but without seriously giving it up." In the scientific phase we acknowledge our uncertainty and insignificance in a vast and complex universe (p. 85).

In his 1956 book *From Medicine Man to Freud,* Jan Ehrenwald commented that "what is left of the magic heritage is being subjected to a gradual process of rationalization . . . secularized and taken over by science . . . steadily receding and scientific psychotherapy is on the ascendancy" (p. 408). The occult is a subject of "methodical scientific investigation" and the claims of the medium are 'put to the test of clinical and laboratory experiments" (p. 409). The cult experience is a challenge to science "to accommodate hitherto neglected aspects of the human mind within a revised and expanded conceptual scheme" and "the therapeutic potentialities of religious experience are once more engaging the interest of the psychotherapist" (Ibid).

NEGATIVE EFFECTS OF CULT INVOLVEMENT

The following is an alphabetical listing of the possible negative or harmful effects of cult involvement based on a review of material from former cult members, their parents, mental health professionals, clergy, and books and articles by professional and lay writers. There is overlap of these harmful effects and their impact and intensity varies with the particular cult, the cult member, and the length of time of exposure to the cult experience.

BEHAVIOR CHANGE can be dramatic and markedly different than the individual's normal baseline behaviors. This is frequently reported by cult member's families.

CONVERSION is a change or transfer of commitment from previous conduct and values and absorption into markedly different beliefs and behaviors of the cult, similar to the religious conversion experience.

CRITICAL JUDGMENT is weakened by vague occult, mystic or unfamiliar Eastern religious or philosophical ideas, or abstract concepts, half-truth, overgeneralization, and oversimplification.

DEPRIVATION, from the normalization process consistent with personal, family, and societal values, and also sensory, perceptual, diet and nutrition, sleep and rest, and privacy. Deprivation alone can contribute to the "seven D's": *distancing* from social, personal, and physical needs not optimally or positively satisfied, creating *stimulus hunger* which can lead to *debilitation, depression, depersonalization,* and *derealization,* these to *delusion* or *dissociation* possibly of psychotic quality and severity.

FAMILY ISOLATION or *break-off phenomena,* where the cult replaces family relationships, breaking off previous support systems, and deliberately alienating the cult member from the family.

FATIGUE is often reported by former cult members, from interrupted sleep, lack of privacy, regimented highly structured routine, long hours of lecture, ritual, discussion, testimonials, or work, and in some cults scheduled restroom breaks and fasting.

FINANCIAL OBLIGATIONS. Some cults work their members morning to night without pay, as an offering or sacrifice and solicit funds as additional offerings from the cult members themselves or their families.

IDENTITY and ROLE CONFUSION. A major characteristic of many cult recruits is identity crisis or deep feelings of uncertainty about their future, inadequacy, or inferiority. The cult offers a completely packaged trouble-free lifestyle, predictable and orderly, and a cult pseudo-personality which is relatively passive and submissive to cult values and beliefs. Children in cults may have role confusion since the usual nuclear family parental role is disturbed by many other unclear or competing role models such as the cult leader and other adults which dissipate normal family relations.

INTERRUPTED life phase and personal growth and development. Most cult members no longer pursue a career or education and total commitment of time and self to the cult interrupts social, sexual, educational, and religious relationships. Therapists have reported *arrested development,* where persons who joined a cult in their teens and left the cult in their 20s were actually functioning at a similar developmental age as when they entered the cult, requiring long-term psychotherapy to restore them to age-appropriate norms.

ISOLATION (see DEPRIVATION).

MENTAL DISORDER. Forms of mental disorder as defined in the DSM or psychiatric diagnostic manual have been reported in cult members without prior mental problems.

PERSONALITY CHANGE is frequently reported, involving increased dependence or passivity, flat affect unable to express affection or maintain an intimate relationship, feelings of inadequacy, guilt, fear, or depression, suspiciousness or guardedness, diminished sense of humor, dramatic change in values and motivation, vocabulary and communications style. Suicides have been reported.

PERSONAL RESPONSIBILITY is diminished in favor of the group norm, a change from an "I" individual orientation to a "we" or "us" which eliminates decisionmaking, increases dependency, and interrupts optimal personal growth and development.

REALITY ORIENTATION can be clouded and confused by "word magic," strange or unusual ideas, beliefs, values, practices, and rituals, and isolation from previous environment and support system.

VALUES CONFUSION. Many cults establish a "we-they" right-wrong, good-evil dichotomy where parents, previous friends, religion, school and career objectives neatly fall on the "wrong" or "evil" side. Some cults actually teach these "others" are agents of Satan. Cult lifestyle and values completely replace all previously held values. This is, however, very difficult to achieve without underlying anxiety, uncertainty, and confusion since it seeks to reverse a life-long pattern of behavior and discredit supportive relationships.

MANIPULATIVE TECHNIQUES

In addition to the effects described above, there are manipulative techniques used to assure conformity to cult norms. The following have been reported by former cult members and parents of active cult members:

ABUSE, mental, physical, or sexual, child and adult, have been reported, child abuse by extremist criminal cults, and litigation by adults has been based on psychological-emotional injury by deceptive manipulation, misrepresentation, and fraud.

ALTERED STATES OF CONSCIOUSNESS can be induced or enhanced by meditation, chanting, speaking in tongues, dancing, rituals, fasting, or drugs. Long hours of lecture or the effect of a charismatic leader in a monotonously repeated daily schedule can contribute to suggestibility, to hypnosis or a hypnotic-like state.

CONFESSION, either in public or in private, to a peer or cult leader, mobilizes and can focus guilt, anxiety, or fear and thus used to reinforce the cult experience.

INDOCTRINATION or PROGRAMMING is the systematic process of learning and conditioning through lectures, rituals, and shared behaviors in rituals and the work of the cult. The use of "word magic," universal ideals, vague, abstract ideas, and strange and unusual concepts provide a verbal screen of doubletalk and doublethink which frustrates reason and critical judgment.

"LOVE BOMBING" is feigned affection and caring used for the sole purpose of influencing behavior, most frequently in cult recruitment and the indoctrination of new members.

"HEAVENLY DECEPTION" is deliberate misrepresentation such as denying a cult's identity or a recruiting cult members affiliation with it, justified on the grounds that if prospective cult members knew the cult connection they would break off contact.

ISOLATION, physically in a markedly different environment, in a milieu of different values and beliefs, practices and expectations, in a different culture.

MANIPULATION (See INDOCTRINATION).

PRIVACY, lack of. Frequently reported is a lack of privacy which is both physical and mental. Sharing rooms and bathrooms, food, work, and rest times intrudes on the mental state of the individual with "psychic noise."

REGIMENTATION by repeated routine, such as shared exercise, meal, lecture, discussion, or work. All time is structured and routinized, reinforcing the cult lifestyle, beliefs, and values.

SEX. The sex drive can be sublimated into work, ritual, and cult routine. One cult uses prostitution as a form of "doing good works."

There are "4 C's" involved in cult conditioning: *Conjuring up* such as with altered states, "love bombing," and repeated ritual; *cluttering up* the mind through regimentation, indoctrination, or planned, intentional abuse; *cleaning up* or "brainwashing," wiping the mind's slate clean rendering it more receptive, by communal living, closely shared activities, sex, public confession, or social isolation; *clouding up* the mind by drugs, altered states of consciousness, or constant indoctrination.

VICTIMIZATION AS PROCESS

Three psychiatrists who have studied the phenomenon of victimization in groups and mass movements are worthy of note: Joost Meerloo,

William Sargant, and Robert Lifton. Descriptions and explanations from more recent books and articles are consistent with their observations and help differentiate constructive from destructive factors in the cult experience. Cults, as we have seen, are many and varied, and like human nature, complex and with many features. Only careful examination of psychological and emotional factors within each and their effect on the individual can differentiate what is "good" and what is "bad" in them.

Joost Meerloo's 1956 book, *Rape of the Mind,* was a natural progression of the content of his 1949 book, *Delusion and Mass-delusion.* He concluded in it that "stealthy mental coercion" is "among the oldest crimes" (p. 13). He referred to ancient practices using masks, chants, special effects, and a "hypnotizing ritual." He considered cult involvement to be a form of *brainwashing, delusion,* and *menticide.* He defined brainwashing as an elaborate ritual of systematic indoctrination, conversion, and self--accusation. Delusion, as he used the term, was first formulated by Johannes Wier in 1563 who reported that witches were scapegoated by "the inner confusion and desperation of their judges and of the Zeitgeist in general" (p. 27). The Middle Ages were a time of ferment and insecurity, of civil and religious unrest, and distrust. Any convenient, conspicuous target was welcome and the "ritual of interrogation and torture on an eccentric old woman charged with witchcraft compelled her to yield to the fantasies of judges and accusers" (p. 26). This coercive process is not limited to witchcraft. Meerloo coined the term *menticide* to describe an organized system of psychological intervention to "imprint the mind to express complete conformity," resulting in "great confusion" so that "no one knows how to distinguish truth from falsehood" (p. 28).

Meerloo used the case of Cardinal Mindzenty, an outspoken clergyman who was brainwashed by careful and deliberate severe stress to publicly confess treason. He was fed "inadequately and irregularly," questioned day and night by rotating interrogators, under unshaded lights, and possibly drugged. He was forced to stand 66 hours which caused swelling and pain in his legs. Meerloo suggested the interrogation process tapped "hidden guilt" which "undermines rational awareness," which exist in everyone. Like Fromm, he saw freedom as two-sided, everyone having "two opposing needs," to be independent, to be oneself, and the need not to be (p. 76). It is Hamlet's soliloquy, "to be or not to be." Not to be is basically masochistic and "at the end all moral evaluations disappear" (p. 88). Compounding this potential confusion and insecurity are our "inner contradictions" which Meerloo considered "part of the philosophical sickness of our time" (p. 29). Young and old, we can come from good homes, with few hardships, yet in every life there is some frustration and discontent which Meerloo felt was a frequent entry point for influence. With "daily propagandistic noise" and "forceful verbal cues" we identify with the "powerful noisemaker. Big Brother's voice resounds in all the little brothers" (p. 47).

According to Meerloo, there are a variety of negative stimuli available to skilled molders of the mind, such as moral and physical pressure, fatigue, hunger, boring repetition, and "confusion by seemingly logical syllogisms." In the concentration camps of World War II "the most upsetting experience" was the "feeling of loss of logic" which led to the disillusioning conviction that "nothing has any validity" (p. 49). He saw this as a state of Pavlovian *inhibition* or *depersonalization* in which former responses are unlearned and new ones adopted, what the Nazis called *gleichschaltung* (levelling). Through this stress conditioning "people often learn to like and do what they are allowed to like and do" (p. 52). In our time this has been called the *Stockholm syndrome* (Harnischnacker & Muther, 1987).

Meerloo suspected the victimization process may involve a form of hypnosis or hypnotic-like phenomenon. "There is no intrinsic difference," he wrote, "between individual and mass hypnosis" (p. 144). He commented that hypnotizability is enhanced by feeling part of a group, sharing common longings and needs, in a highly structured, always repeated, boring routine, monotonous and long speeches full of "specially suggestive words," and slogans monotonously repeated. He saw the mind as affected "daily" by systematized suggestion, subtle propaganda, and "more overt mass hypnosis" which involve the "irrational child hidden in the unconscious" and the "internal conflict between reason and emotion" (p. 73). He cited the example of the mass delusion from Orson Welles' 1938 radio drama *War of the Worlds*, a fictional invasion from Mars.

"Political hypnosis, mob hypnosis, and even war hypnosis can turn civilized men into criminals" and hypnosis can be a "trigger mechanism" to release "repressed infantile dependency needs" into a "waking sleepwalker and mental slave" free of personal responsibility (p. 64). Propaganda "kneads mental dough" through deception, distortion, and delusions of an "omnipotent, ideal state." Thinking "and the brain itself" become superfluous, individuality is renounced, replaced by "the inner emptiness of the savage child" (p. 124). The persuasiveness of cult leaders and activist followers is "verbocracy and semantic fog." The "big lie and phoney slogan" get focussed attention, their repetition dulls and weakens critical judgment and leads to submission to "every suggested myth of happiness." Then people are "capable only of imitation," are incapable of the "inquisitive sense of objectivity and perspective and . . . individual ideas and ideals" (p. 136). It is word magic and the magician exercises power "by increasing anxieties and fears . . . exploiting dependency needs and provoking feelings of guilt and inferiority" (p. 73). Joining a cult initially isolated the individual from family and society and "when sensory stimuli of everyday life are removed . . . the entire personality may change" (p. 78).

Meerloo described the victimization process as occuring in four phases (p. 90):

Phase 1: ARTIFICIAL BREAKDOWN AND DECONDITIONING
The techniques here are intimidation, suggestion, dramatic persuasion, mass suggestion, humiliation, embarrassment, loneliness, isolation, self-pity, or "overburdening the unsteady mind."

Phase 2: SUBMIT TO AND IDENTIFY WITH THE ENEMY
This is the "moment of surrender" in which a "parasitic superego" is implanted, usually facilitated with a "parental attitude." This activates and reinforces regression to infantile thoughts and feelings.

Phase 3: RECONDITIONING TO THE NEW ORDER
This is "taming," systematic indoctrination, filling in the empty slate of the mind, inputting new data into the mental computer, the more strange and unusual the better.

Phase 4: LIBERATION FROM THE TOTALITARIAN SELF
By whatever means, stopping the process which removes all external reinforcers. Meerloo pointed out that this is accompanied by crying spells, guilt, and depression which are temporary.

This process not only victimizes the innocent but it also attracts like-minded leaders and followers: "Charming characters who are easily able to influence others are often extremely susceptible to suggestion," Meerloo observed. This can lead to shared paranoid disorder, or *folie a deux,* still reported in current diagnostic manuals. He recommended that we increase our defenses against suggestion because "strong egos and critical persons are less sensitive to suggestion."

William Sargant, the British psychiatrist, wrote his book *Battle for the Mind* in 1957. He defined *brainwashing* as severe stress conditioning and agreed with Meerloo and others that there is a universal susceptibility to it but extroverts are the most sensitive. Among the examples cited is Maya Deran, who went to Haiti on a research grant to study and film

Haitian dancing. A stranger in a foreign culture, she unwillingly found herself immediately sensitized to and becoming entranced by the music, chanting, and repeated rhythm of the ritual to Erzulie, the goddess of love. She described later how it felt. Her "skull was a drum," she reported, the singing "inside my head," and her body activated: "I cannot wrench my legs free . . . there is no way out" (p. 107).

Sargant described three phases to what he termed *transmarginal inhibition,* a state of physical and/or mental exhaustion where the mind becomes a "perfect blank." He formulated these from a historical study of religious and political conversion and stressors in World War II and the Korean War but also from a study of John Wesley's journals, the founder of the Methodist church:

Phase 1: EQUIVALENCE
  All stimuli, important or trivial, yield the same response intensity. Sargant based this phase on the study of 5000 combat casualties in the Normandy campaign of World War II, marked by constant fatigue not relieved by rest, indifference, psychomotor retardation, and dulled response to all stimuli.

Phase 2: PARADOX
  Weak stimuli get a greater reaction than strong stimuli. In the same 5000 combat casualties, overreaction to stimuli, weak and strong. Some oppositional behavior was noted, such as complying with the request to hold out the hands but unable to lower them while being watched, or paralysis of limbs intensified by the effort to control it. In such a state the most illogical becomes logical.

Phase 3: ULTRAPARADOX OR PROTECTIVE PHASE
  Sudden and complete reversal of behavior and submission. The mind is a blank slate and new ideas and behaviors easily introduced and reinforced.

Sargant described two separate methods, *individual* or Eastern European method (Nazi Germany, Stalinist Russia), and *group* or Asian method (Chinese during the Korean War). The individual method is aimed at getting a confession, to imprison, execute, or for propaganda purposes. As used in and immediately after World War II, a file or dossier is built up, the person arrested, isolated, then interrogated first in a friendly manner, then by increasingly confrontive and abusive techniques.

More relevant to current cult practices is the Asian method, aimed at conversion and indoctrination in a group setting. Daily routine of lectures and visual and auditory propaganda is repeated endlessly, continually reinforced, increasingly effective over time. Korean War prisoners were placed in a controlled environment with no outside contact, "poisonous individualist" leaders or the better educated removed, subjected to continuing physical and mental fatigue and lack of sleep and rest, enforced attendance at long propaganda lectures (4–6 hours) of half-truths and generalizations, indignities (lack of privacy, rewarded self-criticism and informing, screened mail, strange customs), uncertainty and insecurity feelings (interviews at odd hours), guilt over violating rules or causing problems for others, and an atmosphere of extreme seriousness or sacredness to the entire process (no humor tolerated).

Other aspects of the Asian method: strange medical practices such as implanting a quarter-sized chicken liver in the chest and acupuncture; living in mud huts; 40–50 percent loss of body weight; propaganda newspaper entitled *Toward Truth and Peace;* mandatory "school" with subjects such as *The 60 Big U.S. Families, Admission of New China into the U.N., Decline of Capitalism;* oratory contests on selected topics, and the *Lenin Debating Society* on: "The United States started the Korean War," with a loaded negative. The Chinese focussed on what they considered basic American traits: materialism, opportunism, competitiveness, basic laziness, lack of thought and commitment to principle. Their approach was one of mock friendliness and helpfulness, explaining they knew Americans didn't want to be there, would share the same food, and ask them to be neutral and listen. There were 7190 POWs in 20 camps in Korea. Of these, 2730 died while imprisoned. No one escaped despite the absence of searchlights and guard towers and a guard-to-prisoner ratio of 1:100. One of three POWs collaborated by informing or signing false confessions, and 21 refused to return to the United States after the war. It was the highest casualty rate of prisoners and the highest number of refusals to return in American history. Of all American troops, Marines withstood the indoctrination process more than others.

Sargant found Pavlovian personality types to be the most heuristic. These were first formulated by Hippocrates in the ancient Greek cult of Asklipios. Sargant described them in terms of their characteristic reactions to stress conditioning and amount of sedation required to stabilize them:

Pavlov	Hippocrates	Response to stress	Sedation
strong excitatory	choleric	wild, hysterical	5× to 8×
lively	sanguine	controlled, purposeful	
calm imperturbable	phlegmatic	passive	
weak inhibitory	melancholic	fear paralysis	1×

In his 1987 book, Robert Lifton listed eight criteria for "ideological totalism" (parenthetical annotations mine to clarify Lifton's approach): milieu control (no external communication); mystical manipulation or planned spontaneity (leader-selected by design); demand for purity (simplistic, rigid pure-impure right-wrong good-evil dichotomy where only the cult is 100% pure); confession (1-sided, confessor tells all, cult criticizes but concedes nothing); sacred science (pseudo-scientific half-truth, oversimplification, illogical rationalization, invalid generalization); loaded language (literalization, jargon, simplistic, reassuring but cliche-ridden "language of non-thought") doctrine or dogma over the person (conflict between what one thinks or feels and what the cult requires should be thought and felt); dispensing of existence (cult truth is higher than any other or any other person's, therefore those outside the cult are dispensable). This latter "truth" makes animal and even human sacrifice justifiable.

SNAPPING

In their 1978 book, *Snapping, America's Epidemic of Sudden Personality Change*, Conway and Siegelman cited examples from an extensive study of the cult experience nationwide of how people uncertain of psychological-emotional identities, unable to sharpen self-awareness or reach fulfillment in the family, school, job, or religion, turned to ready-made off-the-shelf packaged answers of cults. The individual sees the cult connection as a multi-faceted answer to life's complex questions and "snaps." They define *snapping* as "the sudden, drastic alteration of personality in all its many forms" (p. 13), as if "some invisible switch is thrown," and a person "stops thinking and feeling for himself," breaks the awareness and social responsibilities between personality and the outside world "and literally loses his mind to some form of external or automatic control" (p. 225). From that moment, little or nothing from one's previous life, gets through into consciousness as it did, from family, friends, religion, or former values or goals. It is "blind detachment from the world and self-delusion ... to escape the responsibilities of being human in this difficult, threatening world ... betrayal both of one's individuality and of one's society" (p. 226).

Rather than facilitating personality and self-development, the cult experience further loosens associations, resulting in a "floating" consciousness, like a rudderless ship drifting with wind and tide. The struggling, uncertain personality is discarded for an off-the-rack, one-size-fits-all personality. What is perceived as ecstasy or a mystic experience is really the security of finding a temporary refuge from the outside world. Whether surrendered willingly or by deception, to "some religion, a psychology, or other recipe for living," the mind stops and remains in drifting neutral, without conscience or real consciousness. This mental Shangri-la is not rent-free nor without cost to the individual and the personality. There are new realities in the rigid, enforced belief system of the cult and the monotony of cult routine, "intense experiences (which) may affect fundamental information processing capacities of the brain" (p. 13). Worse, many cults use "powerful tools" with "little or no understanding of their immediate or long-range effects" (p. 14).

Conway and Siegelman cite Patty Hearst as an example of the long-term effects of the "snapping" experience. When psychiatrist and researcher Dr. Martin Orne, asked her about the times she was confined in a closet, he reported seeing "an immediate collapse. A totally helpless person would appear at that time" (p. 210). This vacant stare or empty look, haunted, lonely, and helpless, has been reported by therapists who have treated cult victims, from abused children to adults. Conway and Siegelman concluded "there really is nothing human inside human beings. It's all biology, chemistry, and machinery. Our humanity lies in the space between" (p. 225). They saw awareness, personality, and sense of self as formed by social communication and therefore no greater than the quality of interactions and relationships with others. Even loners and recluses are "raised by someone, given a language, and taught to think and feel" (p. 226). They concluded that we "stand poised at the threshold of a new age" but which we may never see "because our culture seems to be embarking on a destructive new course of manipulation and escapism, of human abdication" (p. 225).

The same year *Snapping* was published, the authors' admonition about a "destructive new course of manipulation and escapism" was tragically confirmed with the suicide of more than 900 followers of the Reverend

Jim Jones at Jonestown, Guyana. Jones directed the mass suicide over the PA system which was connected to a tape recorder. We have his final rationalization, the ultimate manipulation and escape for himself and his followers: "We've stepped over, one thousand people who said we don't like the way the world is. Nobody takes our lives from us. We laid it down. We got tired. We didn't commit suicide. We committed an act of revolutionary suicide protesting the condition of an inhumane world" (Feinsod, 1981, p. 201). Seeing some cult members reluctant to come forth and drink the poison, a woman came to the microphone and said: "Person after person, all ages, all races, rises to add another vote for death . . . to thank Jim Jones for bringing them to this land of freedom, to thank him for this chance to die with our brothers and sisters" (p. 199). Those men, women, and children heard only one side. Isolated physically and mentally, there was for them no other side.

SATANIC RITUAL

As presently practiced, there is a wide range of Satanic ritual taking place. Organized Satanic "churches" and "temples" advertise their regularly scheduled, public worship services which compete with and generally resemble traditional religious services and are relatively innocuous. To some they violate good taste and propriety but do not break the law or offer animal sacrifice. Sermons depict Satanism as rational and traditional religions as irrational. The sex and fraud scandals of televangelists in the 1980s and the bigotry and wars rooted in religious differences, historically and currently, provide them with many examples. Historically, vehement anti-Satanist religious leaders and writers have indirectly stimulated interest in Satanism more than the cults themselves which are small and with limited funds for advertising and promotion. There is no national or international Satanic organization accepted by all Satanists as *the* official authority. Rather, they are mainly small groups with few members and depend on one strong leader who defines beliefs and establishes ritual practices. As groups enlarge, they splinter and weaken. This has been the pattern of Satanic cults throughout history.

An example of how a cult is the product of one person's ideas and leadership is the work of Aleister Crowley who blended Eastern and Western occultism and mysticism, gay and heterosexual sex, and animal sacrifice into what he called "magick" (Crowley, 1969, 1974). He saw sex as exerting a powerful force field that could be harnessed and used ritually ("sex magic"). He ran newspaper ads for deformed people because he believed sex with them released more energy (Kahaner, 1988). He used drugs in an attempt to achieve enlightenment. In 1898 he joined the Hermetic *Order of the Golden Dawn.* In 1904 he claimed his guardian angel Aiwass appeared to him and announced he was "the harbinger of a new age, the eon of Horus" based on "the law of thelema," Greek for "will" (Lyons, 1988, p. 80). A major tenet was a typically Satanic reversal of the Golden Rule: "Do what thou wilt shall be the whole of the law" (Crowley, 1969). In 1912 he affiliated with *Ordo Templi Orientis* (OTO), a German secret society that believed in meditative sex, consistent with his preoccupation with sex. He rose to lead the British chapter. In 1920 he founded *The Abbey of Thelema* on the island of Sicily. There, on one occasion, he ritually killed a male goat having sex with a woman at the moment of orgasm (Lyons, 1988). In the early days of World War II, an Abbey member died after drinking the blood of a cat with distemper and the Italian government deported Crowley. It was one of many exiles for Crowley, who died in 1947. During his lifetime he referred to himself as "666" and "the Great Beast" (Daraul, 1971). OTO chapters continue in the United States and Canada but deny any connection with its European origins (Kahaner, 1988).

Materials commonly used in Satanic rituals are: robes with cowls, though according to original Satanic ritual only the master wears the cowl, black signifies death and for blood rituals or worship, red for sexual rituals; candles (usually black, red for sex, green signifies friendship); amulets inscribed or painted with occult symbols; an altar; Satanic symbols (6, 9, 666, or FFF (6th letter of alphabet); inverted and usually encircled pentagram to signify baphomet, the horned goat or Goat of Mendes; an inverted cross); bell and gong (bell sounds to begin and end the ritual and at incantations); silver chalice (never gold) for wine, blood, holy water, or urine; *athame,* the witch's knife; sword (signifies aggression, points to four cardinal directions called *crowns* or *points;* 6-foot length of rope or stranded cord; *thurible* or incense bowl; *parchment,* written blessings or curses ritually burned in candle flame); *grimoire* or the "book of shadows," recipes for conjuring and cursing; kosher salt (believed to repel demons); bones, whole or pulverized. These materials are also common to witchcraft, the feminist variant of Satanism. The Satanic sign of recognition is the "horned hand," fist raised, palm out, index and little fingers extended.

Melton (1986) described Satanic ritual as a "parody" of Christian practices such as the mass, communion, prayers, and hymns, deliberately desecrating religious objects such as spitting or stepping on the cross, inverting it, smearing feces or urine on the host, saying the Lord's Prayer backwards and reversing spelling (Dog for God, live for evil, Natas for Satan, Nema for Amen, red rum for murder), and in extremist criminal cults, physical and sexual abuse, mutilation, animal and human sacrifice. The most frequent Satanic animal sacrifices are domestic cats and dogs which are usually decapitated, the heads sometimes placed on stakes. It is believed that if the devil returns he will need a head. Satanic ritual takes place around the encircled inverted pentagram which is always present, with the altar to the north, a fire to the south, water to the west, air (nothing) to the east. Sometimes a *witch's tree* is burned by chopping through the bark, pouring and igniting lighter fluid, gasoline, or kerosene. Marihuana might be burned in the fire. Candles for evil hexes are on the altar's left, called *the left path,* candles for "good" on the right.

Ritual abuse and criminal acts occur in smaller, secret cults, committed by psychopaths or other mentally disturbed people who often mark victims and leave ritual objects and symbols at the crime scene. Larger, public Satanic "churches" and "temples" such as the Church of Satan and Temple of Set are not involved in these primitive, illegal acts. The Church of Satan was founded in 1966 by Anton Zandor LaVey, who wrote three books on Satanism (1969, 1971, 1972), and who publishes a newsletter, *The Cloven Hoof.* In his 1969 book, *The Satanic Bible,* he listed nine basic tenets of Satanism: indulgence over abstinence; "vital existence" not "spiritual pipe dreams"; "undefiled wisdom" not "hypocritical self-deceit"; kindness to the deserving, not "love wasted on ingrates"; vengeance instead of "turning the other cheek"; responsibility to the responsible, not "concern for psychic vampires"; man is just another animal, sometimes better, often worse, because of divine spiritual and intellectual development the most vicious animal of all; so-called sins lead to physical or mental gratification; Satan is the best friend the church has ever had because "he has kept it in business all these years." These tenets appeal to nonconformists and rebels in search of a cause. Melton (1986) observed that Satanists have produced "almost no literature" and groups "have come and gone without connecting with previously existing Satanic groups or leaving behind any progeny" (p. 76).

LaVey's "church" has had several schisms over the years and is less prominent because of them. Most Satanic cults disband when the leader dies, or split into less organized transient groups. A growing splinter group is the Temple of Set founded in 1975 by Michael Aquino and Lilith Sinclair, now Mrs. Aquino, which publishes a newsletter *Scroll of Set* and whose rituals are not public. It is named after the ancient Egyptian deity Set, god of night, "evil" brother of Osiris, god of life and immortality, who killed Osiris (Bridgwater, 1968, p. 802). A personification and symbolization of evil, Set was a predecessor of Satan.

Satanism is rich in legend, imagery, and fantasy. It is a persistent and recurring idea which has inspired drama, music, novels, and movies. These are fictionalized, imaginary elaborations of incidents and experiences reported over centuries of time. Most have never been conclusively proven. Few if any would stand the test of scientific analysis or legal rules of evidence. Examples: *The Exorcist, The Omen, Rosemary's Baby,* and such classics as *Faust.* All are fiction, fantasy, grossly exaggerated to arouse and hold interest. Police and the courts, psychic and other researchers, and investigative reporters cannot objectively prove or disprove supernatural, mystic, or occult experiences. This same lack of "hard" conclusive evidence also applies to the growing concern that there may be a network of extremist criminal cults kidnapping and ritually killing animals and people. Local, state, national, and international law enforcement agencies and an increasing number of mental health professionals and researchers are conscientiously searching for it and highly motivated to find it.

WITCHCRAFT

Witchcraft, as we know it today in the West, is a form of Satanism mainly of British origin and a witch inducted into a coven in England has the highest credentials. Maple (1966) described Rochford Hundred, between the rivers Thames and Grouch, in Southeast Essex about forty miles from London, as "the witch country." It is low, marshy ground where many believed "ghosts haunted the fields . . . gaunt black dogs wandered at night" and "the Devil had his chosen spots to raid suffering humanity" (p. 163). There were, according to Maple, "witch villages" and "Wise Men" and "white wizards." The most famous among these was James Murrell, the seventh son of a seventh son, born in 1780 at Rochford, Essex. Without any formal education, he first worked in surveying, then with a chemist, returning in 1812 to Rochford as a shoemaker until he assumed the "profession . . . of a Cunning Man" (p. 165). He fathered twenty children and died in December, 1860.

Murrell's lack of formal education and self-proclaimed leadership role are still typical of most cult leaders. Witchcraft is highly individualized and it is not possible to define it in terms that would apply to all who claim to be witches. Murrell, however, presents a typical pattern of occult beliefs and ritual practice. He lived in a cottage in which the front room was "full of drying herbs which hung in bunches from the ceiling." The "wizard's wooden chest" of magic books and papers was in the corner and there was a table on which was a skull and an assortment of "various mysterious implements." Herbs were prescribed for medical ailments, given with an incantation. The "magical lore of the ages" was available for a shilling to treat demonic possession, witchcraft, or finding lost property. White magic, "summoning forces from the other world," cost a crown. Murrell asked clients if they wanted "high" (spiritual) or "low" (material) treatment. "High" treatment required intercession of "good angels" to combat "bad angels."

For his rituals, Murrell used a "magic mirror" where people reported they saw persons who stole from them or lost relatives. It was believed he could foretell the future. When a woman asked him to predict her future for the next ten years, he limited his forecast to eight years. She died nine years later. He "cured" animal and human illness by laying on of hands, amulets hung around the neck, and herbal or topical remedies, always with an unintelligible incantation. There was a legend that a farm girl surprised an old gypsy woman in the barn where laborers stored beer. Ordered to leave the premises, the gypsy did so, grumbling "you'll be sorry." The girl was "attacked by a series of fits . . . ran on all fours, mewed like a cat, barked like a dog, and was uncontrollable." Murrell was summoned, confirmed possession, brewed a concoction of the girl's urine, herbs, pins, and blood and heated it in a bottle in a darkened room with locked doors, everyone present pledged to absolute silence. There was a knocking on the door and the voice of an old woman crying out: "For God's sake stop. You're killing me." The bottle burst. There was no sound outside the house. The next day they found the gypsy woman dead, her body showing strange burns. The farm girl recovered. Commenting on this case, Maple noted "how little the traditional form of witch belief had altered since the 17th century" (p. 168).

Much of these accounts suggest the possibility of hypnosis or hypnotic-like states. The gypsy woman was obviously still in the neighborhood and could have overheard the ritual aimed forcefully and directly at her. Skin changes such as blistering or hives have been reported with the use of hypnosis and the gypsy's "strange burns" are consistent with this. The "cure" was affected by Murrell but in the context of close family support and caring which could heighten hypnotic susceptibility and effectiveness. After all that effort and multisensory impact, the gypsy had to know she was in deep trouble, and the girl that she could escape the gypsy's "curse." Maple gave us further evidence of possible hypnotic effect. Murrell had bottles made of metal so they would not break in the fire. A boy drank beer from one not knowing its purpose, and when told, he "at once turned deathly pale and went home shaking wit fear and fell dead" (p. 168). In Canewdon, Nellie Button "had the power to hypnotize those she disliked so that they lost the use of their limbs." She "struck down" a girl who offended her with an undiagnosable, untreatable paralysis. After seven days, Nellie "whispered something in the ear of the sick girl who was within five minutes was well again" (p. 172). Witchcraft, voodoo, or any other strange and unusual belief, *can* affect physical and mental health, can kill you, if you believe it can (MacHovec, 1975, 1976).

Group witchcraft occurs in *covens* which originally consisted of thirteen persons, twelve and a leader, designed to profane Jesus and the twelve apostles. Today, those who publicly claim to be witches avoid illegal acts such as animal or human sacrifice, but classical witchcraft ritual requires both. The use of the *baphomet* or goat's head may have arisen from several ancient cults such as the goat-god Dionysus, the goat's horns of Priapus, the ram, stag, and bull of Mithraism, the horned helmets of the Teutons, or the unicorn. These are consistent with the primitivism of the ritual. Devils to personify evil also have ancient roots: Set, the god of darkness in ancient Egypt; Ahriman and Angra Mainyu in Persia; the yin of Taoism; Lilith, the "vampirelike child killer and nocturnal female demon" and legend has it, Adam's first wife, of the Hebrews (Bridgwater, 1968, p. 615); Satan, leader of "fallen angels," is referred to in Judaism, Christianity, and Islam. Other names: Abaddon (destroying angel, Hebrews); Apollyon (destroying angel, Greeks); Baalzebub or Beelzebub (from Baal, Babylonian Bel, originally local gods of Canaan, then fertility god, chief god, later denounced as evil); Belial; the dragon; Lucifer (*Paradise Lost*), Mephistopheles (*Faust*); Old Nick; the serpent or snake.

Esbat, Sabbat, Black Mass

There are three forms of Satanic ritual, the *esbat*, informal, usually unscheduled local meetings, the *sabbat*, a formal, scheduled festival, and

the *black mass,* a blasphemous and profane reversal of the Roman Catholic mass. The *esbat* is the routine business meeting of the coven. Less
ceremonial, no costumes are worn. The agenda consists of sharing activities and any charms or spells which need to be cast. The 13th or 31st days
of the month are popular Esbat dates, using the Kabbalistic numeral 13.

Sabbat festivals occur seasonally such as February 2 (Candlemas Day),
April 30 (Roodmas Day) or May 1 (Walpurgis Day or May Day), August
1 (Lamnas Day), and October 31 (Halloween). Other special dates in the
Satanic calendar: January 1, 7 (St. Winebald's Day) and 20; February 2
and 25; March 1 (St. Eichatadt's Day), 20 (Spring Equinox); April 24 to
May 1 (Corpus de Baahl, Grand Climax); June 21 (Summer Solstice) and
23; July 1 (druidic sexual union with demons) and 25; August 3 and 24;
September 7 (marriage to satan), 20 (midnight host), and 22 (Fall Equinox);
October 29–31 (All Hallow Eve); November 1 (Halloween) and 4; December 21, 22, 24 (High Grand Climax). Special events occurred on these
holidays, classified as blood (specified type of sacrifice), or sex (specified
age range of victim and individual or orgy). Christmas, the birth of
Christ, is reversed in Satanic practice to celebrate death of an infant
sacrifice (MacHovec, 1989).

The sabbat is a major Satanic event marked by feasting, dancing, and
sex following the ritual agenda. The Grand Master presides over the
sabbat, representing Satan, wearing a horned goat-mask with a candle
between the horns, sometimes in the costume of a black ram. Paws of
sacrificial animals are removed and used as symbols of the devil who
supposedly has animal forelegs. Participants usually wear black robes
and carry candles, usually black. A typical sabbat agenda would include:
reports by witches on their activities, usually themes of power, money, and
sex; initiation of new witches; animal sacrifice, preferably a black hen or
goat; ritual of the kiss of shame; orgy of food, dance, and sex. To be
initiated, candidates profess a wish to become witches of their own free
will, disavow the Christian faith (or presumably any previously held
religious belief), complete a pact in their own blood with the devil, and
have a witch's mark (tattoo or symbolic scar). The sacrifice is done on
an altar and there are reports of animals and babies being stabbed lying
atop a nude woman. The "kiss of shame" is on the buttock of the Grand
Master. Hector Berlioz' Symphonie Fantastique (1830) describes a witch's
sabbat.

The *black mass* was first described at the end of the 17th century (Lyons,
1988). In *Justine,* the Marquis de Sade referred to celebrating a black
mass in a cloister. Summers (1974) reported that an elaborate, expen-

sively furnished Satanic chapel was discovered in 1895 in the Palazzo Borghese in Rome (p. 209). He quoted the April 14, 1934 *London Daily Mail* reported "certain London cults practice the black mass where black bread, black wine, and black candles are used and worshippers confess every good deed as a sin" (p. 223). The black mass usually follows the sabbat or is held independently. The ritual is a "carnal reversal" of the Roman Catholic mass, but Satan is substituted for references to God and Christ (Lyons, 1988). Summers (1974) credited Gilles de Rais (Bluebeard), Francesco Prelati, Abbe Cotton, Abbe Lemaignan, and Abbe Guibourg with developing the black mass but Lyons (1988) described the Guibourg version as the major contribution. The altar is a naked woman lying on her back on a coffin or table. Black candles replace the white candles of the church. Since the object is to degrade and defile, stolen chalices, hosts, and holy water are used with urine, feces, animal or human body parts, and blood. If substitute objects are used they are reversed in color and shape, and so the usually round white host may be triangular and black or red and the cross is broken, defaced, or inverted (Summers, 1974). A variation of the black mass was a major feature of the British *Hellfire Clubs* from 1730–1750 (Lyons, 1988).

In 1801, Francis Barrett wrote The Magus or Celestial Intelligence, a book Summers (1974) described as "among the most interesting and most valuable books of English occult lore" (p. 167). In it, Barrett describes the nine "degrees" of devils which equate with the nine "choirs" of angels:

1st degree: *False gods*, led by Beelzebub, god of Ekron.
2nd degree: *Spirits of Lies*, led by Pytho, prince of seance spirits, and familiar of the Witch of Endor.
3rd degree: *Vessels of Iniquity and Wrath*, led by Belial, prince of evil acts, malice, disobedience, and deformity.
4th degree: *Avengers and Revengers*, led by Asmodeus, the "fearful fiend," prince of vengeance who killed the seven husbands of Sara.
5th degree: *Deluders*, led by Balban, prince of conspirators and witches, who possessed Sor Magdalena de la Cruz by imitating miracles.
6th degree: *Aerial Powers*, led by Meririm, who harm the earth, sky, and sea with wind, hail, lightning, fire, locusts, caterpillars, and flys.
7th degree: *Furies*, led by Abaddon (Hebrew) or Apollyon (Greek), "the destroyer" who leads the Apocalypse, which Summers considered "the worst of all the hierarchy of hell . . . the world is under their dominion today" (p. 168).
8th degree: *Accusers*, princes of envy, jealousy, and evil motives, who according to Summers possessed the Pharisees to accuse Jesus of casting out devils by working through the devil.
9th degree: *Temptors and Ensnarers*, led by Mammon, prince who is with

everyone, completing the good angel bad angel interaction of good and evil first formulated by Origen (185–254 AD) and later by Bandinius in the 12th century

AFRO—CARIBBEAN CULT RELIGION

About 300 years ago, West African Blacks were sold into slavery by their chiefs, loaded onto ships, and torn from their land, language, culture, religion, and lifestyle and brought to a strange, markedly different environment on the islands of the Caribbean. Afro-Caribbean cult religions are a reaction to this and a psychological-emotional attempt to return to their African roots. There is considerable variety in these cult religions. Some invoke primarily white or *sympathetic* magic for benevolent purposes, others use more black than white magic, toward evil ends. Most have some of each, gray magic. The best known of these is *voodoo, vodou* or *vodun,* which translates "protective spirit," a mixture of two primitive African religions, from the Yoruba of southwest Nigeria and the Fon of Dahomey (now Benin), and the Roman Catholicism forced upon slaves in Haiti. Increasing in the United States due to immigration, most notably from the 1980 Mariel boat lift from Cuba to Florida, are *santeria, abaqua,* and *palo mayombe.* Other Afro-Latin cult religions are *brujeria* and *curanderismo* in Mexico, *espiritismo* in Puerto Rico, *obeah* or *myalism* in Jamaica, from African Ashanti beliefs, *macumba, candomble,* and *umbanda* in Brazil, *shango* in Trinidad, and *The Religion* in New York and elsewhere in the U.S. This amalgamation process is called *syncretism.* These cult religions are not Satanic, but retain the primitive spiritism and animism of the less civilized African societies from which they came. Distinctive features of primitive cult religions are the number of gods, offerings and animal sacrifices to appease or "feed" them, magic and superstition, spells and sorcery using herbs, charms, amulets, talismans, bloodletting, and animal sacrifice.

There is much overlap and duplication of beliefs and ritual practices across Afro-Caribbean religions but they all believe human events are controlled or influenced by direct intervention of gods. They agree gods who are not "fed" and satisfied are likely to retaliate in some way. These cults are loosely organized, without an overall leader and with no written scriptures or dogma. They are simple, naturalistic, animistic, and primitive. Compared to most major world religions they are unsophisticated, unscientific, and anti-intellectual. On the positive side, they offer close, personal support, an orderly, disciplined with strong, rigid values above and beyond those of the street which tolerate or condone crime and violence. The priest and priestess function as doctor, therapist, and caseworker. Most Afro-Caribbean cults meet informally and privately in groups formed geographically or around a priest or priestess.

They usually get "bad press" because of their strange beliefs and animal sacrifice and are accused of grave robbing, devil worship, even ritual murder. None of the Afro-Caribbean cult religions are Satanic, nor do any of them refer directly to Satan in their rituals. They do not do human sacrifice, though some cult members have as individuals committed crimes. Their major focus is more on common sense than complex theology, more self protective than primitive, more on wellbeing (*salud*) than wrongdoing. Sympathetic magic is used as traditional religions use prayer and good works. Voodoo teaches that doing evil solely for evil purposes will turn back or backfire on the evildoer.

Voodoo is a Haitian import, first entering the United States centuries ago in what is now New Orleans. The slaves adapted Roman Catholic saints to the deities of their own bush religion. French-speaking, Haitian immigrants preferred New Orleans where French was still spoken. Sargant (1957) observed that voodoo "shows with what ease suggestibility can be increased by subjecting the brain to severe physiological stresses" (p. 106). *Loa*, African tribal gods, possess humans during voodoo rituals and "carry out all the detailed behaviors expected of the particular deity" (p. 107). Possession (*chevauche*, "mounted like riding a horse") occurs amid frantic dancing, incessant drumbeating, rum drinking, and cigar smoking of the voodoo ritual. Those who have experienced it report they first feel a "force" inside them, then uncontrollable trembling like shivering, loss of motor control, falling, seizureform writhing, as "the god takes over." This process can be prevented by reorienting them by eye contact, conversing or dancing with them, or ringing a small bell in their ear. There are similarities to hypnosis: susceptible persons are in a highly suggestible state, do not recall behaviors while possessed, awaken feeling relaxed and relieved, and possession is easier after the first time.

Le Bon Dieu (God), the Creator, according to voodoo legend got bored with the world and created minor deities to take over. They were given human qualities and motives, some fun-loving, others fierce, some warm and wise, others war-like. There were many of them, as numerous as the gods of the ancient Greeks, Romans, and Egyptians. *Erzulie* (Virgin Mary) is the goddess of love who prefers decorated cakes and creme de menthe as offerings. *Damballah* (St. Patrick) is the god of fertility and prefers champagne as an offering. Some voodoo gods accept Coca-Cola®. A deeper analysis of this imagery sees them as Jungian primordial archetypes or cosmic forces given names and simplified to be more easily understood. Made famous in horror movies is voodoo use of a doll with the victim's name written on it or on an attached note, a candle in its head, and pins stuck in it to cast a spell. Actually, dolls are used more frequently to symbolize a person in need of help, the pins locating body areas or functions needing help. Sewing herbs into to doll's stomach is believed to relieve an upset stomach.

Santeria (pronounced Santa-Reeyuh, means "saint worship") is an Afro-Cuban cult religion which has adapted selected Roman Catholic saints to the primitive spiritism and rituals of the Yoruba region of southwestern Nigeria. Most *santeros* consider themselves Roman Catholic and attend Catholic services and santero rituals. It is said the church "takes care of the soul" (salvation) and santeria "takes care of life" (protection). Estimates of the number of santeros in the United States vary from less than a million to three million, as many as 100 million worldwide. It is estimated there are 50,000 santeros in the Miami area, more per square mile than in Cuba (Erickson, 1988). New York, northern New Jersey, and Los Angeles also have large concentrations. Most came to the United States during the 1980 Mariel boat lift.

According to santeria belief, *Olodumare-Olofi* is the Creator, so powerful he is not worshipped directly and so there are no idols or pictures of him. There are many minor deities called *orichas* or *oricha saints*. They combine African gods with Catholic saints. According to santeria belief, everyone has a personal guardian that can harm or heal, harass or protect. They can be bought by witches but neutralized by magic and rituals. They need to be regularly "fed," with the blood of roosters or goats. *Otanes* are sacred stones which not only represent the oricha saints or gods but are believed to actually contain them. Otanes contain *ache* (Ah-Chay), the basic power of the universe. Ache is also in santero priests, persons possessed by oricha saints, herbs, prayers, rituals, and religious objects.

There are *Seven African Powers,* major deities shared by most Afro-Caribbean religions (adapted from Wetli and Martinez, 1981):

Deity	Associated power	Special Objects	Animal Sacrifice
Eleggua Esu (St. Anthony; Christ child; Guardian Angel)	Communicates with orichas; trickster god, mischievous, complex, popular, demanding, needs frequent offerings, controls roads and gates	rum, corn, cowrie shells candy, cigars	blood of decapitated black rooster smoked possum
Obatala (Risen Christ; Holy Eucharist; Our Lady of Mercedes)	Father of orichas and humanity, patron of anxious and depressed, wise and pure, curses are blindness birth defects, paralysis	pearls white things	white pigeon white canary female goat
Chango Shango (St. Barbara)	Thunder, lightning, fire, curses of death and suicide by fire; warrior deity; fiery and quick-tempered	apple, banana, axe, sword castle, cups	red rooster, lamb, goat, rodent
Oshun (Our Lady of Charity or Cuba)	Beauty, culture, love, sex, good marriage, money, gold, curses are home, social, or stomach problems	gold, copper, mirrors, river water, seashells, pumpkin	yellow hen, male goat, sow
Yemaya (Our Lady of Regia)	Women, fertility, motherhood, sailors and the sea; curses of respiratory illnesses	watermelon, boat,	duck, female goat, turtle
Babalu-Aye (St. Lazarus)	patron of the sick, especially skin diseases; curses of leprosy and gangrene	cigars, pennies, glass of water	--
Oggun (St. Peter)	Warrior god; metal, tools, weapons, patron of miners truck drivers, mechanics, working people; curse is a violent death (car crash)	railroad track or spikes, steel knife	blood of red or white rooster, male goat, feathers

In addition to these Seven African Powers there are other deities such as Orunla (St. Francis of Assisi), patron of diviners, Osain (Archangel

Raphael), patron of herbologists, Los Ibelli (St. Damian and St. Cosme), patron of good luck, Ochosi (St. Norbert), patron of the bird hunt, Agallu (St. Christopher), patron of seaports and harbors, Oya (Our Lady of La Candelaria), patroness of cemeteries, and El Negrito Jose, who guards the Seven African Powers and allows communication with them. According to santeria belief, everyone has one of these deities as a guardian spirit which must be appeased and "fed" by animal sacrifice. Pictures or symbols of them are frequently in the home or at ritual sites, as follows (Martinez & Wetli, 1982):

Elleggua: A clay head or face with eyes, nose, and mouth of cowrie shells, corn, rum, red and black beads.

Obatala: Anything white, typically white clothing, a white cloth, pearls or white beads.

Chango: A sword or double-edged axe, apples, bananas, red and white beads.

Oshun: Mirrors, seashells, river water, honey, gold, copper, white and yellow beads.

Yemaya: Black madonna holding white baby Jesus, watermelon, white and blue beads.

Babalu-Aye: Old man on crutches with sores on his legs, accompanied by dogs, cigars, pennies, glasses of water, white and purple beads.

Oggun: Metal necklace with 10–12 pendants of miniature garden tools, railroad track, steel knife, black and green beads.

Orunla: Spring water or white wine, prunes, the Ifa divination board, green and yellow beads.

Osain: A clay head or face of a Black man with one eye, cigars, rum, green and black beads.

Los Ibelli: Two carved wood figures of people, candy, red and white beads.

Ochosi: Deer antlers, bow and arrow, brown and green beads.

Agallu: Statue of St. Christopher, white, red, and yellow beads.

Oya: A sapphire, cemetery, hurricane, lightning, brown and white beads.

El Negrito Jose: Old Black man sitting in a chair, pennies, cigar.

Santera groups range in size from a few members to more than a hundred, mostly women. Each group is led by a santero priest or priestess who control the group's beliefs, practices, and rituals. Santero priests cast spells (*embrujamiento*), exorcise evil spirits (*despojamientos*), foretell the future, cure illness and the evil eye, and conduct animal sacrifice. They are believed to be able to induce a state of cosmic transcendence. Sandoval (1977) reported santeros believe problems and diseases result from five causes: magic, either imitative or contagious; loss of the soul; spirit intrusion; object intrusion; and anger of the gods. *Fiesta santera* is a ritual held weekly or more often if needed which includes chanting incantations and rhythmic drumbeating (believed to call the gods), rum drinking, and cigar smoking (including women). A chicken, pig, or goat is usually ritually killed and offered to the oricha saints, along with select fruits. During the ritual, someone is possessed by an oricha saint, usually the priest. This resembles a seizure, falling to the ground, writhing and tremoring, then getting up and wandering through the group, touching others and mumbling as if speaking in tongues. Someone, usually another santero priest, is designated interpreter and translates the oricha saint's messages. Possession is terminated by calling the name of the possessed so the soul can return to the body as the oricha saint leaves. Alonso and Jeffrey (1988) reported that on occasion this technique fails and the possessed person may "enter a frenzy and remain in that state for hours." In such situations, mental health professionals are rarely consulted.

The longest and most elaborate santeria ceremony is the *asiento* which lasts about seven days and costs $4,000 to $7,000 (Erickson, 1988). The santero priest candidates have their heads shaved and eat only coconuts, smoked possum, herbs, and the blood of sacrificed animals. More than a hundred animals and birds are killed. After one asiento, police found thirty pots in each of two rooms, a goat or sheep head in each pot, and the bodies of about fifty chickens in a neat row in the hallway. In simpler rituals, a hen, dove, or canary is rubbed over the body of the faithful to transfer evil spirits to the bird which is then killed and bled into a coconut shell as an offering. The most common ritual to appease or intercede with the gods is to cut a rooster's throat and bleed it into a bowl together with honey, rum, and some feathers. *Botanicas* are stores that sell herbs, roots, leaves, oils, incense, sprays, statues, bones, stones, and sometimes sacrificial birds and animals.

It has been estimated that a santero sacrifices about 35 animals and birds a year (Erickson, 1988). The bodies of the dead birds and animals are often left in secluded areas as offerings to the gods. The June 22, 1981 *Newsweek* reported Miami River "cleanup boats" removed an average of 100 decapitated doves and chickens a week. Local newspapers in 1988 described how "pig entrails dangle from the branches of sacred trees, and great skulls, decapitated pigeons and offerings of fruits, pennies, and cigars can be easily unearthed in area parks and cemeteries," the discovery of mutilated bodies of fifteen animals and birds, lamb, sheep, and roosters in New Jersey, seizure of a calf, pig, goat, doves, hens and roosters from a santero priest in Washington, D.C., and of sickly, lice-ridden goats, chickens, a lamb and pig in California. Mistreating birds and animals is denied by santero priests who point out that sacrificing sickly animals is an "insult to the gods." Animal sacrifice has caused the most public concern and raised serious legal and constitutional questions. In 1987, a Florida city passed ordinances prohibiting animal sacrifice. A santero priest filed suit claiming violation of freedom of religion. The Humane Society maintained this freedom is exempted by the state's right to prevent cruelty to animals. The American Civil Liberties union supported the priest on the grounds animal sacrifice is acceptable religious practice. It seems likely the case will go to the U.S. Supreme Court. Meanwhile, the Humane Society of the United States is encouraging the passage of ordinances prohibiting animal sacrifice (see Appendix B).

Some journal articles have defended santeria as "a collaborating institution for matters of the soul" just as mental health professionals treat the mind (Sandoval, 1979), an "adaptive mechanism," folk psychiatry, readily available source of personal and emotional support (Lefley, 1981), counseling by divination, help through ritual, cure by priest's intervention (Sandoval, 1977), and "a voluntary stress-reduction mechanism" (Perez y Mena, 1977). Local and national visual and print media, however, have in most instances been critical of santeria, mainly because of concern about uncontrolled, frequent bird and animal sacrifices.

Abaqua is a well organized, closeknit, highly selective group that investigates prospective members and votes on their acceptance. The ideal candidate is *varon,* "having manly traits." Fidel Castro did not interfere with abaqua. *Babalao* are the priests and *motanza* is the major ceremony, taken from the name of the province in Cuba where the sect originated. Objects used are: coconuts, fruits, water, and flowers. There is animal sacrifice but Kahaner (1988) reported no bloodletting or ritual drinking of blood and sacrificed animals are cooked and eaten. Abaqua does not kill black birds or animals. Specially observed dates are December 4, the feast of Saint Barbara (Chango) and December 17, the feast of Saint Lazarus (Babalu-Aye).

Palo Mayombe, also known as *Palo Monte,* is another Afro-Caribbean cult religion from Cuba that blends the primitive spiritism of the Bantu region of the Congo with Catholic saints. Its followers quite often also use santeria beliefs and rituals. It is not unusual to find objects of both cults in the same home, but not in the same room. Santeria is used mostly for good or neutral purposes (white magic) but Palo Mayombe is "primarily oriented towards malevolent sorcery" (Wetli & Martinez, 1983). St. Lazarus is the mayombero patron saint, actually Babalu-Aye, depicted on crutches, with sores on his legs, and dogs licking them. Interestingly, this was a common practice in the ancient Greek temples of Asklipios, the cult where Hippocrates was a priest-physician. It is also interesting that the late Desi Arnaz, a Cubano, sang a best selling record of the song *Babalu* (Kahaner, 1988).

Palo Mayombe practitioners are *paleros* or *mayomberos* and are often referred to as "Padre" or "Madre." Those who perform good works are *mayomberos Christianos* and those who do evil are *mayomberos Judios.* To be initiated, mayomberos must wear clothing buried three weeks in a grave and are presented with a sceptre of a human tibia bone wrapped in black cloth with which they "rule over the powers of darkness." The mayombero keeps a *nganga* or "sacred cauldron," a black iron pot which contains human bones (black or dirt-encrusted skull and sometimes long bones), animal bones (skulls, birds, sometimes turtles), cowrie shells, feathers, colored beads, wood, herbs, small garden tools, sacred stones, candles, gunpowder, sulfur (incense), mercury (quicksilver), and ashes. Mayombero Christianos include a crucifix; mayombero Judios add rail-road spikes and bullets. The ritual involves asking the nganga to satisfy the needs of the faithful. The skull is *kiyumba* and is used in the belief it holds the intelligence and spirit of the deceased. It is "fed" sacred stones and sometimes blood.

Palo mayombe and santeria worship the same gods, but with different names, according to Wetli and Martinez (1983). Mayomberos call their gods *nkitas* or *mpungus* but represent them with the same Christian saints as the santeros:

Mayombero god	Santero god	Catholic saint
Tata legua, Nkuyu	Eleggua	Christ child, Guardian Angel, St. Anthony of Padua
Mama Nsasi, Nkita Nkitan Kitan	Chango	St. Barbara
Mama Kengue, Yola, Yeye	Obatala	Risen Christ, Holy Eucharist, Our Lady of Mercy
Mpunga Mama, Wanga Choya, Wengue	Oshun	Our Lady of Charity
Mboma Mama, Kalunga Mama,	Yemaya	Our Lady of Regia

Mbumba Mama,		
Mamba		
Pengun Futila,	Babalu-Aye	St. Lazarus
Tata Funde		
Zarabanda,	Oggun	St. Peter
Pungo Dibudi		

The Religion is a Black American version of African tribal religion which seeks to return to beliefs and practices in southwestern Nigeria at the time of the slave trade 300 years ago. Some Caucasians have joined this movement. Members are better educated than most other Afro-Caribbean cults, often college graduates with majors in anthropology and social work. They assume African names, eat special foods, wear West African beaded necklaces and clothing, and make offerings and sacrifices to African deities. Priests are paid fees for their services which range from $20 to several hundred, depending on the ritual and its complexity and components. Only *babalao,* high priests, "throw and read the shells," much like reading *I Ching* yarrow sticks in ancient China (MacHovec, 1971). There is a commune of this cult religion in a 9-acre reconstructed Nigerian village in southeastern South Carolina where the Yoruba language is taught, African artifacts and clothing are sold, and the public can tour. Polygamy is practiced and tribal symbols are cut on the faces and backs of the faithful. Unlike typical Nigerian villages, this American version has electricity, plumbing, modern furniture, and television. **Gullah** is a predominantly Protestant Christian Afro-American subculture of former slaves who live along the South Carolina, Georgia, and north Florida ocean coast. They were brought directly from Sierra Leone and Angola to the southeastern United States without stopover in the Caribbean. Perhaps because of this Africa to Protestant America connection, there was no syncretism with Catholic saints. Gullah beliefs and rituals are primarily Protestant Christian, such as baptism by immersion, and with little continuing African content.

Brujeria is a Mexican variation on Afro-Caribbean religion but which mixes Aztec beliefs with witchcraft and Catholicism. A *bruja* is a witch and *brujeria* is witchcraft or the use of black magic or evil rituals. Their patroness is Our Lady of Guadalupe, but Kahaner (1988) reported this is actually the ancient Aztec goddess Tontantzin. Cemetery dirt, herbs, astrology, and a Tarot deck are used in brujeria rituals. Evidence of santeria and palo mayombe are common in brujeria, such as the use of seven pennies to symbolize the Seven African Powers.

The 1987 movie *The Believers,* starred Martin Sheen as a police psychotherapist whose young son is chosen as a human sacrifice by an extremist African cult. It contains specific references to santeria, brujeria, and African bush religion, but in quick takes with very little elaboration or explanation. The film takes the most dramatic extremes of ritual practices and human behavior, combines them with far-fetched plot, and blends them into a forcefully dramatic, bizarre drama. Like *The Exorcist,* it distorts and exaggerates reality but contains some truth. *Exorcist* showed the authentic exorcism rite but combined dramatic symptoms of possession never reported in one person. *Believers* provides a comparison of white and black magic and their rituals, how African gods and Catholic saints are fused and imbedded in Latino culture, and how santeria is misunderstood. The film *is* worth viewing, best done by videotape to play back easily missed references to santeria, its beliefs, rituals, and religious objects.

Summing up, Afro-Caribbean cult religions use animal sacrifice to appease or "feed" the gods to protect the faithful, not to inflict pain or harm others. These folk religions are benevolent and not violent and the primary goal is to seek wealth and well-being here on earth rather than eternal salvation in the hereafter. All variations of these religions include African gods with human traits, much like the pantheons of Rome, Greece, Egypt, and other ancient civilizations. Most cult members are devoutly religious and do not commit crimes. Those few that are involved in crime, usually drug dealing and murder, sometimes leave symbols and ritual objects at the crime scene. Bodies of birds or animals sacrificed before the human victim was killed have been found. In these cases, the criminal happens to be in the cult—the cult is not criminal of and by itself. Criminals in cults sometimes rely on cult beliefs such as wearing a protective necklace and sprinkling powder at crime scenes to prevent detection and apprehension by police. These are ancient and primitive practices. Centuries ago American Indians, African tribesmen, and Polynesian islanders would charge armed troops believing these devices rendered them impervious to bullet and sword.

POLLS AND STATISTICS

Ben Wattenberg, in his book *The Real America* (1974) reported statistics of church attendance and religious beliefs which relate to growing involvement with cults (pp. 261–263). A 1973 Gallup poll reported a decline in attendance at weekly religious services from 49% in 1957 to 40% in 1973. Only two in five Americans regularly go to church or temple. Still, a 1968 Gallup study showed worldwide Americans are more active than West Germans (27%), the French (25%) or Norwegians (14%) and have a greater belief in God: 98% as opposed to 81% in West Germany and 73% in France and Norway. Conversely, when asked if religion is increasing or losing influence, there was a very significant change in opinion in the United States from 1957 to 1970: in 1957 14% saw it as increasing to 69% who viewed it as decreasing in influence; in 1970 75% saw religion's influence waning to only 14% who saw it increasing. Since that time we have had nationwide fiscal and sex scandals of TV evangelists which would suggest further erosion of the perceived influence of religion. Cults have moved into this vacuum.

Wattenberg also reported polls by Daniel Yankevich among college students 1969–1971 who were asked if in their opinion it was morally wrong to have extramarital sex, homosexual sex between consenting adults, and casual premarital sex. Polls in 1969 to 1971 yielded the following comparative data: extramarital sex was morally wrong for 77% in 1969 but only 57% in 1971; homosexual sex was wrong for 42% in 1969 and 45% in 1971; premarital sex was wrong to 34% in 1969 and to 25% in 1971. This is the population most vulnerable to cult recruitment (MacCollam, 1979) and Yankevich's polls suggest a softening or lowering of moral values which suggests increased susceptibility to the order and structure of cult life and practice.

In Dr. Marcello Truzzi's introduction to Albert Lyons' 1988 book *Satan Wants You,* he reported the results of a 1982 Gallup poll in which 70% of adult Americans questioned believed there is a devil, 34% as a "personal being who directs evil forces and influences people to do wrong" and 36% as an "impersonal force that influences people to do wrong" (p. xiii). Truzzi also reported a 1968 study which found 60% of Roman Catholics and 38% of Protestants agreed it is "completely true the devil actually exists" (p. xiv). There was a wide variation in the Protestant results: 92 percent Southern Baptists; 77 percent Missouri Synod Lutherans; 13 percent Methodists; 6 percent Congregationalists.

THE VATICAN ON CULTS

In 1986 the Vatican Secretariat for Non-believers and the Pontifical Council for Culture issued *The Vatican Report on Sects or New religious Movements: A Pastoral Challenge.* It acknowledged the "rapid proliferation" of "new religious or pseudo-religious movements, groups, and practices" which were considered "a serious matter." It noted difficulties differentiating cults, sects, and religions and preferred the term "sect" as having a less negative connotation. The report identified the typical target population as "youth . . . unemployed, not active in parish life . . . from an unstable family . . . ethnic minority group or living far from the Church's reach . . . well-to-do and highly educated . . . or irregular marriage situation" but "very few . . . join a sect for evil reasons" (*Cultic Studies Journal,* 1986, *3,* p. 117). The growth and success of cults was attributed to needs and aspirations not met in "mainline churches," recruitment and training tactics, economic advantage, political interest, or initial curiosity. Contributing factors were cited, such as "the growing interdependence in today's world . . . the depersonalization structures of contemporary society . . . multiple crisis situations" (Ibid).

Cults claim to be uniquely relevant to these basic needs and aspirations and the *Vatican Report* observed that they function on both cognitive and affective levels but "in a way that deadens the cognitive faculties." It listed nine "needs and aspirations" most involved in the cult experience and pointed out that there can be overlap:

1. *Quest for belonging (sense of community),* a reaction to disrupted lifestyles, broken homes, and loneliness. Cults promise warmth and support, sharing and attention, safety and security, "resocialization of marginalized individuals." In exchange, the report commented "the sect often does the thinking for the individual" (p. 119).

2. *Search for answers,* to those feeling insecure, inadequate, or uncertain of their identity, role, or place in the world. Cults offer "simple and ready-made answers to complicated questions and situations, simplified and partial versions of traditional truths and values," through magic, supernatural, or subjective proof, claims of unique moral superiority, trance, mediumship, prophecies, possessions, etc. (p. 119).

3. *Search for wholeness (holism)* by those who feel alienated, isolated, from home, family, or society. Cults offer harmony, togetherness, a substitute family joined in a "gratifying religious experience," body and spiritual healing, all in one place and time (p. 119).

4. *Search for cultural identity,* to overcome dissociation from the world community, especially for Third World peoples who lose traditional social cultural, and religious values. Cults offer "plenty of room" for diversity and "a style of prayer and preaching closer to the cultural traits and aspirations of the people" (p. 120).

5. *Need to be recognized, to be special,* "not just a number or a faceless member of a crowd," to have a clear identity and to "rise out of anonymity." Cults promise caring and concern, sharing and equal opportunity in an elitist group (p. 120).

6. *Search for transcendence,* a spiritual need to venture and experience beyond the obvious, the quest for the ultimate meaning of life, a sense of mystery and mysticism. Cults offer being saved as one of the chosen, "gifts of the Spirit," meditation, and spiritual growth, clear though oversimplified answers to life's seemingly unanswerable questions (pp. 120–121).

7. *Spiritual guidance,* a reaction to a perceived lack of leadership and inspiration in home, school, and church. Cults offer "strong, charismatic leadership . . . binding the disciples . . . even an almost hysterical devotion" to the leader (p. 121).

8. *Vision,* to offset worry about the future, despair, and feelings of powerlessness to control the present or future. "to make the world better." Cults offer a "new vision," a new mental ball game, unhampered by anything in the past—religion, family, or societal values—and the promise of a "new age, a new era" (pp. 121–122).

9. *Participation and involvement,* to be an active, sharing part of the whole. Cults offer a "mission for a better world," worthy of self-discipline and sacrifice (p. 121).

Recruiting techniques, the *Vatican Report* observed, are "often highly sophisticated . . . often staged" and may use "abusive behavior-modification techniques." Cultists, firmly committed and with missionary zeal, "go out of their way" to find and solicit potential recruits "warmly, personally, and directly." They "reinterpret one's experience" and "reassess values," reshape them into the cult's mold, saved by its simplistic goals and mission (pp. 122–123). The report completely ignored extremist Satanic cults which are far from "warmly personal." It noted deceptive recruitment and indoctrination and self-imposed isolation of cults from mainstream religion and their refusal of ecumenical dialog. Cults can be "destructive to personalities and disruptive to families and society," and in some "powerful ideological forces . . . are at work . . . using the 'human' for inhumane purposes" (p. 127), but recommended an attitude of "openness and understanding, not of condemnation . . . it is imperative to remember the respect due to each individual" (p. 118).

The *Vatican Report* concluded with specific recommendations for coping with cults. Youth should be better informed of the risks, with backup counseling support and legal protection "by appropriate measures on the part of the state." Cults are a challenge "to stimulate our own renewal" and should not "diminish our zeal for true ecumenism among all Christians" (p. 128). It would have been more helpful had the report embraced all religions, not just Christianity, since Jewish youths are also prime targets for recruitment. It complained (as I have) that we desperately need more information and suggested these study areas: theology (religions, use of the Bible, esoteric, mystical, and human potential sects); interdisciplinary studies (history, anthropology, sociology, with theology); psychological and pastoral studies (on recruiting, training, deprogramming, after-effects, needs); the family (reactions of, effect on), women (male and female dominance effects), acculturation and inculturation (geography, history, and cross-cultural aspects); youth movements (from before World War II to the present); religious freedom (ethical, legal, theological aspects); and public opinion (imagery, reactions, effects).

JEWISH COUNTERCULT RESPONSE

The Commission on Cults and Missionaries of the Jewish Federation Council of Greater Los Angeles published *Cults and Consequences: The Definitive Handbook* (Andres and Lane, 1988). Longer and more detailed than the *Vatican report*, it was originally intended to help Jewish families cope with cults, but is now offered also "to educate the public on the dangers of destructive cultism" describing its deceptive proselytizing, unethical conduct, and political activities." It contends the First Amendment was not established to protect religious *organizations* but rather the freedom of *individuals* who organize together to worship as they freely choose. A cult using "fraudulent means to entrap them into a belief system" without free choice and personal autonomy violates freedom of religion and freedom of thought" (p. 1-1).

Rabbi Stephen Robbins, Chair of the Commission on Cults and Missionaries, and Vice Chair of the Union of American hebrew Congregations National Cult Task Force, recommends a tightening of legal restrictions over religious organizations using deception, fraud, and manipulation. He is quoted in *Cults and Consequences* as explaining the "Jewish attitude" on the First Amendment as protecting these rights "in the most intense way" even when those protected are "inimical to those of the Jewish community" (p. 1–18). Contemporary cults, however, are "a new situation," a "cover" for direct proselytizing using deception without informed consent. "Freedom of religion is not a license to behave in any manner one chooses," he wrote, but is freedom to "practice religion within the constraints that do not violate civil or criminal law and the general social compact . . . " (p. 1–19). When religions produce "aberrational or illogical activity," society has the right to intervene by law and with free, open dialogue make known its concerns. The "essence of freedom of religion," he concluded, is the right of the proselytizing religion to respond to these concerns and it is also the right of the proselytized religion to defend and protect itself.

Later in the book, Rabbi Robbins explained the number of Jews who become cult members. Most cult converts are white, middle-class, and well educated, recruited mainly from large college campuses. "Jews fit that niche," he observed, "in greater numbers proportionately than other religions and ethnic groups" and not because Jews are more susceptible (p. 2–15). Rabbi Yehuda Fine attributed Jewish representation as due to Jews being present and alone where cults are active, and to increased vulnerability from weakening family, religious, and traditional values. He pointed out that there are major cult organizations in Jerusalem, where tension, danger, and hardship are "a fertile ground" to recruit Israelis who when trained can go to the United States and Europe. He recommends that cults have a legal obligation to obtain informed consent after disclosing requirements of communal living, income limits, arranged marriages, and lack of medical and retirement benefits which can be weighed against interrupted school, career, family, and home life (p. 2–28 to 2–31).

Cults and Consequences contains an article by Norman Cousins, former *Saturday Review* editor, entitled "The Right of the Religious Fanatic." He described how government officials knew of fraudulent practices and physical dangers in the People's Temple in Jonestown but did not intervene because it was protected as a religion under the First Amendment. He criticized this "curious paralysis" when "confronted with any knave or fanatic who wraps himself in the mantle of religion . . . a mindless assumption . . . that religion is deserving of special respect and privilege." He pointed out that anyone can form a cult, prey on members, and use tax-exempt funds, deceit, misrepresentation, and theft "disguised as religious undertakings." Cousins contended that our founding fathers never intended religious organizations be immune from the law. "There is more than one Jonestown," he warned, and the "same dangerous nonsense is being peddled today by a dozen or more religious cults." When we provide "unlimited hospitality" and tax exemptions to "imposters and spurious organizations" just because they claim to be religions, we should not be shocked at "the horrors that are their natural progeny" (p. 1–17 and 1–18).

CONCLUSIONS

There are as many reasons why people get involved in cults as there are cults and personalities. Cult religions "defy analysis . . . it is difficult to generalize about them" (Allen, 1982, p. 215). Cults and the cult experience are complex, multidimensional, and multifactorial. "Straight arrow types live alongside the dropout . . . low and high IQ types," and we can't "pinpoint a universal or general motive for joining" (Allen, op. cit.). For some, it is out of curiosity, in a superficial, game-like spirit of adventure, or fascination that requires some active experimentation. These are the "dabblers" who do not necessarily have identity problems or need for a full-time support system external of themselves. When the cult experience becomes serious, more time is invested in it, and this raises the risk of increased personal commitment, gradual indoctrination, and assuming more of a cult identity. For them, cultism is a convenient packaged self, a one-size-fits-all, ready-made personality which quickly resolves an identity crisis.

Nonethnic communal cults are "pop religions." Most have a simplistic, unsophisticated belief system. If not overly involved in the supernatural or unduly disruptive to normative personality development they can be emotionally supportive, reducing anxiety, fear, and insecurity. Likely reasons for the growth of cults are the increase in population itself, insecurity from world tension, technology and rising complexity of living, hypocrisy, loneliness, meaninglessness, identity crisis or confused self concept, dissatisfaction with traditional religion, less concern about social sanctions to join, and increased interest and fascination with the supernatural, the occult, and mysticism. It is interesting that atheists, agnostics, and "secular humanists" generally do not join cults but Catholics, Protestants, and Jews do. This may be due to the former being more skeptical and critical, or with less need for an external support or value system.

Though unpopular, animal sacrifice is more civilized and a step beyond human sacrifice. Afro-Caribbean folk religions are based on the state of

African tribal religions at the time of slavery 300 years ago. They are fixed at that period in history and sophistication in a language and culture foreign to the United States. They require rigid discipline and regular offerings and sacrifices, for if the gods are not satisfied they can retaliate. The best sacrifice is blood, not symbolic as in the mass or communion, but real blood from birds or animals. The bigger the animal, the better the offering. Modern society considers this to be cruel and inhumane. In the December 2, 1979 *New York Times,* De Montalembert, a voodoo practitioner initiated in West Africa who moved to New York, observed that American voodoo differs markedly from that of Africa. He described African voodoo as "very tender and very loving," with a more quiet dignity and character. He considered American voodoo to be crude and aggressive. American cults have separated themselves from and do not mix with mainstream society. Deception, fraud, isolation from families, school, and career, and animal sacrifice are serious obstacles not only to public acceptance but also to integration into society and culture.

Chapter Four

WHEN CULTS HURT

Every age has its own collective neurosis
and every age needs its own psychotherapy
Victor E. Frankl
Man's Search for Meaning

RISK POPULATIONS

The cult experience can be classified by three major risk populations each with its own distinguishing characteristics and vulnerabilities: children, adolescents, and adults. Young children are usually unwilling victims of extremist criminal cults. Teenagers are involved in Satanic ritual or antisocial acting out, alone or in small groups. Adults (those over 18) are prime prospects for recruitment into nonethnic communal religious cults or cult-like organizations that compete with traditional religions. Estimates of the number of cults range from several hundred to several thousand, with total membership up to three million (Allen and Metoyer, 1988; Melton, 1986).

CHILDREN

Child Ritual Abuse

Generally, ritually abused children show age-inappropriate behaviors or knowledge, an excessive preoccupation or marked aversion to certain places, objects, colors (usually red or black), foods, or persons who are or are similar to those involved in the abuse. Therapists who have treated victims of ritual child abuse, describe a wide variety of behaviors which deviate significantly from a child's baseline norms, such as one or more of the following: mood swings; low stress threshold; aggressive physical or sexual acting out; hypersensitivity or hyperactivity; antagonism or temper tantrums; crying spells; marked anxiety and/or fear; inadequacy, difficulty concentrating, poor school work; rocking; nailbiting; bedwetting; speech disorder; withdrawal; nightmares; insecure and clingy; imaginary playmates; multiple personality disorder; accident-prone or self-mutilation. Children's play behavior is an excellent indicator of their mental state and the ritually abused have destroyed their favorite toys, pulled off arms or legs from dolls, acted out rituals with toys, peers, and pets, sketched ritual symbols, objects, and people, and referred to cult rituals in their self-talk.

A frequent criminal cult practice is to frighten children into silence by threats their parents will be killed, their house burned down, or that they themselves will be hurt, mutilated, or killed by animals, poisonous insects or snakes, teachers, doctors, nurses, police, strangers, or fantasy figures (nursery rhyme, cartoon, or movie characters). Often, the feared figure resembles the abusing masked or costumed cult member. If drugs are used, abused children may have a phobic fear of medicines, alcohol, or "poisoned" candy, or may actually abuse alcohol and drugs. If they were bound or locked alone in a cramped space, they are likely to show excessive anxiety and fear and ask never to be left alone, tied up, hung upside down, thrown or tumbled, or put in closets, elevators, or stairwells. If rituals involved sexual contact, there may be fear and anxiety removing clothing, or paradoxical seductive mannerisms when doing so. Some unusual behaviors may be an occasional, spontaneous, normal variant. These generally have less dramatic affect and usually fade of and by themselves. Ritual abuse is sudden, unexpected, confusing, and not understood by most children. It therefore has great impact and very high potential for inflicting profound trauma. When the child recalls the abuse or is in a play or real-life situation which seems similar, there is likely to be a noticeably emotional reaction.

Dr. Catherine Gould (1988), a California licensed clinical psychologist who has treated many ritually abused children, offers the following signs and symptoms which she has observed in her practice. Sexually abused children tend to talk about sex, in conversations with others, at play, or in self-talk, or show age-inappropriate knowledge of sexual behavior, fear of being touched or disrobing. They may behave seductively or attempt to initiate sexual contact, masturbate compulsively or publicly, have a relaxed rather than the usual reactive tightening of the anal sphincter on medical examination. There may be anal or vaginal pain, soreness, or injury, semen, blood, or feces on underwear, or venereal disease. They may be afraid to use the bathroom to the point of constipation or soiling themselves, and resist washing and personal toileting hygiene, play with, smear or eat excrement. They may show a paradoxical preoccupation with cleanliness. Ritual abuse differs from physical or sexual abuse by the additional involvement in religious, occult, magic or mystic practices. This is often evidenced by a child's exaggerated fear of masked, costumed, or fantasy figures perceived as real. Ritually-abused children have described what the fantasy figure did to them, or recalled and described the ritual or its objects, symbols, costumes, chants, songs, prayers, or sayings. The child may improvise a mask while playing, wear something red or black, or disrobe and dance in circles, write backwards right to left with inverted or reversed letters, draw circles or symbols, invert a crucifix, or show abnormal fear when seeing any of these ritual objects in movies or Halloween costumes. Some abused children have associated ritualistic behavior with traditional religious services and show fear and anxiety in church, synagogue, at funerals, or in cemeteries.

DEFINITION: Intentional mental, physical or sexual injury inflicted by a secret ceremony or ritual as part of a belief or delusional system. The setting can be religious, educational, social, or political or a combination of these. *Examples:* Abusive rituals to God, Nature, Satan, the sun, moon or stars, popular, to historical or legendary figures, or to demonstrate a misguided belief such as children being evil by nature, to defile innocence or virtue, or to symbolize religious, economic, social or sexual extremism.

TYPICAL VICTIM: Children, ages 2–6, usually 3 to 5. They are smaller and easier to kidnap and restrain, offer an innocent ideal to be defiled and indoctrinated. Unsophisticated, their weaker ego strength and coping skills make them more sensitive to the severe stress conditioning of sadistic ritual. Their testimony in court can be discredited as childhood fantasy or a variation of normal development.

PURPOSE is to indoctrinate ideologically and to shape behavior to conform to cult philosophy and practice, by severe stressors such as fear and terror, degradation, humiliation, social and emotional isolation, and intense physical pain.

PLACE is usually secluded and isolated, after dark (midnight to 3 AM) such as a park, beach, junkyard, cemetery, forest, cave, quarry, abandoned home, building, church, or school.

MATERIALS reported in cult and ritual abuse are: knives (especially a ceremonial knife), guns, sticks, bells or gongs, candles, herbs, oils, knotted ropes or cords, toys, costumes (robes, Santa Claus, Disney characters, other cartoon characters), bowls, crucibles, or mortar and pestle, live and dead animals or animal parts, human bodies or body parts (skull, femur, little finger, vertebra), blood, feces, urine, semen, and drugs (psychotropics, potions, psilocybin mushrooms). Satanic rituals use silver, never gold which is associated with Christ or God.

PHYSICAL ABUSE is in most cases sadistic and painful, to degrade and evoke terror, by being thrown, repeatedly spun around, beaten, or ritually cut. The child is abused directly by one or more adults, forced to attack another child or watch another victim being abused. Reported degrading practices are being smeared with blood, feces and urine, forced to eat or drink these or human flesh, being placed inside a dissected animal, in a casket with a corpse, in a garbage can or closet, electric shock, "Russian roulette," or the child's hand is placed on the knife used by an adult to kill an animal or human sacrifice.

SEXUAL ABUSE is most frequently done forcibly, violating the person by anal, vaginal, or oral penetration by person or objects (pencils, sticks, penis, or animal or human body parts), adult to child, forced child to child, or adult to adult witnessed by the child. Some have reported this abuse is sometimes videotaped.

ANIMAL CRUELTY is often reported in child ritual abuse, which involves cutting or killing the animal by bloodletting, smearing or drinking the blood, or eating some of the animal's flesh. Most frequently used animal parts are the tongue, genitals, anus, and front paws—the devil is said to walk on animal forelegs. Animal bodies found at cult ritual sites are usually mutilated and bloodless, the blood drunk, poured over objects, or smeared on victims or cult members.

HUMAN SACRIFICE can be real or symbolic, sometimes staged or faked to terrorize the child who is then implicated or blamed for the death. Some children have reported stabbing a baby or another child by being forced to use a ceremonial dagger, an adult cult leader's hand over theirs inflicting the wounds.

MAGIC POWER is suggested by special multisensory effects such as a bonfire, candles, colored lights, smoke, incense, costuming, signs, symbols, repetitive chanting, drumming, or rhythmic music, and special props (goat or animal heads, skulls, bones, etc.). Bones and blood are believed to contain the spirit of the bird, animal or person. The larger the sacrifice, the more blood and bones, and the more powerful the offering. According to this primitive logic, a human is the highest sacrifice, being the most developed of creatures, and the innocence and purity of a human baby add to sacrificial value.

EMOTIONAL DYNAMICS of child ritual abuse are *fear and terror* by being awakened from sleep, usually after midnight, physically thrown from one adult to another who stand in a circle, stood up and spun around, sometimes smeared with blood, urine, or feces, physically and sexually attacked, then locked away alone or placed in a casket, closet, or other uncomfortable, frightening place. Sensory and emotional deprivation add to the confusion, terror, and pain of the physical and sexual abuse and personal degradation. Child victims are told if they report the abuse no one will believe them, they or their families will be killed, or their house will be burned down. These have been effective deterrents. *Confusion* is created by using names and costumes of popular figures such as Santa Claus, Disney or TV cartoon characters, the Easter Bunny, clergy, doctor or nurse, teacher or police officer. Adult cult members dress up in costumes and assume the role of any of these trusted figures. Not only does this add to the child's bewilderment and shock, but it makes it more difficult to identify the abuser and the child's account is less credible.

Children in Court

Recent court cases involving child or ritual abuse in daycare centers have raised concern about the effect of court proceedings on children "of tender years." These children have been preschool or of primary grade age, impressionable, suggestible, and sensitive and for these reasons poorly prepared for vigorous, public cross-examination. They tend to be easily led, anxious to please, likely to fear rejection or reprisal, self-conscious or embarrassed, and because they do not understand the abuse or reason for it, may also feel somehow responsible for it. Because of the short attention span characteristic of their age, the stress of the abuse, and the new, added stress of court, many of them have difficulty remembering their own previous testimony as well as specific details required in examination and cross-examination. Their testimony is often inconsistent, uncertain, or confused. In most cases, there are no other witnesses to corroborate a child's statements.

Children in court are in a strange, different world of grownups who may seem cold and impersonal, rigid and judgmental. They testify alone, in public view, on sensitive subjects, reliving the trauma as they recall and recite it. Most therapists feel strongly that young child abuse victims should be spared the risk of additional trauma of direct confrontation of the alleged offender in open court. Ironically, there is almost no empirical data to substantiate this opinion and no convincing followup studies of negative aftereffects in children who have testified (Applebaum, 1989, p. 14). Some therapists maintain that open court testimony can be therapeutic, giving the child the opportunity to "tell it like it is," see justice done, vent their frustration and hurt, and begin to process the experience. In some cases, concern over possible adverse effects on a child has led families and attorneys to decline prosecution even when convictions were highly probable (p. 13).

About half the states allow videotapes, closed circuit TV, or closed court testimony of young children even though the Sixth Amendment requires alleged offenders be confronted with witnesses against them. Lower state courts have been inconsistent with their rulings about child testimony, sometimes requiring direct confrontation in open court, sometimes relaxing that requirement. In 1988, the U.S. Supreme Court ruled unconstitutional the use of one-way mirrors for children's testimony (Coy vs. Iowa, 56 USLW 4931). This may signal a trend toward more open court confrontation and away from TV, closed court, and other devices which interfere with face-to-face adversarial proceedings. Justice Scalia interpreted for direct confrontation regardless of a witness's age. Justice O'Connor dissented and held that while direct confrontation is preferred, provision should be made for an exception if there is a specific finding of substantial risk to the mental health of a child of tender years. This dissenting opinion allows for a battle of expert witnesses over the relative vulnerability of a child witness to psychological harm from open court procedures.

Child custody hearings involving a parent who is a cult member require investigation and evaluation of cult beliefs and practices, the structure of the organization, its daily routine and the quality of its environment. These factors are over and above the usual physical, psychological-emotional, and economic-financial considerations of the child living with one of the two parents. The court must determine the effect of the cult's lifestyle on a child at a formative and impressionable stage of life. Cults that consider parents and the family setting evil are at a distinct disadvantage in contested child custody proceedings. There have been court cases where parents who were cult members separated and one left the cult seeking custody of the child.

Attorneys representing noncult parents have successfully argued that the cult is the adversay. This has been facilitated when the whereabouts of the noncult parent and child were kept secret under the attorney-client privilege to prevent reprisals. Such secrecy is claimed justifiable if harmful physical or psychological-emotional practices have been alleged. The cult connection in a child custody case requires more time in court and in preparation because of these added factors. To this end, it is helpful to have testimony by former cult members and case studies of children physically or emotionally injured in the cult, augmented by expert witness opinions. The most effective expert witnesses and expert consultants have been mental health professionals, behavioral scientists, and social science researchers with forensic training and experience to be most effective in court.

Interestingly, cult leaders have been subpoenaed by the plaintiff to explain cult beliefs and practices. This has demonstrated the cult parent's relative lack of control over the environment, possibly also a lack of free, mature, rational or reasonable, independent judgment over self or the child. Submission to a cult's structured lifestyle can prevent or restrict parental function and responsibility. The time required by most cults restricts time between parent and child, can diminish the quality of home life, and the concentration of people in the cult can cause role confusion and blur parental imagery. Cult life can interfere with socialization and normalization by isolating children from peers and role models outside the cult, from healthy competitiveness, achievement, and the enrichment of diversity which is the hallmark of American society. Litigation involving cult members can require a separate hearing to ascertain the relative dangerousness of the cult to the child's normal or optimal development.

ADOLESCENTS

Adolescent Ritual Abuse

TYPICAL VICTIM: While there are exceptions, most teenagers who get involved in cult rituals are not living up to their potential, have serious unmet needs (Maslow, 1970), and difficulties at key life stages (Erikson, 1950). They tend to be socially alienated, feel lonely, and are experiencing significant identity crisis or confusion. The motives former teen cult members give for their involvement is a quest for power, sex, or money. There is no connection with adult or larger cult organizations. There have been many cases of solitary male teenagers who committed ritual acts and crimes. It is difficult to determine whether the cult ritual was a major influence on them, used intentionally to "cop a plea" of insanity, or was merely a convenient vehicle for preexisting homicidal intent.

PURPOSE: The purpose or function of nonviolent ritual is to express a search for self, to test limits of experience or reality, experiment with altered states with or without drugs, or a combination of these motives. For violent acting out, the motivation is most likely venting sadomasochistic impulses, repressed rage, or for psychopaths, domination, absolute and total control over another person.

PLACE: Adolescent ritual behaviors usually take place in a secluded and secure location, in the outdoors at night away from public contact such as parks, forests, cemeteries, school or church grounds, or at home when parents are away, in basements or garages.

MATERIALS: Inverted crucifix, pentagram or drawings of these on walls (sometimes spray painted) or sketched in soil, Satanic symbols (666, OTO, 9-foot circle around pentagram), reversed words (DOG for GOD, NATAS for SATAN, LIVE for EVIL, etc.), animal paws, tongue, ears, or genitals, human bones, black candles and robes with cowls, silver chalice, tattoos or ritualistic scars, and "black metal" rock music with Satanic and violent references.

PHYSICAL ABUSE: Cutting symbols on the chest, legs, forearms, or arms, binding with cords or ropes.

SEXUAL ABUSE: Some former teen cult members have reported "homosexual tantra" or "sex magic." Heterosexual or group sex (orgies) are rarely reported.

ANIMAL CRUELTY: Many teenagers who "dabble" and experiment with the occult eventually mutilate or kill animals. A mutilated or bloodless body with missing parts suggests Satanic ritual.

HUMAN SACRIFICE: Ritual murder occurs rarely and is usually the result of preoccupation which progresses through obsession into paranoia or delusion. A bloodless body, mutilated or marked with symbols, painted or smeared, with candle wax in the eyes or mouth, bound with rope or cord, and with penetrating stab wounds in the stomach not through the body, and a stab wound in the neck to bleed the victim into unconsciousness and for ritually blood use, suggest satanic cult murder. Stomach contents may show drugs, feces, urine, or a herbal potion.

MAGIC POWER: Teen cults are usually improvised and unsophisticated, a mixture of occult and mystic practices with primitive religion, Satanism or witchcraft, from readings.

EMOTIONAL DYNAMICS: "Normal" teenagers who became involved in extremist criminal cults report they were first drawn by a natural curiosity which led to fascination and an urge to experience something "weird" or "different" or in the pursuit of power, sex, or money. Teenagers who are depressed, feeling inadequate and insecure, with problems at home, in school, or on the job, are especially vulnerable to a destructive or criminal cult experience.

ADULTS

Adult Ritual Abuse

TYPICAL VICTIM/MEMBER. Adult cult members are mostly 18 to 25 years old, though children, parents, and grandparents actively participated in the Jonestown commune. There is a high number of college-educated, middle class Caucasians. Idealists and intellectuals, they tend to be enamored of simplistic solutions to complex problems and the adventure of a crusade. The lesser educated range from school dropouts and street people to "self-identified failures" from families of overachievers, and those with personality disorders (MacCollam, 1979, p. 36). They seek escape, a refuge of safety and security. Adult cult involvement differs with the type of cult and there are three major groups: non-communal ethnic groups such as the Afro-Caribbean folk cult religions; communal nonethnic groups; extremist criminal cults.

NON-COMMUNAL CULTS

Adult involvement in noncommunal cults can be by isolated individuals, small informal or organized groups, or large ethnic cult-like religious groups.

An example of an alleged adult cult member convicted of serial murder is Henry Lee Lucas. He claimed to be a member of "The Hand of Death" cult which operated in the United States and Mexico and claimed he was paid $1000 "a load" for kidnapped children who were sold to wealthy Mexican families, forced into prostitution, ritually murdered at cult meetings, or raised by cult families. Asked why there is no hard evidence of ritual murder, Lucas stated: "We are trained not to leave evidence." He added that cult members "pass" as everyday citizens who "are just like you and me." He said that ritual killers always mark the victim's body and sometimes place it in a distinctive position (Norris and Potter, 1985). There was no external corroborating evidence for Lucas's claims.

An example of an individual who appeared to be obsessed or delusional about Satanic beliefs is Richard Ramirez, the 25-year-old, Mexican-American "night stalker" who had the Satanic pentagram tattooed on his left hand, wore only black, carried a black suitcase, was obsessed with heavy metal music with Satanic references, and painted pentagrams and Satanic symbols on the walls of his victim's homes. No connection to an organized Satanic cult was conclusively proven.

Afro-Caribbean folk religions function as noncommunal ethnic cults. Therapists should realize that those who believe in oricha saints and magic and supernatural forces may seem delusional but unless grossly exaggerated are exhibiting a cultural variant. It can also be a defense mechanism against the stress of a new and different environment in a search for security and identity. On the other hand, it can be a vehicle for the excessive religiosity common in many thought disorders. Alonso and Jeffrey (1988) recommend an assessment of "the adaptive function of their belief in possession," ability to function optimally at work and at home using reasonably good judgment, and their realization of the limitations of belief. Another useful measure is the DSM Axis V global assessment scale which compares present function with that over the past year. In treatment, it is helpful to reassure the client that therapy is to improve coping skills and strengthen the self-concept and will not interfere with religious belief, though participation in fiesta santera has caused dissociation and psychotic decompensation in susceptible individuals.

Alonso and Jeffrey (1988) describe four cases where santeria belief and practices contributed to mental disorders that required professional consultation and treatment:

CASE 1 was a 32-year-old Cubano woman refugee who had to leave her husband and two children behind. She became deeply involved in santeria rituals, praying to oricha saints to reunite the family. She was found confused and wandering on the street, hospitalized, and treated for bipolar affective disorder, manic, DSM Axis IV stress rating 5, Axis V global assessment 35 (current) and 80 (past year). Discharged on chlor-promazine and lithium, she continued with santeria rituals, discontinued taking medications, decompensated, and was rehospitalized.

CASE 2 was a 40-year-old Cubano woman and teacher who attributed her successful marriage to the help of oricha saints and was trying to have a family. Toward this end she sacrificed chickens and spoke in tongues. She began having troubled sleep and auditory and visual hallucinations involving the dead and oricha saints. Her santero priest told her she was possessed. Previously diagnosed histrionic personality disorder, she was hospitalized with an admitting diagnosis of brief reactive psychosis, Axis IV stress rating 3, Axis V global assessment 35 (current), 80 (past year). She improved on medication but still believed she was possessed.

CASE 3 was a 59-year-old unmarried Puerto Rican woman who lived in Cuba thirty years before coming to the United States. She had a history of alcohol dependence, difficulty holding a job, and she believed she was possessed and could hear voices of the oricha saints. Touched by a possessed santero priest during a fiesta santera where she consumed a large quantity of rum, she became agitated and was admitted to an inpatient alcohol detox program diagnosed organic delusional syndrome secondary to alcohol dependence, Axis IV stress rating 3, Axis V global assessment 40 (current) and 50 (past year). Discharged improved but with mild organicity, she continued to believe she had been possessed and continued to drink at fiesta santeras.

CASE 4 was a 70-year-old Cubano woman living with her daughter who was a santero priestess. She was referred to an outpatient clinic because of a continuing delusion her other daughter was kidnapped and was going to be killed by the Russians. She and her priestess-daughter performed many santeria rituals to seek help and protection from the oricha saints but without success. She was diagnosed shared paranoid disorder, Axis IV stress rating 2, Axis V global assessment 50 (current) and 80 (past year). Both women were treated with low doses of haloperidol. The older woman's hallucinations stopped within a week and her delusion cleared soon after. Both remained active in santeria.

COMMUNAL NONETHNIC CULTS

The following two cases are taken from the opinion of a 1988 case argued before the California Supreme Court. The experiences of the male and female plaintiffs were recruited into a large, nationwide cult typical of most communal nonethnic cult organizations.

CASE 5 was a 27-year-old unmarried male Caucasian and a recent law school graduate. He was approached at a bus stop by two male peers who struck up a casual conversation with him. They told him they lived in an "international community" that met evenings after dinner to discuss important issues to which he was invited. He asked if they had "a religious connection" and they told him they did not. He asked their occupations and they replied: "social workers." He agreed to go with them. During the meal he was "held in constant conversation and isolated from other guests." A slide show and narration promoted a "farm" outside town as a "rural getaway where people from the house went for relaxation and pleasure." He was invited to visit and told a van would leave in a few minutes. He said he had no personal effects, he was assured these would be provided and urged to go. He agreed and signed his name, address, and phone number.

At the farm a group member was with him at all times wherever he went. The daily routine was rigidly structured, from exercises before breakfast to lectures on morals and ethics followed by discussion, lunch, more exercise, more lecture and discussion, a break for showering, supper and testimonials, group singing, and a final discussion period. On the second day he was tired and uncomfortable and he told his two initial contacts he wanted to leave. He was informed he was free to do so but the bus left at 3 AM. They urged him to stay because important information would be discussed in the days to come. He asked the name of the group and was told it was "The Creative Community Project." The following days were repetitions of the first. Lectures were repeated verbatim.

On the 5th day the group went for a weekend to a camp. When he returned to the farm he became increasingly depressed and asked if the group was involved with a larger organization. He was then informed, for the first time, on the 12th day of continuous involvement, the name of a nationwide cult organization. He became angry and confused and was told deception was necessary because "people who hear negative stories about it tend to be unreceptive before hearing what it had to say." He agreed to stay to work out his anger and confusion. The same daily routine was repeated for another five weeks. Concerned about him, his parents visited but could be with him only a few hours and always with other cult members present. The cult taught that parents are agents of

Satan. He donated $6,000 to the cult. He was abducted by deprogrammers hired by his parents and taken to a motel. After three days of deprogramming he terminated cult membership and later sued the cult for fraud and deceit, intentional infliction of emotional distress, false imprisonment, and restitution of his $6,000 "gift" (88 CDOS 7320, California Supreme Court).

CASE 6 was a 19-year-old unmarried Caucasian female college student. During a bus trip to a smaller college she was considering transferring to, she was approached in the bus station by a female peer who struck up a casual conversation with her. She said she was waiting for a friend returning from Switzerland. They discussed travel and skiing, mutual interests. The friend arrived and they discussed "The Creative Community project" where they lived and worked and "did good works such as giving food to the poor." Invited for lunch, sightseeing, and dinner, they assured her she could catch a later bus. She asked if they were "part of a religious group" because she "did not want to get involved with them if they were." They replied that the people in the group "all came from different religious backgrounds." She accepted their invitation. At the house she was "kept apart" from other guests and "held in constant conversation" with other group members. There was a lecture and slide show about a nearby "farm" and she and others were invited to visit there. No cult connection was mentioned. She went.

At the farm there was a routine of exercise-lecture-discussion. The next day she asked if the group was part of a cult and was told it was not but was "a form of Christian group" being kept quiet for a while so as not to "frighten people away." After two days at the farm she agreed to go to a "camp" for a "two-week seminar." The routine and schedule there was the same. She again asked if the group was a cult and was assured it was not. On the 22nd day she was informed it was indeed a cult. She remained two more months during which her family visited and urged her to leave. She remained another month for "advanced lectures." She was then abducted by deprogrammers hired by her parents who "successfully persuaded her to leave the cult." She later took part in a class action suit against the cult.

DEPROGRAMMING OR EXIT COUNSELING

Deprogramming is a method and technique used to restore a cult member to previous behavior and personality function. It has been called "repersonalization" (MacCollam, 1979), "reverse brainwashing" by cultists, and "exit counseling" or "exit therapy." It serves the same purpose as psychotherapy for victims of crime, war, personal crisis, or natural catastrophe, whenever there has been severe or prolonged stress which interrupts or interferes with optimal personality function. Clinical and research literature on crisis and stress management and the treatment of posttraumatic stress disorder and phobias have been effectively used to facilitate recovery from the cult experience.

Deprogramming or exit counseling should be bound by the same legal and professional standards and expectations as psychotherapy since it is, in fact, a form of psychotherapy. This means undue force should not be used, nor should there be any violation of rights such as deprivation of food, water, bathroom, clothing, legal counsel, and such. Legal rights of parents of minors or a court order for adults provide sufficient authorization for initiating the treatment program. The deprogramming process is a difficult time for parents emotionally and physically and "commitment must be complete or failure is almost assured" (MacCollam, 1979, p. 129).

Legal justification for intervention by family, guardian, or friends for custody of minors or conservatorship ex parte or court order for adults has involved disruption of the family unit, personal or family relationships, progressive or sudden behavior or personality change and mental injury by stress conditioning or deprivation, and lack of informed consent. Cults argue that cult membership is voluntary and as a religious organization is protected by the freedom of religion provision of the First Amendment. Some courts have ruled in favor of family rights to intervene in the cult experience with a variety of opinions, on the grounds the situation is a danger to health and welfare, or to self, inability to make a free, voluntary decision (competence), the cult member has been rendered mentally disordered (is mentally ill and in need of treatment), or reasonably justified by "maternal solicitude." These decisions vary from state to state.

There has been a growing consensus against the use of force or coercion. Hargrove (1980) pointed out that abduction and forced indoctrination reinforces the view that the former cult member is incapable of making decisions or using free will. Galanter (1983) observed that the therapeutic value of forcible rehabilitation "remains unanswered." Maleson (1981) cautioned that therapists who get involved in involuntary deprogramming risk their independence, objectivity, and effectiveness. Sage (1976) reported that deprogramming has in the past "turned brutal when those abducted tried to resist."

Professional involvement should be by ordained clergy (ministers, priests, rabbis of established religious denominations) and mental health professionals (preferably experienced, licensed psychiatrists, psychologists, social workers, counselors, or nurse practitioners) are justified because of the nature of the problem which involves the mental health and integrity of the basic personality of the cult member. Untrained practitioners may miss signs of major mental disorder and the individual's basic personality dynamics and further exacerbate existing problems. It is very helpful to have the assistance of former members of the same cult, preferably in the same city, recently, and of the same age group.

Goals of deprogramming are to interrupt the cult experience, return the individual to former life style, personal and family relationships, restore deteriorated personality function, and strengthen ego defenses, autonomy and integrity, personal responsibility, and self esteem. In cases where the individual escaped the family to take refuge in a cult, the deprogramming should include recontracting with others to improve personal autonomy, integrity, and free choice. It is possible the deprogrammed individual will freely choose to return to the cult or a life-style differing from both the family or the cult. Many Vietnam veterans returned home and chose to remove themselves from anything military or governmental and also from their families.

Methodology varies with individual needs and the nature of the cult experience, its scope, depth, intensity, and duration. These variables are the same as for any mental disorder, but most relevant to posttraumatic stress disorder and phobias (MacHovec, 1984 a and b, 1985). It has been found effective to use a team of clergy and mental health professionals as noted above. Treatment dynamics generally involve four stages which I call the SURF method: STOP or interrupt the cult experience, UNDO or UNWIND, RESTORE or RE–ENTRY, and FREE, autonomous personality function. The STOP phase removes the direct reinforcers of active cult involvement and limits defenses to those learned and conditioned by the cult and, increasingly, those natural to the personality. Defenses *of the individual* are strengths to be improved, and recognizing and enhancing them is another indication of the need for professional involvement. The UNDO phase isolates the individual in a new environment between cult and family and in time insulates the person from undo influence by either so that the true personality can again function.

RE–ENTRY or RESTORE is to again exercise more autonomous behaviors such as decisionmaking and orientation to societal or moral values and school, career, and life goals. Group counseling and re-entry into home, family, and community life replaces the programmed monotony of the cult (Thomas, 1979; Galanter, 1983).

Treatment techniques should vary with individual needs as for any form of counseling or psychotherapy but the most effective reported deprogramming of adult cult members has included:

1. *Factual confrontation,* accurate and precisely focussed, on cult practices and effects, preferably using former cult members. Stick to facts, don't debate what is logic or truth. It didn't do Pilate or Socrates much good! Effect of cult experience on the mind or soul and behavior are acceptable if handled by a trained and credentialled professional. Statements of former cult members help, such as "My parents gave me my life back ... I'm myself again not a smiling puppet/robot ... I'm somebody now ... " Examples of deception and misrepresentation and physical or mental abuse or coercion have also been effective.

2. *Reasonable decisionmaking* exercised in decisions as to daily routine, choice of food and clothing, and in whatever is discussed. Some cults teach deprogramming defenses such as making demands. The key here is the word *reasonable.* No demand should be honored without a reasonable trade-off, one demand for one expectation, similar to hostage negotiation.

3. *Experiencing freedom.* This is perhaps the most important and also the most effective technique. Decisionmaking is using freedom of choice, one way to transfer or generalize into free thought, to free the mind itself from the tracking, channel, or mental frequency of the cult. The basic clash of free vs. forced (shaped or coerced) should be emphasized and reinforced by example, using the deprogramming method itself as an example. Some cults are teaching members to use this freedom by choosing not to converse with deprogrammers. Silence and time are on the side of the deprogrammer since the cult member is entirely alone. In such an event, an eavesdropping technique can be used, where deprogramming staff talk with each other on the intended subject. A former cult member is very helpful here.

4. *Groups* of ex-members and *family sessions* help adjust to previous personality functioning and lifestyle.

Time required will vary with individual needs but averages four to six weeks in a residential rehabilitation setting. This is similar to the time and intensity of alcohol and substance abuse programs, another type of habituated and dependent behavior including a week or two of brief therapy or crisis intervention equivalent to the detox phase of a substance abuse program. Some cult members have required only a week or two. Case 5 described earlier in this chapter required only three days. Usually these are people who either have not been in the cult a long time or who had some reservations about it and did not commit themselves to the cult experience. Success of deprogramming generally depends on the length of time in a cult and level of satisfaction with the experience (Thomas, 1979). There should be outpatient followup on a regular basis until such time as the individual is functioning autonomously. In many cases, a year or more of outpatient therapy was required.

Cost will depend on length of time and the fees of participating professionals but is comparable to expenses incurred in a good substance abuse program plus costs not usually part of such a program. As an average rule of thumb, cost would range from $5000 to $10,000, which includes room, board, fees, phone bill, legal and court costs.

Problems and pitfalls. Deprogramming can only be as good as those who do it. Because it involves the mind and the possibility of mental illness, and moral values prior to the cult experience, only those licensed and qualified in these areas should provide services. Missionary zeal, anger, or impatience are to be avoided since they are more likely to entrench defenses than eliminate them. Playing exorcist is best left to actors and actresses and the movies, though in rare instances a formal exorcism rite has helped (MacCollam, 1979, p. 133). Being yourself and knowing what you're doing is far better. Assuming all cults, leaders, and members are the same is a strategic error which can cost time, money, and increase risk of failure. Using physical violence or restraint is not effective, as has been proven in prison and military settings and in raising children. A rule of thumb as to what to avoid is to ask how you would respond, how you would like or dislike what is proposed, and whether it would likely pass the legal test of being *reasonable*. Most people would benefit from a good deprogramming sequence since it provides the opportunity of examining individual values and identity.

As Plato so aptly observed in his *Dialogues* (300 BC), "the life which is unexamined is not worth living." He also wrote that "false words are not only evil in themselves but they infect the soul with evil."

EXTREMIST CRIMINAL CULTS

These are the cults which engage in physical or sexual abuse, animal and human sacrifice. There is very little documented evidence of their existence, but an increasing number of psychotherapists are reporting cases of adult and child survivors of ritual abuse (Kahaner, 1988; Norris and Potter, 1985; Smith and Pazdar, 1980). The descriptions of the nature of the abuse are consistent, and some consider these similarities to prove the existence of a national or international criminal cult network. Critics point out that these similarities could be the result of being cued or led by questioners who projected their own beliefs onto the victim being interviewed. This is the "credulous" vs. "skeptical" effect cited in experimental research which can skew results one way or another depending on the expectations or wishes of the experimenter (Sutcliffe, 1960). It has been empirically documented in hypnosis research, where experienced hypnotists could not differentiate between persons really hypnotized and those who faked it (Orne, 1971).

There appears to be a group of believers in a criminal cult network despite the lack of evidence to the contrary. Police officers, parents, and friends of victims have attributed murders to ritual cult practice even when there was little or no evidence of any ritual taking place. Confronted with this fact, they replied: "That just shows you how clever they are." Sacrificed babies are not found because the cult cremates the remains. These rationalizations suggest Festinger's *cognitive dissonance* theory (1957). That theory is based on a research on UFO cultists who predicted the end of the world on a certain day which did not occur. Faced with this reality, they explained that the world must have realized its imminent danger, changed its attitude, and therefore won a stay of execution. When a prominent televangelist was involved in a sexual encounter and misappropriation of funds, his devout followers accepted his explanation that Satan had tempted him.

While criminal cults composed of intelligent psychopaths may be eluding detection, it would seem highly likely that at some time there would be a defector who could set up a "sting" operation to expose the cult. It is also true that in time, victims' accounts should lead to the accumulation of more details of cult operations to make apprehending them possible. Allen and Metoyer (1987) reported that street gangs in the Los Angeles area were contacted by extremist criminal cults but refused to get involved with them. Gang leaders, asked about cults, replied: "You're not looking for gang members. You're looking for those weird people who hang around the graveyard, play records backwards and do what the devil tells them to do." Most police authorities admit to considerable frustration about the lack of evidence: "A family fight call would be easy duty in comparison to conducting an occult crime investigation" (p. 3). If extremist criminal cults exist, there is a Pulitzer Prize awaiting the investigative reporter who convincingly exposes them.

CULTS IN COURT

Though most contemporary cults claim protection as religions under the First Amendment, there is a substantial body of data from case law for claims of wrongdoing even when acting according to sincere religious belief. In these cases, courts used "the balancing test" of the state's interest balanced against the burden of that interest on religion. The greater the burden, the more compelling must be the state's interest. Here is a sampling of such cases:

Religiously motivated injurious acts: O'Moore vs. Driscoll, 135 Cal App 770, 778 (1933).

Polygamy: Reynolds vs. United States, 98 U.S. 145, 166 (1878).

Social Security enrollment: United States vs. Lee, 455 U.S. 252, 261 (1932).

Religiously-based racial discrimination: Bob Jones University vs. U.S., 461 U.S. 574, 604 (1983).

Minimum wage coverage for employees of religious organizations: Tony and Susan Alamo Foundation vs. Secretary of Labor, 471 U.S. 290, 305 (1985).

License for religious parades: Cox vs. New Hampshire, 312 U.S. 579, 575 (1941).

Minimal education standard: Wisconsin vs. Yoder, 406 U.S. 205, 215 (1972).

Public sale or distribution of religious literature: Heffron vs. International Society for Krishna Consciousness, 452 U.S. 641, 654 (1981).

Effects of shunning: Bear vs. Reformed Mennonite Church, 341 A.2d Pa. 105, 107 (1975).

Alienation of affection from husband declared "full of the devil": Candy H. vs. Redemption Ranch, M.D. Ala. 563, F.Supp. 505, 516 (1983).

"Brainwashing" in religious settings: Petersen vs. Sorlein, 299 N.W. 2d 126 (1984) and also Meroni vs. Holy Spirit Association, 125 Misc.2d 1061, 1067 (1984).

False imprisonment: Van Schniack vs: Church of Scientology of California, Inc., D.Mass. F. Supp. 1125, 1135 (1982).

Fraud and intentional emotional distress: Molko and Leal vs. Holy Spirit Association for Unification of World Christianity, Cal.Sup.Cit., 88 CDOS, 7320 (1988).

Religious use of peyote is illegal and so not protected by the First Amendment: Oregon Department of Human Resources vs. Smith, 56 U.S.L.W. 4357 (1988).

Deprogramming of adult members of nonethnic communal cults has resulted in court action. In Katz vs. Superior Court, the California Court of Appeals issued parents temporary conservatorships for their five adult-age children for deprogramming "of ideas instilled in a religious cult." There must be sufficient evidence or cause for conservatorships to outweigh subjecting cult members to deprogramming against their will or kidnapping. Parents have used a *choice of ends* rationale, a reasonable attempt to avoid a greater evil, *necessity,* reasonable belief deprogramming is necessary to prevent physical or psychological harm, or *compulsion,* reacting understandably to a crisis situation. Deprogrammers act as agents of the parents, rendering services the parents themselves cannot provide. While lower courts tend to be sympathetic to traditional family values, needs, and roles (Schwartz, 1978), conservatorships are rarely successful because most adult cult members are legally competent and not commitable for inpatient treatment of DSM mental disorders. Ungerleiter and Wellisch (1979) reported two cases where deprogramming failed. Both had strong dependency needs and difficult social relationships not diagnosable as serious mental disorders.

CULT INVOLVEMENT SCALE (CIRS)

Interest and participation in a cult ranges from superficial conversational pastime to total commitment. It can be a solitary obsession, shared group behavior of a few friends "dabbling," an extremist criminal cult, or large international "new religion." The following involvement scale describes the varying intensity of cult involvement:

0 or "normal" interest

DISTINGUISHING FEATURE: Temporary fascination
RISK POTENTIAL: Minimal
PEAK NEGATIVE: Deepening interest

"Normal" curiosity, fascination or interest as reflected in social conversation, reading an article or book on the subject, but not pursued further.

+1 or dabbler stage

DISTINGUISHING FEATURE: Preoccupation
RISK POTENTIAL: Mild
PEAK NEGATIVE: Dabbling experimentation

Mild intensity or interest beyond normal, with some definite additional action taken such as solitary experimentation or group activity, participating in "soft" nonviolent ritual, with an intensity equal to that of a traditional religious worship service, or seeking out and talking with a cult leader or member, or attending one cult meeting out of curiosity.

+2 or joiner-doer stage

DISTINGUISHING FEATURE: Obsessive preoccupation
RISK POTENTIAL: Moderate
PEAK NEGATIVE: Participation

The stage of serious commitment, joining a cult, with interest of moderate intensity, clearly beyond dabbling, taking an active part in cult ritual but not in a leadership role, by "going along with" but taking part, or passively assisting in ritual abuse such as animal sacrifice, human mental, physical, or sexual abuse. Usually, there is also extensive reading and studying of cult materials, use of tattoos, or significant personality or behavior change.

+3 delusional stage

DISTINGUISHING FEATURE: Delusional, psychopathy
RISK POTENTIAL: Maximum
PEAK NEGATIVE: Ritual abuse, mutilation, murder

These are the hardcore cultists with psychopathic or sociopathic commitment to the cult, in an active leadership or blindly loyal follower role, an obsessive preoccupation with the cult's ideas and practices. For criminal cults, there is active participation in antisocial, unlawful acts such as mental, physical, or sexual abuse, mutilation, dismemberment, or murder. Criminal cultists at this level can decompensate to a delusional or psychotic degree dangerous to self and others. Regularly repeated ritual abuse suggests psychopathy not unlike serial killers, an addictive hunger for violence, sadism, and excitement.

CULT CLASSIFICATION INVENTORY (CCI)

In the interest of standardizing the classification of cult organizations and to provide a checklist for a more objective study of them, the following is suggested:

Name of cult

Leader (biographical data and personal history, education, training, previous occupations, publications)

Scope (local, state, national, international)

Basic beliefs, goals, objectives

Rationale (type of cult, historical and theoretical roots, scriptures, texts, and references)

Behavioral norms (lifestyle, practices, rituals, jargon)

Typical membership (sex, age, race, education, occupation, social status, life situation, personality pattern)

Legal history (civil or criminal proceedings, out-of-court settlements, substance abuse)

Complaint history (adverse newspaper-TV references or investigative reports, parent and former member reports)

EFFECTIVE INTERVIEWING

As for all counseling and therapy cases, a careful history should be taken, including a mental status examination and diagnostic workup according to the latest DSM diagnostic manual using all five axes. Special care should be exercised to avoid direct questions, make assumptions, or lead the client. This is most important when interviewing children, whether or not later court testimony is involved. Instead, open-ended questions should be used to encourage the client to do the talking with as little intervention as possible by the interviewer. *Never* ask: "What did he do with his hand?" *Preferred:* "What happened then?" Children, and some confused or traumatized adults, can be very sensitive to verbal and nonverbal cues, *what* you say and also *how* you say it—eye contact, tone of voice, speed of delivery, pauses, posture, gestures. Anxious to please or end the pain of recalling a painful event, they may exaggerate or confabulate, "fill in the blanks" in their responses. Staged illusion, drugs, fear, trauma, and dissociation, together with the child's tender age and limited life experience, cloud memory and mix with childhood fantasy. Forensic training and experience enhance objective inquiry. If there will be courtroom testimony, consult with legal counsel about the advisability of videotaping interviews to avoid charges of bias or leading the witness. If videotaped, the entire session should be taped, from arrival of the client to departure, to eliminate the charge that the witness was prepped beforehand.

Interviewing children is greatly facilitated by the use of play therapy, anatomically correct child, adult, and animal dolls, toys, drawing, and role play, encouraging free expression with minimal input and control. Randomly presented pictures in children's books or magazines, or cards from projective tests such as the Rorschach or Apperception Tests (CAT or TAT) have facilitated spontaneous verbalizations with minimal intervention by therapists. Spector (1986) used Tarot cards to make therapeutic suggestions to a 15-year-old male preoccupied with Satanic occult imagery. Unusual references or mannerisms showing sensitivity to words, actions, situations, symbols, colors, and the like, should be noted using the client's exact words. It is helpful to note any nonverbal behaviors which accompanied the verbal responses as well. These responses can be researched after the session and used in further questioning, future therapy sessions, or in court if there is a hearing or trial. This book's index, appendices, and references can help you do so.

Some ritually abused children have named fantasy, cartoon, or movie characters who abused them, possibly adults in mask and costume. Some have used words not age-appropriate nor used in school, by peers, or parents (e.g., baphomet, the goat of Mendes, sabbat), repeated unusual sayings or values ("evil is good, death is life, pain is pleasure, Satan is God, do what thou wilt"), word reversals (Natas for satan), strange practices (inverting a cross, the Satanic horn-sign of forefinger and little finger extended), or described animal or human sacrifice or acted them out in play, alone and with others.

Child ritual abuse adds an overlay of bizarre cult ritual over physical or sexual abuse. This introduces additional variables to be assessed to obtain a correct diagnosis and then formulate the most effective treatment plan. Physically, sexually, and ritually-abused children can be without symptoms, or misinterpreted as normal age-appropriate variants of an imaginative child. Children who have not been abused can feign symptoms or be led by unskilled interviewers to create symptoms. Detecting child abuse is difficult and detecting child ritual abuse moreso, requiring careful observation of verbal and nonverbal behaviors, taking a thorough personal and family history, and a working knowledge of cult and ritual practices and materials. A major characteristic of ritual abuse which differentiates it from the nonritual type is the intentional, direct, degradation of the person physically and the personality psychologically and emotionally.

Adult survivors of extremist criminal Satanic cults describe a systematic shaping of thinking and behavior which begins with a simple pairing good (relief from pain) with evil (inflicting pain). Later, the child is rewarded for initiating violent acts on others, then by forced participation in animal sacrifice, then faked or real human sacrifice. Children who resist or refuse are told a pet, peer, sibling, or parent will be hurt or killed or their house burned down. "Magical surgery" has been reported in which the child is shown an electronic component imbedded in a dissected animal or body part. Told it will be surgically implanted in the child's brain, heart, or stomach, he or she is drugged, passes out, and when awakened is covered with blood. If the child tells anyone of the cult's rituals, the implant will cause trembling, pounding heart, or churning stomach, or told the brain, heart, or stomach will explode. If a child even thinks about confessing what was seen and done, or is asked about it by anyone outside the cult, normal psychosomatic symptoms of mild tremors, rapid heart rate, or nervous stomach are misperceived as due to the implant. Survivors reliving these in therapy are usually so terrified or were so young at the time of trauma that recall is clouded and it is not possible to separate real from imagined. Therapists who have treated adult survivors of child victims shortly after the trauma report very dramatic emotional reactions, a degree of terror that is very unlikely to have been faked.

Believe the Children, a California-based ritual awareness organization with chapters throughout the country, reports that sexual abuse occurs very frequently in child ritual abuse and coerced sexual contact between children in the majority of cases. Degradation and demoralization to convert, change, or transform an innocent child into evil is the prime motive. Sexual pleasure of adult cult members or the child victim is secondary. Child molesters are predominantly male but child ritual abusers are mostly female. Both molestation and ritual abuse are repeat offenses inflicted by the same perpetrators. There are three major difficulties in detecting child ritual abuse. First, criminal cults abusing children operate in secret and condition children to maintain secrecy. Second, many children have a rich fantasy and if led by an unskilled interviewer can distort reality and obscure what really happened. Third, the sensitivity of parents, some police, teachers, agency staffs, and therapists can have high risk of exaggeration and hysteria. Interviewers should be aware of how ritual practices differ from normal age-appropriate play, ideas, and fantasies in three major areas:

NONVERBAL BEHAVIORS: Drawings of sexual or ritual practices or occult symbols; dramatic emotional reaction to symbols, colors, places, masks, costumes, to certain people or specific places; sadomasochistic acts or play (bondage, sacrifice, stabbing, torture); writing backwards ("devil's alphabet"); seductive pose for photos or fear of camera; avoiding bathrooms or disrobing; abnormal fear of ghosts and monsters; accident prone; unexplained aversion or phobic reaction such as to tomato soup or sauce (blood), enclosed spaces (closets, cages), immersion in water (bath, tub, pool), guns, knives or penetrating objects, drugs, graveyards or coffins, fire, school, religious rituals, masks or costumes (robes in church or court), of normally trusted people (authority, hero, fantasy figures), unusual sadistic, aggressive, or sensual behaviors; nightmares or flashbacks.

VERBAL BEHAVIORS: References to body painting, "my other daddy/mommy/friend, fantasy figures they insist they've seen, or "bad people" who hurt animals, kill people, or burn houses; dramatic or strongly worded threats; age-inappropriate language or knowledge not otherwise explained; preoccupied with urine, feces, or blood, the devil, or magic; odd songs, chants, or sayings; talk of a "bomb" or "wires" or "ropes" inside the body or "bad medicine": describes places not part of school, home, or church activities.

PHYSICAL SIGNS: Marks or bruises in a pattern; rope burns; bedwetting; soiled underwear; rectal or vaginal irritation, inflammation, lacerations or scarring.

Some of these may be normal variations but several together warrant further investigation. As in all criminal cases, there must be corroborating evidence from other sources in order to confirm cult ritual abuse. A child's verbal statement is not enough to obtain a conviction.

CULTS AND MENTAL DISORDERS

Stress and trauma can cause anxiety and agitation vented at the time or reactive behaviors beytond the victim's conscious awareness (MacHovec,

1985). As Freud discovered, a traumatic event can be real or imagined, exaggerated in the memory or symbolized and fantasized in the imagination. Involvement in an adult nonethnic communal cult can directly and indirectly place significant additional stress on the individual, by the dramatic change in environment, sudden isolation from previous support systems, and a new and different lifestyle, beliefs and values, and rigorous daily routine (Andres and Lane, 1988; Galanter, 1985; Hassan, 1988; Kaslow and Sussman, 1982; Langone, 1988; MacCollam, 1979; Ross and Langone, 1988; Ungerleider and Wellisch, 1979). In noncommunal ethnic-religious cult religions, cognitive commitment in beliefs and emotional involvement in practices and rituals can lead to the excessive religiosity seen in classical psychotic thought disorders (Alonso and Jeffrey, 1988; Eth, 1985; Galanter, 1983; Martinez and Wetli, 1982; Prince, 1979). The severe psychological trauma of child or adult ritual abuse can cause adjustment, anxiety or dissociative disorders, and even when only partially integrated, serious obstacles to optimal personality development (Hollingsworth, 1986; Kahaner, 1988; MacFarlane and Waterman, 1986; Smith and Pazdar, 1980; Summit, 1983; Terry, 1987).

Shapiro (1977) considered "destructive cultism" to be "a distinct syndrome" which includes "behavioral and personality changes, loss of personal identity, cessation of scholastic activities, estrangement from family, disinterest in society, and pronounced mental control and enslavement by cult leaders." He concluded that harmful cults were a "sociopathic problem" that requires "confrontation, rehabilitation, sociologic, psychotherapeutic, and general medical measures" (p. 80). These symptoms and effects are typical of adult cult members but do not satisfy the criteria for involuntary commitment to an inpatient mental health facility as a danger to self or others, unable to care for self, or in need of the more restrictive environment of an inpatient facility. They also do not satisfy the forensic criteria to establish legal incompetence according to present standards and precedents.

Ethically and legally, the standard of care and practice for mental health professionals is to follow current, established diagnostic criteria and treatment methodology. Diagnosis should follow the latest edition of the *Diagnostic and Statistical Manual* or "DSM" of the American Psychiatric Association. Common DSM diagnoses of cult victims, child to adult, have run the gamut from what I call *reactive disorders* (adjustment, anxiety, dissociative disorders) to classical psychotic mood and thought disorders. Some disorders cluster according to age and the nature of the cult experience, such as multiple personality disorder (MPD) and post-traumatic stress disorders (PTSD) child ritual abuse victims, and a wide range of diagnoses for adults involved in cults. For example, diagnoses varied in the four Afro-Caribbean cases cited by Alonso and Jeffrey (1988): bipolar affective disorder manic (Case 1); brief reactive psychosis and histrionic personality disorder (Case 2); organic delusional syndrome with auditory hallucinations secondary to alcohol dependence (Case 3); and shared paranoid disorder with hallucinations and delusions (Case 4).

Three of the more commonly reported diagnoses associated with cult involvement will be described further: dissociative, anxiety, and personality disorders. Psychopathic or sociopathic personalities, which I consider personality disorders, are not listed in the DSM manual and have been described earlier in this book (check index).

Dissociative Disorders

Common among abused children but also occurring in adults, these disorders were previously known as hysterical neuroses, dissociative type. They can be mild to severe, transient or chronic, and sudden or gradual onset, frequently based on physical, sexual, or psychological-emotional abuse in early childhood. They are characterized by disturbed identity, memory, or consciousness. If the major dynamic is identity or role confusion, previous identity is replaced by a new personality (multiple personality disorder or MPD). If the major dynamic is impaired reality teating and orientation, there are feelings of unreality (depersonalization), amnesia, or fugue.

Multiple Personality Disorder (MPD). For this diagnosis, two or more different, relatively intact and enduring personalities coexist, one in total control of the person at any given time, each with unique memory and distinctive behaviors. In young children seen soon after a precipitating trauma, the other personalities are not fully developed. Multiple personalities become more concrete and entrenched with the passage of time and continued traumatization. Change from one to another is sudden in most cases, usually in stress situations, but can take hours and in rare instances, days. Other trigger situations are personal need states, conflict between the personalities, environmental cues (similar situations, persons, or objects to the traumatic ritual), use of hypnosis, or sodium amytal.

The personalities or "alters" can differ markedly from each either and can even have different prescriptions for eyeglasses, handwriting, responses to medications and psychological testing, and differ in age, sex, sexual preference, race, religion, family of origin, knowledge, and taste in food and clothing. There is often a pattern in these alters, such as one with painful memories and secrets, another with no such knowledge, a naive child, an adult avenger or protector, an abuser persecuting the others, a sexual, physical, or verbally assertive-aggressive alter, a passive-dependent "anesthetized alter" who may even be "dead"; and an alter who fulfills job or school responsibilities. They usually have their own names which frequently have symbolic meaning to the previous, original personality. They usually do not know of each other but are aware of unexplained gaps in time when another personality has taken over. Awareness of the others is a therapeutic breakthrough and a dialog can be established to work through differences. Hypnosis has been helpful to facilitate smooth transition from one alter to another, much like placing a phone call to each. About half of cases reported with this diagnosis have less than ten coexisting multiple personalities, but there have been cases of more than a hundred personalities in one individual. These people are high risk for suicide, self-mutilation, antisocial acting out (child abuse, rape, assault), and substance abuse. Common misdiagnoses have been borderline personality disorder, impulse disorders, religious possession or excessive religiosity, psychosis, and malingering.

Early diagnosis and intervention are recommended by most therapists experienced in treatment of MPD. They caution against undue reliance on medications since the alters do not respond equally, rushing the treatment process, and group therapy until the personalities have been integrated. It is important to establish trust and to use but not abuse the transference. Ground rules should be established early, to set limits ("nobody gets hurt or killed or we all die"), agree on expectations, and assure that all alters get equal care and time (even the obnoxious ones). Alters should identify themselves when speaking and therapists should make it a practice to frequently refer to them by name. Treatment goal is one reality, eventually one integrated person. Assets and strengths of the alters should be applied to the treatment process.

Ross and Norton (1989) studied over 236 MPD cases of therapists in the Canadian Psychiatric Association and the International Society for the Study of Multiple Personality and Dissociation. The study confirmed higher incidence of MPD among females than males (207 to 28; one report did not specify sex). Other studies have estimated 4:1 to

9:1 female-male ratios. All 236 cases exhibited two or more distinct personalities, each in total control at a particular time with unique, distinctive behaviors and social-interpersonal communications style. Not all cases had amnesia for all personalities and there was diversity in the number of personalities, frequency of hospitalization, length of treatment, choice of medications, previous diagnoses, suicide attempts, self-mutilation, and antisocial acting out. More females (71%) than males (50%) attempted suicide by drug overdose and self-inflicted cigarette burns (58% females; 40% males). More males (29%) than females (10%) acted out antisocially and were tried, convicted, and were incarcerated. Incidence of headache and wrist slashing were similar by sex. Frequent misdiagnoses: personality disorder, affective disorder (65% female; 48% male), anxiety disorder, schizophrenia, substance abuse, adjustment disorder, somatization disorder, eating disorder, and organic mental disorder. Males were correctly diagnosed earlier in treatment than females (4–5 years vs. 6–7 years).

Psychogenic Fugue is a dissociative disorder characterized by sudden, unexplained travel, for hours, days, and rarely weeks or months, during which the individual assumes a different identity who is unaware of any previous identity. Later, there is an inability to recall events which took place during the fugue state. The fugue identity can be a completely new personality but who passes as "normal," might establish a different residence and lifestyle, and is usually more extroverted and socially active. Most fugues are brief, the new identity not complete, and are limited to seemingly calm, purposeful, solitary travel, a "soft escape" from reality or the unpleasant past. Example: A Vietnam veteran who did three tours in Nam as a gunship pilot and was never treated for any mental disorder, rented a plane under his real name, took off, then went into a fugue state and flew across the country until the fuel ran out, landed, checked into a motel, and "awakened" three weeks later wondering how he got there and why he was in a city far removed from his home.

Psychogenic Amnesia is a dissociative disorder the central feature being inability to recall personal information (name, address, age, occupation, etc.) clearly beyond normal forgetting. Unlike fugue, there is no new identity assumed. Most amnestic persons have considerable anxiety about this disorientation and memory gap. Instead of purposeful travel, there is confusion and aimless wandering, as if in a bad dream lost in a strange world. Perceptually, that is precisely what seems to be happening. Onset is sudden, frequently following severe stress, intensity can be mild to severe, and recovery is usually rapid, complete, and permanent. There are several types: *circumscribed amnesia* is the most common, no memory of events during a specific time period (two cases will be described later in this chapter under hypnosis); *selective amnesia,* limited, incomplete recall of some but not all details of an event; *generalized amnesia,* less common, lifelong memory loss; *continuous amnesia,* total memory loss of past and even present events.

Depersonalization disorder is a dissociative disorder in which there are episodes of altered self perception in which reality orientation is significantly changed. Typically, persons with this disorder describe the episodes as feeling "this is not happening to me."

Anxiety Disorders

Formerly anxiety or phobic neuroses, current DSM classification and criteria include panic disorders with and without agoraphobia, social and simple phobias, generalized anxiety disorder, obsessive-compulsive disorder, and post-traumatic stress disorder (PTSD) in this category. Of these, PTSD is more commonly seen in victims of ritual abuse and will be described further.

Posttraumatic Stress Disorder (PTSD) has been called "survivor syndrome" because it and multiple personality disorder are common ways the mind reacts to severe stress. PTSD can be acute (within 6 months of trauma; duration less than 6 months), chronic (within 6 months of trauma; duration more than 6 months), or delayed (occurs more than 6 months after trauma). There are five major factors to meet diagnostic criteria: a significant severe stressor; reexperiencing the ritual abuse in dreams, frequent flashbacks of spontaneous recall, or apprehension it will happen again; psychological-emotional numbing or withdrawal by distancing from others; decreased interest in previously favorite or pleasurable activities; constricted affect, reduced emotional spontaneity and responding, blunted or flattened. Common misdiagnoses: Adjustment disorder, atypical psychosis, paranoid schizophrenia; mood disorder or dysthymia (depressive neurosis).

Frequently reported PTSD symptoms are: exaggerated startle response; disturbed sleep; survivor guilt; impaired memory and concentration; phobic dread, dramatic avoidance, or intense anxiety in situations or activities, with people, or seeing places, objects, or symbols similar to the ritual abuse. Other common PTSD symptoms are anxiety, anger or hostility, antagonism or irritability, suspiciousness and distrust, hypervigilance, insomnia, compulsive overindulgence, apathy or lethargy, fatigue, depression, low self-esteem, poor coping skills, emotional numbing, difficulty concentrating, poor memory, disturbed sleep, substance abuse, and suicidal ideation and attempts. Not everyone has all these symptoms, and those are most significant which depart from a person's normal baseline behaviors and are inconsistent with their established personality pattern. Feinsod (1981), one of a few survivors of the Jonestown religious cult mass suicide, described survivors "shared the same problems: nightmares, severe depression, insomnia, and an unshakable compulsive desire to hide from the outside world. Few were able to work steadily" (p. 218). These symptoms suggest PTSD.

Rocklin and Lavett (1987) reported ten cases of adult survivors of child physical abuse who did not abuse their own children. They concluded that it is "assumed incorrectly that abused children will grow up to be abusive parents." None of the ten cases developed a dissociative disorder but all of them showed symptoms of anxiety disorder, specifically post-traumatic stress disorder. They had an exaggerated fear of violence to a phobic degree. They could not read of violence nor watch anything violent in a movie or TV drama. They were hypervigilant, with intense concern for security and safety. They suffered from anxiety which could be so severe as to be disabling. They experienced flashbacks in vivid nightmares. They had guilt feelings for having been abused. Rocklin and Lavett reported that all ten survivors shared a "pervasive mistrust ... as if having experienced betrayal by those responsible for their care, they expect it from practically everyone" (p. 769). *Trust or distrust* is Erik Erikson's first of eight life stages. Maladjustment at this stage can adversely affect subsequent development. Rogers and Mewborn (1976) suggested that the impact of child abuse is most severe when the victim experiences fear and terror and cognitively sees no escape, being trapped, helpless, and unable to "ward off danger" (p. 60).

Personality Disorder

Kohut's work on the narcissistic personality (1971) is relevant to adult cult members (1971). He observed that to reach maturity, to realize one's self, requires a passage from primitive, infantile imagery of idealized "selfobjects" to a more realistic relational view, integrating what is of value from the past into a self-sufficient whole. Kriegman and Solomon (1985) applied Kohut's approach directly to the cult experience. They see evidence of narcissism in both cult leaders and cult members. Former cult members, their families, and therapists who have been involved in deprogramming, describe personality traits and behaviors which are consistent with narcissistic personality disorder. This is not a sharply defined personality, and there is overlap with histrionic, borderline, and antisocial personality disorders. Narcissists are less impulsive than antisocial or borderline personalities and less emotional and dependent than histrionic types.

DSM criteria for narcissistic personality disorder are a "pervasive pattern of grandiosity" in fantasy or behavior, an exaggerated perception of self-importance or achievements, of being "special" even without achievement, understood only by other "special" people, hypersensitivity to evaluation by others, and a lack of empathy from early adulthood in a variety of contexts. There can be alternating feelings of exaggerated self-importance and "special unworthiness." They are often "driven" with insatiable ambition, unfeeling and indifferent, preoccupied with "fantasies of unlimited success, power, brilliance, beauty, or ideal love" but with "fragile self-esteem," a sense of entitlement, unrealistic expectations of favor, an exhibitionistic need for constant attention, sought with charm or cool self-assurance, exploitive and manipulative (American Psychiatric Association, 1987, p. 349–350).

It takes a great deal of energy to remain "psyched up" for grandiosity. Negative emotions are common, mainly envy for anyone seen as more successful and rebound depression from the emotional investment in continuing efforts to look good, the unending quest for power and success, rationalizing failures, and faking feelings to impress and use others. Anger or shame are masked by a seemingly icy indifference, like the TV commercial message "never let'em see you sweat." It is as if admitting to or venting emotions detracts from the godlike grandiosity and somehow renders the personality vulnerable. Five of nine criteria must be met to qualify for a diagnosis of narcissistic personality disorder:

1. Reacts to criticism with feelings of rage, shame, or humiliation usually not directly expressed
2. Manipulative and exploitive, selfishly uses people
3. Grandiose, exaggerated "special" self-importance unsubstantiated by actual achievement
4. Perceives problems as unique and understood only by other "special" people

5. Pre-occupied with unrealistic fantasies of unlimited power, brilliance, beauty, love, or success
6. Sense of entitlement or special favor, with unreasonable expectations (e.g., start at the top)
7. Constantly pursues attention and admiration
8. Lacks empathy
9. Preoccupied with envy

THERAPIES AND TREATMENT VARIABLES

Therapy needs of persons who have been involved in or with cults vary with the diagnosis, the nature, depth, and severity of the cult experience, and the individual's personality strengths and dynamics. No single psychotherapy method is universally appropriate to all therapy needs. Child and adolescent victims of ritual abuse are best treated by crisis intervention brief therapy followed by continuing supportive therapy as needed. Adults who leave cults have been successfully treated with a wide range of interventions from a few days of deprogramming as in Case 5 described earlier in this chapter, to ongoing individual and group psychotherapy. For victims of physical and sexual abuse, a primary concern is to restore the personality to pretraumatic function. Commonly used treatment techniques have been those effective for post-traumatic stress disorder. For adult former cult members, treatment has focussed on restoring optimal personality development, making up for lost developmental time, realizing and strengthening a sense of self by improved decisionmaking and critical judgment, and increasing autonomy and self-confidence.

Behavioral, psychoanalytic, and humanistic therapies have been used to treat mental disorders associated with cult involvement. Behavioristic techniques such as thought stopping, systematic desensitization, and behavior rehearsal provide immediate help in overcoming cult conditioning and reinforcing critical judgment, decisonmaking, and increased autonomy. Psychoanalysis effectively probes unconscious processes for deeper roots of factors that led to cult involvement, their scope, depth, and meaning to the individual. Humanistic therapies focus on present (existential) and experiential (primarily emotions and feelings) factors to quickly overcome loneliness and isolation, facilitate transcending the past and experiencing a strengthened self. All three of these basic theoretical approaches to therapy have within them many variations and supplemental techniques which are shared across theoretical boundaries such as hypnosis. We will examine three "spinoffs" from traditional therapies which seem uniquely suited to treating cult-associated mental disorders: *actualization therapy, self therapy,* and *syzygy* or START therapy.

Actualization Therapy

Everett Shostrom (1967), a humanistic psychologist, developed *actualization therapy* from his work in the human potential movement in California. He described ten therapeutic approaches to self-actualization:

CARING. Similar to Carl Rogers' *unconditional positive regard,* Shostrom's *caring* is to regard, value, and care about a person, actively or passively, neither manipulatively nor phoney. Example: "I like you but I don't like what you're doing" or "what happens to you matters to me."

EGO STRENGTHENING, developing thinking, feeling, and perception to improve coping skills, patience with self and others, and self-direction. In these ways, the individual is more a "pilot" and "less a robot" as Freud implied with instinctive drives and hidden, secret but powerful unconscious (p. 204).

ENCOUNTERING, "another word for contact," which is substituted for external control, when both therapist and client are *being* and *expressing* real feelings.

FEELING is experiencing, sharing, and venting feelings in a "psychologically safe relationship" which previously may have been "too threatening to experience freely." Cults stifle the expression of true feelings, some deliberately faking them in "heavenly deception" and "love bombing."

INTERPERSONAL ANALYSIS is evaluating games manipulative people play on each other, actively and passively.

PATTERN ANALYSIS is evaluating a person's philosophy of life and "unworkable patterns of functioning" to help change to "adaptive patterns of functioning."

REINFORCING, where growth-enhancement and socially adaptive behaviors are reworked positively shaped and negative, self-defeating behaviors fade and extinguish.

SELF–DISCLOSURE, the free, open sharing of the therapist's own patterns of living to encourage the client to realize uniqueness and self.

VALUE ORIENTING, reevaluating the client's loosely formulated value orientation and assumptions of self and others.

REEXPERIENCING of past learnings and desensitizing their pathological effects.

Shostrom's therapy process is a "progression in awareness" occurring in three stages (pp. 218–221):

Stage 1. DESCRIBE PRIMARY MANIPULATION

This stage is to detect and identify basic manipulative patterns such as helplessness, avoidance, seduction, control, exploitation or structuring (using up) time, and doing a short- and long-term, cost-benefit gain-loss analysis. Active manipulation is coercive; passive manipulation is seductive.

Stage 2. RESTORE INNER BALANCE

In this stage, the foolishness of manipulation is understood and replaced with actualization behaviors. Exaggeration and paradox, role play and rehearsal of new, opposite, different, or alternate coping skills facilitate free choice of more authentic behaviors. Shostrom wrote: "Exaggerated expression of any manipulative principle indicates repression of opposite potential" (p. 220).

Stage 3. INTEGRATION

This final stage assimilates active and passive principles into a unified working whole which expresses potentials and "skates naturally from one potential to another."

Self Therapies

Most self psychology theories and therapies are well suited to the understanding and treatment of cult-related problems and disorders. Simply stated, they view the self as a wholistic functional entity above and beyond the variety of observed or tested personality traits and abilities. Is self therapy a bonafide therapeutic system? It meets three criteria: it systematically describes and explains the therapeutic process; can be taught and learned in the absence of the founder; is successful after the founder's death (Kohut, 1971). These same criteria separate harmful or destructive cults from those that endure for centuries and are ultimately integrated into society. It is interesting to note that systems of psychotherapy have had cult aspects, flourishing during the founder's life, waning afterwards. Studies confirm most therapists continue the theoretical bias they were taught despite the so-called scientist-practitioner model of independent objectivity. Specialized systems of psychotherapy which isolate themselves from others and fail to assimilate research findings function much like cult organizations. Such therapies, by that feature alone, are contra-indicated for the treatment of cult victims because of the risk of substituting one cult experience for another.

The work of the late Heinz Kohut focussed on realizing and strengthening the self as the end goal of psychotherapy. Kohut's basically psychoanalytic approach joins with and complements humanistic psychologists such as Rogers, Maslow, Shostrom, and Branden. Syzygy theory (MacHovec, 1984, 1986) includes all theoretical and therapeutic approaches. Such an eclectic synthesis, together with a brief therapy model to minimize dependency makes self therapy an effective method for the treatment of ritual abuse victims and re-entry of former cult members into mainstream society.

Kohut (1971) saw therapy as both scientific and inspirational and his treatment goal was to reshape narcissistic structures and integrate them into the personality. This, he taught, is more valid than the person's "precarious compliance with ... change of narcissism to object love" (p. 224). This requires the client to seek, test, select, retest, or validate, then incorporate role models (selfobjects) increasing the risk of over-dependency. Kohut cautioned that there can be a "tenacious transference bondage" and he quoted Freud as also commented about the "temptation for the analyst to play the part of the prophet, savior, and redeemer ... in the place of the ego ideal" (p. 164). In an article on treating Afro-Caribbean cult members, Lefley (1981) emphasized the need for acceptance, rapport, warmth and friendliness by the therapist who functions *initially* and *briefly* as an authority figure in a *short-term* and *problem-oriented* treatment plan of *specified measurable goals.*

There is a delicate balance between guru and guide, mentor and master, and considerable skill is required to use and not abuse the transference to move the client from dependence to independence, from submissive self to self-sufficiency. Kohut (1971) observed that therapists who step beyond interpretation risk becoming "the patient's leader, teacher, and guide" and this tends to render interpretations abstract, less relevant (p. 222). The "messianic or saintly" personality of the therapist, his or her life history and lifestyle, play an active role in the therapeutic process, helping the client fulfill the myth of having "like Christ risen from death ... there can be little doubt that a therapist's quasi-religious fervor or his deep feeling of inner saintliess provides a strong therapeutic leverage" (p. 223). To facilitate this rebirth of self, Kohut encouraged therapists to accept initial *partial* dependence of clients in an "idealizing transference" which later is integrated into the emerging self (Kriegman and Solomon, 1985). Kohut commented that to initially "remain non-interfering while a narcissistic transference establishes itself" without taking action to foster "a realistic therapeutic bond" can be "the decisive factor on the road to therapeutic success" (1971, p. 208). This is a very delicate judgment call, especially so because of the danger of repeating the dependency of the cult experience.

Kohut described treatment goals as a "remobilization of incestuous affective ties" previously imbedded in "regressive narcissism" and "freeing of formerly repressed object libido" in a secondary transference (p. 297). Therapy is a "systematic working through" for "greater refinement" and "emotional deepening" through increased availability of "idealizing libido." The "love experience" is clarified as to its meaning, romantic, sexual, ideal, "fondness of another" and "devotion to cherished tasks and purposes." The individual develops an enriched capacity for object love in a variety of settings which "increases the cohesiveness of the self." Kohut held that the more certain the sense of who one is, the more internalized the values, the more able to "offer love without undue fear of rejection and humiliation" (p. 298). This is the beginning of self-sufficiency and realizing ego strength in striking contrast to the "packaged personality" of most cults.

Infantile, unrealistic parental and egoistic imagery fade as the individual realizes his or her true self, a reasoned, stable autonomy. The *idealized parent imago* is constructively integrated into the superego and ego. The archaic, regressive *pre-Oedipal imago* gradually weakens, is neutralized, then integrated as a basic drive channelling and controlling the ego, merged initially with the idealized therapist. The *Oedipal imago* is more highly differentiated and is assimilated as values and standards providing internalized order, consistency, leadership, and approval. The *grandiose self* also gradually changes from infantile to insightful, more realistically ambitious, self-confident, and purposeful. The *archaic exhibitionistic libido* fades into ego-syntonic success and pleasure marked by the gradual acquisition of empathy, creativity, humor, and wisdom. This emphasis on optimal personal growth and self-realization are in marked contrast to the conformity and submissive dependence of the cult experience. By thus assisting in the birth of the real self (being) and facilitating its unrestricted continued development (becoming), self therapy effectively meets treatment needs of those harmed by cults.

Empathy. Kohut taught that to be without empathy is pathological and evidence of faulty, prerational, animistic, "perceptual and cognitive infantilism." Lack of empathy is also due to "narcissistic fixations and regressions" in archaic stages of development" or from "early disturbances in the mother-child relationship." These prevent the perception and healthy, constructive integration of an idealized parent imago. Most cults isolate the individual from the family and rely on archaic parental imagery (the divinely inspired or commissioned cult leader). This is regressive, fixated at an early or archaic phase, preventing mature integration of parental imagery or an empathic relationship with parents. Empathy is an important clue to a person's selfhood, and also for the therapist since "scientific empathy is "a mode of observation" (p. 300).

Creativity. "Some of the greatest works of art are not new creations," Kohut wrote, "but the reflection of something preexisting rendered immortal" (p. 309). It flows from within the individual, spontaneously and effortlessly. The mundane, ordered routine of communal cults are not conducive to creative expression.

Humor. Genuine humor strengthens values and ideals, according to Kohut. It is "a sign of the transformation of archaic pathogenic narcissistic cathexes." Humor which is not genuine can be defensive, such as when used sarcastically, or an infantile preoccupation to avoid or escape reality. Unhealthy humor is cold, divisive, or mechanical, while healthy humor is spontaneous, unifying, and warming. Kohut saw healthy humor as evidence of the "silently increasing dominance which the patient's ego has achieved . . . over the grandiose, idealized self" (p. 324). Humor is widely reported as a sign of mental health (MacHovec, 1988).

Wisdom is "one of the peaks of human development" as well as "a cognitive and emotional position." Data from the self-study of therapy accumulate, "ordered and fitted together into a broader and deeper knowledge of the cohesive functioning of the mind and the continuity between past and present" (p. 326).

Kohut was a realist. This enabled him to look deeply into psychoanalytic theory and practice, extract what is valid, relate it to current needs, and shape it into an effective system of therapy. Because the cult experience intrudes upon optimal personality development as well as interpersonal relationships with family and friends and life goals, therapy must touch on all these factors. While brief therapy has the advantage of minimizing or preventing overdependence, its brevity limits its depth, less time to probe into deeper, important material and little or no time to process what is discovered. Still, Kohut continued to recommend the brief therapy model, realizing its shortcomings. His description of terminating therapy reflects his treatment philosophy: "Without sarcasm or pessimism, the analyst and patient admit as they are parting . . . not all has been solved . . . some conflicts, inhibitions, and symptoms . . . old tendencies toward self-aggrandizement and infantile idealization remain" BUT "are now familiar . . . can be contemplated with tolerance and composure" (p. 328).

Self esteem (Branden, 1983) is an aspect of the self and a major factor in all varieties of self therapy. Branden described self esteem as "the evaluation component of the self concept" (p. 23). While he did not refer specifically to cults, his theoretical approach and therapy method are quite relevant. Anything that interferes with "self responsibility . . . victimizes us with regard to our own life, and leaves us helpless" (p. 55). Anything that gives us *pseudo-self-esteem* is an "anti-anxiety device" with "defense value . . . motivated by fear and aimed at supporting an illusion of psychological equilibrium" (p. 81). He recommended critical evaluation of the client's values and goals, past and present. He concluded that we "may need to challenge important aspects of the implicit philosophy of the culture in which we live." This involves a need to "check and confront many of the basic premises that almost everyone takes for granted . . . a subtle and difficult task" (p. 183). Doing so has been therapeutic in his practice: "The most radical transformation occurs after the client's realization that no one is coming to the rescue" (p. 54).

Syzygy is a new self therapy which includes internal and external factors and forces which affect the individual and shape personality (MacHovec, 1986a, 1988). There are three basic forces which interact within the individual, in society, even in nature and the universe. This triangulation of force fields converge (in syzygy) for optimal personality development much like red, green, and blue colors for a full-color TV picture. *Stasis* or ST is stability, resistive to change, the "old order" of custom, tradition, and precedent, such as religion, law, institutions, family, and mores. *Action-reaction* or AR is change, the "new order" of advances, discoveries, and breakthroughs in science, technology, or self, "avante garde" art, music, fads, and fashion. ST and AR are in dynamic interplay, a sine wave push-pull, within the individual, society, and the universe. The sparks of their friction ignite the fire of *Tao* or T, the third basic force, what Westerners term transcendence, transmutation, or transformation, wisdom, insight, intuition, creativity, artistry, enrichment, elegance of thought, originality, wholeness, authenticity. It is the "Eureka" or "Ah hah" Zen "mystic leap" into the self, from the mundane to meaning, which exceeds the simple sum of its parts, what is caught, not taught.

Societies (and cults) that have survived for centuries and "real, genuine, authentic" personalities that endure, combine all three of these basic factors in syzygy, like three stars in apposition, separated and unique yet viewed in one configuration. When in balance, personality growth flows naturally to self-realization and self-sufficiency, a three-legged stool or tripod. Focussed on only one of the three, or two of three, there is imbalance and instability. Syzygy as therapy encourages critical thinking to fully explore and experience the ST and AR within the self and in society. Often this involves a ping-pong effect of action and inaction, assertiveness and submission, used to move from experiencing to discovery to transcendence. Paradox, psychodrama role reversal and gestalt empty chair, exaggeration, and humor facilitate the "jump" from ST and AR to T, which in syzygy therapy is to START the self process. The value of this theory is its compatibility with the arts and sciences, ancient and modern, bridging science and religion. It does not simply return the individual to precult function and adjustment, but allows for a transitional self in a natural progression to selfhood.

Family Therapy

Schwartz and Kaslow (1982) recommend family therapy to facilitate reentry of former cult members to their previous environment and lifestyle. They maintain that since family background and relationships contribute to "vulnerability to the cult's invitation to join" and also "extrication" from cults "family involvement in treatment is essential" (p. 25). They see family therapy by a team of well qualified therapists familiar with cults as "a benign alternative" to confrontive deprogramming. They claim similar results to active deprogramming "using less drastic and traumatic measures" even with a "cult buddy" present. They have found that former cult members are "relieved to be back in the outside world" and often wonder how they ever got "hooked" into the cult. Individual or family group therapy are held regularly as needed, then less frequently as the ex-cult member "reestablishes other friendships" and "anchor points in the community."

They see network family therapy as sufficiently similar to the cult experience to provide a "familiar and treasured part of the cult atmosphere into the session making the transition a little easier." The "lead therapist" temporarily replaces the cult leader and the family network gradually replaces the cult. The therapy process is to find a "viable balance between togetherness and separateness and . . . tangible assistance" such as finding a job or returning to school. Group therapy becomes a "kinship group," satisfies the "good Samaritan instinct," a sense of purpose, and concern for others, in the "loyalty born of family ties" (p. 25). These replace the security, continuity, and acceptance of the cult.

Schwartz and Kaslow report that former cult members in family therapy often describe an initial "floating phase," sometimes with altered states of consciousness, withdrawal symptoms from the "cult high," loss of identity or purpose, or a sense of loss of the closeknit, structured cult lifestyle and possibly resentment toward parents who interrupted it. More often there is "profound and prolonged depression" or humiliation over being duped by the cult and discouragement about lost time from school, career, or life goals. They recommend that each case be "carefully evaluated before the treatment of choice is determined" because of the "complexities of these situations, the fragility of the family relations, fears and hurts that have been sustained" (p. 25). It has been helpful to assign to the former cult member a caring, sensitive therapist who can be an authority figure less demanding than the cult and an ego ideal outside the family. If "everyone is willing to work together" the family is seen as a group. If there is antagonism and mistrust, family members see different therapists who collaborate and are careful not to violate therapist-client confidentiality. Group therapy of former cult members concurrent with individual or family therapy builds a support system of fellow feeling from "those who have been there" and further weakens ties to the cult. Treatment variables unique to cult involvement are: guilt over leaving the cult; fear of reprisal; need for reassurance they will achieve personal autonomy; cope with "floating" and dissociation; encouragement to continue their "spiritual quest" and make up for lost time in pursuing school, career, life goals and personal growth; a good medical workup and continuing health care. Therapists should remain optimistic, judiciously self-disclose but remain objective and consistent with ethical, professional standards.

Calof (1988) has treated adult survivors of child physical, sexual, and ritual abuse with an integrated model of individual and family therapy. He observed that "family denial over generations has eclipsed widespread child abuse and family dysfunction," and that many abusing families have failed to develop adequate parenting and relationship skills. They have impaired perception, poor judgment, and their reality is "quite hypnotic and elastic, a series of smoky mirrors, trapdoors, and pulleys" by authority figures trusted by the child who is hostage to them, isolated from other role models and the outside world. A father who raped his 3-year-old daughter rationalized it with the comment: "She's only a piece of shit I created . . . I didn't hurt her or even mark her up any." Trapped in such a situation, the mind defends itself with the only escape possible, dissociation. The abuser's weak rationalization is also dissociative and enables him to continue the abuse. Family dissonance further denies reality and compartmentalizes it. The abused 3-year-old was 40 when she sought therapy!

Traumatic memories and resulting powerful emotions seek outlet which, if frustrated, may "coalesce into an alternate personality." Calof has found that many adult survivors tend to "severely minimize their histories of abuse and present therapists with secondary symptoms." The original abuse is seldom reported initially. Instead, there are one or more presenting symptoms such as anxiety or anxiety attacks, phobias, conflict avoidance, passive overdependence or social isolation, obsessions, compulsions, or preoccupation, depression, suicidal ideation or attempts, mood swings, substance abuse, eating disorder, confusion, disturbed thinking, or somatic complaints. Many of these symptoms are symbolic or conversion phenomena.

Calof combines individual and family group methods, the intrapsychic and interpersonal, to "craft the tools of survivorship." The recovery process "should be family oriented" and multigenerational but also "adequately address the issue of selfhood," provide personal autonomy and the opportunity to "leave home," a process of integrative, dehypnotizing reprogramming. Family loyalties can be powerful antitherapeutic forces and should not be engaged in "direct battle." "Conjoint work" is used only after individual therapy has removed denial, integrated previous trauma, and bolstered the self. Boundaries should be established in survivors "before working on the wider system, if at all." The purposes of involving the family are that they may understand and learn from what has occurred in the past, its impact and aftermath, future goals to prevent "intergenerational transmission" of abuse, and to provide help to other family members if needed.

In Calof's model, recovery occurs in stages usually sequential but which can overlap or coexist: break denial and process the past; move beyond guilt; learn to live with (real) feelings in a (real) body; resocialize and improve interpersonal skills; manage stress and problem-solve; identify and respond to new values and goals; resolve spiritual themes and issues; and closure. Transference issues involve fear of abandonment, contaminating the therapist, being judged evil, disbelieved, or invalidated. Countertransference issues are therapist codependency from overstriving to compensate for abuse or loss, to feel needed or special, guilt for the pain of the therapeutic process, impatience or irritation with slower recovery than expected, or assuming a persecutor role (being an abuser). There can be "web-like manipulation" by indirection, misdirection, blame, unresponsiveness, devaluation, triangulation, seduction, staff splitting, histrionics, or self-destructive acting out. Other potential problems are differences racially, sexually, or in physical appearance, values or lifestyle, crises and additional time required, family interference, overgeneralization, or the threat and risk of violence.

Hypnosis

Hypnotherapy has been successfully used to facilitate brief therapy in the treatment of dissociative disorders (MacHovec, 1984a, 1985, 1986b). Goodman (1975) suggested that the cult experience involves trance behavior and "millenarian expectations" and "Satanic temptations" were remembered longer than other cult concepts and practices. He attributed this to the quality of trance during the cult experience. This may explain why hypnosis has been so effective in treating cult victims and former cult members. It is especially important when using hypnosis on ritual abuse victims or former cult members, to explain the process (all hypnosis is *self* hypnosis) and obtain full informed consent. This helps build ego strength and self-confidence and minimizes overdependence on the therapist. Also, the treatment plan is developed by mutual discussion and consent, treatment methods chosen and explained, and time provided at each session for reflection, discussion, evaluation, and integration. These procedures reinforce the individual's personal responsibility and self sufficiency. The most effective role of the therapist is as a "friend or confidant more than a surrogate or symbolic parent, more accepting than authoritarian, allowing the individual freedom to experience and a high degree of control over the process" (1985, p. 12).

A technique which has been successfully used is "the envelope" (MacHovec, 1986b) consisting of initial progressive relaxation with a 30-1 countdown, guided imagery to a suggested preselected "peaceful scene" for deeper relaxation, reinforced with a 10-1 countdown, then processing material specific to the individual as agreed in advance, amnesia for any traumatic material, guided imagery and suggested relaxation, then awakening on a 1–5 count. In subsequent sessions, the individual was given the opportunity to remember some or all details of the traumatic event, and in most cases did so gradually, the recall correlated to emerging ego strength. The following two cases illustrate use of this technique. Age regression was used to isolate traumatic incidents, both of which occurred at age 5 and 6, within the age group frequently reported for traumatic ritual abuse. Neither of these persons recalled any trauma in early childhood and age regression was used because nothing of clinical significance was found in the current life situation or by history.

CASE 7 was a 24-year-old twice divorced female Caucasian who sought help for what she called a "personality problem." She was attracted to older men in positions of authority, became emotionally involved with them, but once married to them, became critical and demanding. She was planning her fourth marriage when she sought psychotherapy. Initial diagnosis was passive-aggressive personality disorder. Three sessions were spent exploring details of her life history but yielded nothing clinically significant. Hypnosis was used first for relaxation, then for age regression to search for any repressed material. At age 5 she tensed, cringed, and recalled sitting on a swing pushed by her father. He mistook her increasing panic for joy and he pushed her higher and higher. She twisted, lost her balance, and fell to the ground, striking a rock concealed in the grass below. She remembered the pain and the terror and her bewilderment and growing rage at her father who brushed her off, saying: "It's all right, you're not hurt." It was *not* all right, she was in pain and the person who hurt her was the father she loved and trusted. This blocked memory was revivified in subsequent sessions with marked relief. She was given the opportunity to remember "none of it, some of it, or all of it," and declined to do so until the seventh hypnosis session. Therapy was terminated at the tenth session. Followup two years later showed her happy in her fourth marriage without continuing her previous behaviors toward her husband (MacHovec, 1985, p. 9).

CASE 8 was a 27-year-old unmarried male Caucasian who sought psychotherapy because he "couldn't hold a job" or maintain social or sexual relationships though he said he wanted very much to "marry and settle down." He was having anxiety attacks without any apparent cause. His face was a mask of fear. He was underweight, restless, and couldn't sleep well. Extensive medical examination and tests yielded nothing, nor did a careful history and mental status examination. Hypnosis was used to relieve his anxiety and he responded well. In the third session age regression was used to search for any repressed material. At age 6 he grimaced and shifted restlessly in the recliner chair, moaning and wincing, grabbing his right foot and calf. He recalled his mother putting him in the chicken yard to punish him while she went to town to shop. The roosters pecked at his feet and when his mother returned he was terrified and bloody. She did not comfort him. Given the opportunity to recall the event or to remember little or none of it, he opted for total recall. Hypnosis was continued for relaxation and to ensure thorough venting of the event. Therapy was terminated after nine sessions and followup two years later found him working at the same job and engaged to be married (MacHovec, 1985, p. 10).

Treatment variables have emerged from the use of hypnosis as adjunctive treatment of dissociative states (MacHovec, 1984, p. 20). The time interval between trauma and treatment ranges from immediately after to twenty years or more. The number of sessions required to effect recall varies from one to some individuals who do not choose to recall and rely on the therapist's judgment. Hypnotizability seems to correlate with therapeutic need. Some who have been curious about hypnosis and have sought to be hypnotized by stage entertainers or habit control (smoking, overeating, drinking) were not able to do so but responded to hypnosis in psychotherapy. It is, of course, possible they were not hypnotized in therapy but merely thought they were. They responded to hypnotic suggestion, however. A "standard" induction such as "the envelope" was effective and in an era of accountability, peer review, and risk management would seem to be a worthwhile practice. The patient's active involvement as a partner in the therapeutic process is ideally suited to treating cult victims or former cult members and is conducive to progressive self-reliance.

Fixing the seal. It has been my practice since 1970 to routinely "fix the seal" on everyone hypnotized (MacHovec, 1989b). It dates back at least to 1930 and is very likely much older. While there is no research to establish it is effective in all cases, it is in the individual's best interest, especially for cult victims since it bolsters their self-confidence. It is a posthypnotic suggestion that "no one will ever be able to hypnotize you unless you want to be or need to be, unless you know and trust the person doing it and know that he or she is qualified, because we're dealing with your own innermost thoughts and feelings, serious matters to be treated seriously" (MacHovec, 1986). Many have reported to me with a wry smile that ever since their hypnosis experience they were "instantly aware" of anyone's attempt to manipulate them, such as salesmen, politicians, religious extremists, or even overly enthusiastic friends. It may be a very helpful preventive for cult recruitment.

Balson, Dempster, and Brooks (1984) reported that "autohypnosis techniques are an effective strategy for limiting the potential harm from coercion" (p. 252). They also observed the high incidence of posttraumatic stress disorder among victims of "coercive persuasion." They listed three distinct "response patterns" each involving submitting to and imitating the expected behavioral role: "without identifying with it; assimilates or identifies with the prescribed role; and resists both submitting and identifying." They found that the third type used "autohypnotic phenomena to defend against persuasion" (p. 254). This involved "a naturally occurring ability to dissociate hypnotically and evoke hypnotic fantasy" (p. 255). Such persons can diminish psychological and physiological reactivity, similar to use of hypnosis to attenuate the perception of pain, increase stimulus threshold to tolerate high input without overload, remain "psychologically intact," and insulate the self against physical and verbal attacks.

These authors reported a variety of methods used to "substitute autohypnotic experiences for reality during direct coercive persuasion" such as fantasy, illusion, dissociation, revivification of sights, sounds, smells, and tactile memories (ocean, birds, wind, sun, rain, food, traffic, voices). Some have successfully defended themselves mentally by engaging in an ongoing "soap opera" in their mind, continued each day. "Vivid reveries" and "deep meditation" were also used successfully. The victim, in effect, can "provide many of his own reinforcers" and deprives the interrogator or manipulator of "his greatest weapon . . . the capacity to be the primary source of reinforcement (p. 257). They recommend including autohypnosis self-defense techniques in training for foreign service, private industry with officials abroad, and military personnel. Simulation training would provide behavioral rehearsal of this technique, augmented with interactive videodisc technology. These authors concluded: "We may have an ethical commitment to provide the best psychological protection possible for potential victims" (p. 259).

Summing up, treating ritual abuse victims and former members of destructive cults is an opportunity to synthesize the most effective theoretical approaches and treatment techniques. *Cognitive* aspects are taking a detailed history noting all potential contributing factors and their relative effect on the individual, evaluating the present mental status, strengths and weaknesses, listing and rank-ordering current problems, negotiating a meaningful treatment contract and scheduling regular evaluations of it. *Affective* considerations are overcoming guilt, isolating traumatic events and revivifying them, venting current negative feelings, improving coping skills to better deal with anxiety, frustration, depression, and insecurity, and to restore basic trust, self-esteem, and self-confidence to continue on the rocky road to self discovery and self identity.

Successfully treating the cult experience suggests 6 E's and 4 R's. The first three E's are cognitive: *exploration, evaluation,* then *experimenting* (e.g., critical thinking, decisionmaking, thought stopping, coping behavior rehearsal, testing limits or paradox, self analysis, systematic desensitization, etc.). The last three E's are affective: *existential* (focus on the here and now), *experiential* (identify and verbalize real feelings), then *express* them (vent, abreact, process, anticipate next stimulus and response). The four R's are: *reentry,* to reinsert the individual into the optimal pre-cult environment and lifestyle; *restore* "normal" functioning there; *renew* strengths and positive factors; *reinforce* these with gradually decreasing therapist contact and medications as the true or real self emerges. This requires three A's: *autonomy,* to stand alone and know where to get help if and as needed (basic trust, of self and worthy others); *authenticity,* that what is there is real, probably for the first time, and to like it (identity, self-esteem); *assertiveness,* ability to verbalize this process, what has happened, is happening, or might happen. This brief paragraph describes a long and sometimes painful process. Time will vary with individual treatment needs from a few sessions to ongoing weekly sessions. Therapy continuing more than a year should be evaluated for possible over-dependency in both therapist and client. Some therapists transfer clients through specialized supplemental treatments by others, such as self-help or peer groups, psychodrama or other group therapy, hypnotherapy, biofeedback, or pastoral counseling. Attending selected workshops, readings, or coursework can also be effective.

PREVENTION

What can be done preventively to reduce vulnerability of children, teenagers, and adults to harmful cults? Anti-cult organizations of former cult members, families, and friends of cult members have published recommendations for resisting cult recruiters and relating to close friends or family members who have joined a cult. First, some general suggestions:

1. BE AWARE and KEEP INFORMED about cults, cult-like groups or those that may be cults but deny it. Know what they represent. Study about cults in books, journals, magazines, and newspapers, on TV and over public radio, to separate fact from fiction, and to update what you know. Share this information with family, friends, neighbors, and at church, service, and fraternal meetings.

2. PROMOTE public awareness programs at schools, churches, offices, and by civic, service, and fraternal groups. Presentations by former cult members are especially effective. Add books, articles, and reference materials to libraries.

3. BE WARY of "training" workshops, seminars, suggested, offered or required by employers, schools, and other organizations. They may be an overt or cover cult activity.

4. BEWARE OF STRANGERS and newfound friends. Never accept an invitation for a meal, visit, course, or to join a "special interest group" or charity, or any club or group until you have thoroughly checked it out.

5. NEVER GIVE MONEY to anyone unless you know what it is for and where and where and how it will be spent. If in doubt check it out!

6. CHECK LAWS AND REGULATIONS about solicitation and zoning permits for restrictions on public solicitation, on single or multiple dwellings, and public meetings.

7. WRITE legislators, local, state, and federal, and inform them of your concern about destructive cults, that it is based on animal and human rights, deception and fraud, and risks to mental health, not religious belief.

Seven Do's

1. Record all names, addresses, and phone numbers of persons associated in any way with the cult.

2. Keep a *written* chronology of events associated with the individual's involvement in the cult.

3. Answer all correspondence from the individual sincerely and without recriminating language. Don't drive them further into the cult.

4. Collect cult-related items from newspapers, magazines, and other sources, and all available materials from the cult.

5. Keep cool, stay loose, avoid threats. Be friendly but firm, open to and continuing 2-way communication. Don't slam the door.

6. File a written complaint with public officials. Help build a "substantial body of data" and "public information" on the cult.

7. Seek help and support, with other families and friends in similar situations.

Six Don'ts

1. DON'T send money to a cult member or to the cult. Needs are often falsified to obtain funds.

2. DON'T give originals of documents unless required by law and even then consult a lawyer. Provide copies only.

3. DON'T pay any "professionals" until you have verified their credentials, qualifications, and fully understand what they will do for you.

4. DON'T GIVE UP! Every cult member has had affection, care, education, health needs from family and friends, memories that can never be erased permanently.

5. DON'T feel alone. Thousands of families are experiencing the same loss and frustration. There are hundreds of cults with membership totalling millions. Every cult member has family and friends somewhere.

6. DON'T feel guilty. No one is a perfect parent or friend. Hindsight is always 20-20 vision. Cults use deceptive manipulation to recruit and retain members.

Seven Possible Signs of Cult Involvement

1. CHANGE in personality, emotions, motivation, values, goals, plans, or habits.

2. CHANGE in school behavior, lower grades, acting-out behaviors, attitude.

3. MOOD changes. Irritated, frustrated, anxious, or depressed.

4. ISOLATION and WITHDRAWAL. Prefers to be alone.

5. REJECTS parental, social, or religious values.

6. REJECTS friends.

7. UNUSUAL interest in strange beliefs (occult, mysticism, meditation, chanting, Satanism, Eastern religions).

8. SYMBOLS, OBJECTS. Pictures, posters, record albums, objects, or jewelry with occult or Satanic symbols.

9. OBSESSED with heavy metal, hard or punk rock.

10. CHANGED VOCABULARY of new, different, strange or unusual occult, mystic, or Satanic terms not previously known or used.

Some of these can signal drug abuse, an identity crisis, or the changing moods and low stress threshold of adolescence and child victims of physical or sexual abuse not at all related to cult involvement. The list is based on reports by teenagers who have been involved in Satanic cult experiences.

Somehow we need to insulate or inoculate children, teenagers, and adults from deception, manipulation and "hard sell" tactics which surround us. Uninvited, unwanted telephone solicitation, incessantly repeated TV and radio commercials, televangelists, and junk mail invade our homes and our minds. Billboards and ads fill our eyes, flyers and tracts are pressed into our hands, gift and money giveaways attract our attention, and all these invasions of privacy and insults to our intelligence and to our integrity help distract us from other more useful thoughts. It is as difficult to prove these things harmful as to prove what is indecency, obscenity, or profanity.

The lack of legal restrictions increase vulnerability of our children and ourselves to cults that have been nothing more than mental cages. Both cults and media manipulators are protected by First Amendment rights of freedom, of the press and of religion. The public has no such protection. The Bill of Rights doesn't include a right to privacy, of home or mind. Usually, controls come when there is blatant excess and public outrage. When 913 people died tragically and unnecessarily in Jonestown, Guyana, including a Congressman there on a factfinding tour, there was great public concern but no controls resulted. *We* are our only defense. We can reexamine our values, as our founding fathers did and join in a similar renewal of ideas and ideals. Perhaps we need a new—or renewed— *Declaration of Independence.* The 1776 original clearly listed "life, *liberty,* and the *pursuit of happiness* as "unalienable rights." Cults deprive members of liberty and the free and unrestricted search for happiness. In 1800, Thomas Jefferson vowed "eternal hostility against every form of tyranny over the mind of man." In his first inaugural address in 1801, Jefferson said "error of opinion may be tolerated where reason is left free to combat it."

CONCLUSIONS

Cults and cult-like organizations have both positive and negative aspects. There are promises and costs. Many are anti-intellectual, offering security, structure, and support at the cost of independent judgment and established relationships and values. If optimal personal development requires gradually maturing self-awareness and decisionmaking, the enforced conformity and communal lifestyle of cults is clearly deficient. Shared lectures, meals, work, rituals, and practices shape a cult or group personality, frequently as extension of the cult leader's model of behavior. Leadership is a one-way street from the leader downward and all decisions are unilateral. There is a narrow, polarized world view of rigid dogma and restricted socializations a system of absolutism and totalism. Adult cults function as a "velvet trap," into a bland, lifeless recipe for reality in an infantile "land of the Lotus eaters."

Reentry of former cult members and the recovery of cult ritual abuse victims is complex. The effect is catastrophic on young children who have been ritually abused. It intrudes on their minds and personalities with the most intense shock and terror, destroys trust, confuses values, and adds guilt and insecurity to an already fragile personality structure. Teenagers involved in Satanic cults engage in behavior consistent with the complex of forces and needs within them: identity crisis, role confusion, uncertain career and life goals, unrealistic expectations of self and others, insecurity about the future, inferiority, suspended precariously between childhood and adulthood, dependence and independence, responsibility and reckless disregard. Added to these are physiological changes in body chemistry and physical appearance, an awakened sex drive, an impressionable child in an adult body. The German poet-philosopher Goethe called such a developmental stage *sturm und drang* (stormy turbulence). The effect on adults is either immediate fixation by a quick mental disconnect fixed at present mental and personality function, or a regression to infantile submission and primitive mental imagery.

To prevent child ritual abuse, teenage obsession with fantasy, and adult susceptibility to cult escapism, we must somehow encourage the development of critical thinking, intelligent decisionmaking, and reasoned judgment. To do so we will have to know and understand what we believe and how and why we behave as we do. We have the ability and the capability of applying what we know in the behavioral sciences, the theories and the therapies, to what has in the past been called religion.

We need to expand the scope of the behavioral sciences to include social, religious, political, and popular movements and especially to conjointly explore the interface of science and religion. Deprogramming without appropriate scientific *and* religious components is incomplete and more likely to result in a return to the cult or to the same life situation and relationships that made the individual vulnerable to the cult experience to begin with.

We can pair the science of human behavior with the religion of human nature to transcend minority and majority and even cultural and national differences to focus on common needs and values. The lesson of the behavioral sciences, of anthropology and history is that we are more similar than we are dissimilar, across time, geography, and culture. From this can come a realization of shared values, such as to protect the innocence and preserve the trust of children, in themselves and in us, and to respect and value life, of animals and humans. We can begin by examining more closely what we say and do, what we think and feel. As Shostrom pointed out, "psychology was never meant to be a justification for continuing . . . behavior that does not permit the individual to live up to the maximum of his potential." He added that the goal of psychology is also "not merely to offer explanations of behavior" but "to help us arrive at self knowledge, fulfillment, and self-support" (p. 34).

What can be concluded from this worldwide, cross-cultural, historical and contemporary exploration of the cult experience? Science has produced a substantial body of data demonstrating that the cult experience can precipitate mental disorders according to current diagnostic criteria. Religion has established an equally substantial body of data that there is a universal need for spiritual expression. Cults can intrude upon and disrupt both areas. Effective therapy should restore optimal and unobstructed psychological and spiritual growth. To satisfy this need, mental health professionals and researchers need to know more about religion. The clergy need to know more about personality development, mental disorders, and the scientific method. Both clinicians and clergy have a mission. One is committed to the search for the self, the other to the search for meaning. Are they separate pursuits?

The best protection against manipulation and exploitation by cults or any other force has not changed since the days of the ancient Greeks who inscribed a simple antidote on the Temple of Delphi: "Know thyself." The search for self, in therapy as in life, is an exploration which ends mysteriously, magically, where it began, but at a higher level of awareness and insight. That's also true for therapy that transports a child, teenager, or adult not just to the "former" self, uncertain and vulnerable, but to the "true" self, joyously alive and well, passing from darkness to light. And that is a fitting end to this book, which was an exploration of inner space through the dark side of personality, emerging now in the clear, fresh air, and sunlight. T. S. Eliot (1888–1965) described it well in his *Four Quartets* (1935):

> *We shall never cease from exploration*
> *And the end of all our exploring*
> *Will be to arrive where we started*
> *And know the place for the first time*

May it be so for you and all you meet and help along the way!

APPENDIX A

SOURCES OF ADDITIONAL INFORMATION ON CULTS

American Family Foundation
P.O. Box 336
Weston, MA 02193
(Phone: 617-893-0930)

Believe the Children
P.O. Box 1358
Manhattan Beach, CA 90266
(Phone: 213-379-3514)

Center for the Study of the Self
3804 Hawthorne Avenue
Richmond, VA 23222
(Phone: 804-329-9418)

COMA (Council on Mind Abuse)
Box 575, Station Z,
Toronto, Ontario, Canada
  M5N 2Z6
(Phone: 416-484-1112)

Cult Awareness Network
(also WATCH Network)
2421 West Pratt Boulevard
Suite 1173
Chicago, IL 60645
(Phone: 312-267-7777)

Humane Society of the
  United States
2100 L Street NW
Washington, DC 20037
(Phone: 202-452-1100)

Justice for Children
P.O. Box 42266
Washington, DC 20015
(Phone: 202-686-1035)

National Center for Missing
  and Exploited Children
1835 K Street NW, Suite 700
Washington, DC 20006

National Center for the Prosecution
  of Child Abuse
American Prosecutors Research Institute
1033 North Fairfax Street, Suite 200
Alexandria, VA 22314
(Phone: 703-739-0321)

National Children's Advocacy Center
(and National Resource Center
  on Child Sexual Abuse)
106 Lincoln Street
Huntsville, AL 35801
(Phone: 205-533-KIDS)

National Committee for Prevention
  of Child Abuse
332 S. Michigan Avenue, Suite 950
Chicago, IL 60604
(Phone: 312-663-3520)

National Victim Center
307 West 7th Street, Suite 1001
Fort Worth, TX 76102
(Phone: 817-877-3355)

APPENDIX B

MODEL ANIMAL PROTECTION ACT

(Courtesy, Humane Society of the United States)

Section 1. Definitions

a) "Animal" means any member of any species of the animal kingdom.
b) "Slaughter" means the killing of any animal for food purposes.
c) "Ritual slaughter" means the preparation and killing of any animal for food purposes in accordance with (cite your state's ritual or kosher slaughter statute).
d) "Animal sacrifice" means the injuring or killing of any animal in any religious or cult ritual or as an offering to or propitiation of a deity, devil, demon, or spirit, wherein the animal has not been injured or killed primarily for food purposes, regardless of whether all of any part of such animal is subsequently consumed.

Section 2. Prohibited Acts

a) No person shall engage in or perform animal sacrifice.
b) No person shall own, keep, possess, or have custody of any animal intending to use such animal for animal sacrifice.
c) No person shall sell, offer to sell, give away, transfer or provide any animal to another person who intends to use the animal for animal sacrifice, if such intent is known or reasonable should have been known by the selling or transferring person at or before the time of the sale, offer to sell, giving away, transfer or provision. There shall be a rebuttable presumption that the sale or transfer of any animal to or from a so-called botanica, occult supply store, or any enterprise a substantial portion of whose business is in religious, ritual, or occult articles is made in violation of this section.
d) The presence of any animal carcass or animal parts or blood found in conjunction with evidence of any religious or cult ritual shall be prima facie evidence of a violation of this Act.

171

Section 3. Exemptions

Nothing in this Act shall be construed to prohibit any person or establishment lawfully operating under the laws of this state from lawfully engaging in the slaughter or ritual slaughter of animals.

Section 4. Enforcement and Penalties

a) Any person found to be in violation of this Act shall be fined not less than $100 nor more than $1000 for each offense, imprisoned for not more than six months, or both. Each violation of this Act shall be considered a separate offense and may be separately charged.

b) Agents of animal control departments, law enforcement officers, and investigators of any private organization incorporated for the prevention of cruelty to animals shall have the authority to investigate suspected violations of this Act.

Section 5. Civil Actions

Any person, on behalf of any animal involved or being used in any acts prohibited under Section 2 of this Act, may bring a civil action in any court of competent jurisdiction to enjoin violations of this Act.

Section 6. Severability

This Act is severable. If any provision or part is ruled invalid, the remaining provisions or parts shall still be valid.

Section 7. Effective Date

This Act shall take effect immediately upon enactment.

REFERENCES

Aceves, J. B., & King, H. G. (1978). *Cultural anthropology.* Morristown, NJ: Silver Burdett.

Allen, C., & Metoyer, P. (1987). Crimes of the occult. *Police,* February 1987, 38–45.

Allen, S. (1982). *Beloved son: A story of the Jesus cults.* Indianapolis, IN: Bobbs-Merrill.

Anderson, S. M., & Zimbardo, P. G. (1984). On resisting social influence. *Cultic Studies Journal, 1,* 196–219.

Andres, R., & Lane, J. R. (1988). *Cults and consequences.* Los Angeles, CA: Jewish Federation Council of Greater Los Angeles.

Alonso, L., & Jeffrey, W. D. (1988). Mental illness complicated by Santeria belief in spirit possession. *Hospital and Community Psychiatry, 39,* 1188–1191.

Allnutt, K. R. (1985). Cults: Organized, armed and protected by the First Amendment. *Police Product News,* October 1985, 29–33.

Allport, G. W. (1964). The fruits of eclecticism: Bitter or sweet. *Acta Psychologica, 23,* 27–44.

American heritage dictionary (1985). Second edition. Boston, MA: Houghton-Mifflin.

American Psychiatric Association (1987). *Diagnostic and statistical manual (DSM-III-R).* Third edition. Washington, DC: Author.

Annon, J. S., Crossley, T., DeVault, S., Liebert, D. S., Reiser, M., Rogers, M. L., & Webster, S. L. (1988). The psychological interview in criminal cases. *American Journal Forensic Psychology, 6,* 5–90.

Appel, W. (1983). *Cults in America.* New York, NY: Holt, Rinehart, and Winston.

Appelbaum, P. S. (1989). Protecting child witnesses in sexual abuse cases. *Hospital and Community Psychiatry, 40,* 13–14.

Aquino, M. A. (1983). *The church of Satan.* San Francisco, CA: Temple of Set.

Aquino, M. A. (1986). *The crystal tablet of Set.* San Francisco, CA: Temple of Set.

Asch, S. E. (1952). *Social psychology.* Englewood Cliffs, NJ: Prentice-Hall.

Bainbridge, W. S. (1978). *Satan's power: A deviant psychotherapy cult.* Berkeley, CA: University of California Press.

Bandura, A., & Walters, R. (1963). *Social learning and personality development.* New York, NY: Holt, Rinehart, and Winston.

Banner, P. (1989). Law enforcement's response to Satanism. *The National Sheriff,* December 1988–January 1989, pp. 58–64.

Barker, E. (Ed.) (1982). *New religious movements: A perspective for understanding society.* New York, NY: Edwin Mellen Press

Barker, E. (1984). *The making of a Moonie.* Oxford, England: Blackwell.

173

Barry, R. J. (1987). Satanism, the law enforcement response. *The National Sheriff,* February–March 1987, pp. 11–14.

Becker, H. (1963). *Outsiders.* New York, NY: Free Press.

Benedict, R. (1961). *Patterns of culture.* Boston, MA: Houghton Mifflin.

Berry, G. L. (1961). *Religions of the world.* New York, NY: Barnes and Noble.

Bettelheim, B. (1977). *The uses of enchantment.* New York, NY: Vintage.

Bloom, A. (1987). *The closing of the American mind.* New York, NY: Simon & Schuster.

Boisen, A. (1960). *Out of the depths.* New York: Harper & Row.

Branden, N. (1983). Honoring the self: The psychology of confidence and respect. New York, NY: Bantam.

Bridgwater, W. (Ed.) (1968). *Columbia Viking Desk Encyclopedia.* New York, NY: Viking Press.

Bromley, D. G., & Richardson, J. T. (1983). *The brainwashing/deprogramming controversy.* New York, NY: Edwin Mellen Press.

Brown, R. *He came to set the captives free.* Chino, CA:

Buber, M. (1951). *The way of man.* New York, NY: Wilcox and Follett.

Budge, E. A. W. (1930). *Amulets and talismans.* New York, NY: Macmillan.

Bugental, J. F. T. (1965). *The search for authenticity.* New York, NY: Holt, Rinehart & Winston.

Bugliosi, V. (1974). *Helter skelter.* New York, NY: Norton.

Call, M. (1985). *The hand of death.* Lafayette, LA: Prescott Press.

Calof, D. (1988). Adult survivors of incest and child abuse. *Family Therapy Today,* 3, 1–3.

Cavendish, R. (1967). *The black arts.* New York, NY: Putnam.

Connor, J. W. (1980). The projected image: The unconscious and the mass media. *Journal of Psychoanalytic Anthropology, 3,* 349–376.

Conway, F., & Siegelman, J. (1978). *Snapping: America's epidemic of sudden personality change.* Philadelphia, PA: Lippincott.

Crewdson, J. (1988). *Sexual abuse of children in America.* Boston, MA: Little, Brown.

Crowley, A. (1969). *The confessions of Aleister Crowley.* New York, NY: Hill and Wang.

Crowley, A. (1974). *Magick in theory and practice.* New York, NY: Gordon Press.

Daraul, A. (1971). *A history of secret societies.* New York, NY: Pocket Books.

Dollard, J., & Miller, N. E. (1950). *Personality and psychotherapy.* New York, NY: McGraw-Hill.

Drapela, V. J. (1987). *A review of personality theories.* Springfield, IL: Thomas.

Ehrenwald, J. (1956). *From medicine man to Freud.* New York, NY: Dell.

Eliot, C. W. (Ed) (1909). *The Odyssey of Homer.* Harvard Classics, Volume 22. New York, NY: P. F. Collier.

Ellis, A., & Harper, R. A. (1974). *A guide to rational living.* North Hollywood, CA: Wilshire Book Co.

Erickson, S. (1988). Santeria: Alive and well in the U.S.A. *Humane Society News,* Fall, 12–16.

Erikson, E. H. (1950). *Childhood and society.* New York, NY: Norton.

Eth, S., & Pynoos, R. S. (1985). *Post-traumatic stress disorder in children.* Washington, DC: American Psychiatric Press.

Feinsod, E. (1981). *Awake in a nightmare, Jonestown: The only eyewitness account.* New York: Norton.

Fenichel, O. (1945). *The psychoanalytic theory of the neuroses.* New York, NY: Norton.

Festinger, L. (1957). *A theory of cognitive dissonance.* Stanford, CA: Stanford University Press.

Festinger, L., Riecken, H., & Schachter, S. (1952). *When prophecy fails.* New York, NY: Harper and Row.

Frankl, V. E. (1963). *Man's search for meaning: An introduction to logotherapy.* New York, NY: Washington Square Press.

Freedom, L., & Hunter, E. (1957). *Brainwashing: The story of men who defied it.* New York, NY: Farrar, Straus and Cudahy.

Freud, S. (1911). Psychoanalytic notes upon an autobiographical account of a case of paranoia (dementia praecox). *Collected Papers of Sigmund Freud. Volume III.* London, England: Hogarth.

Freud, S. (1921). Group psychology and the analysis of the ego. *Standard Edition of the Complete Works of Sigmund Freud,* Volume 18. London, England: Hogarth Press.

Freud, S. (1950). *Totem and taboo.* New York, NY: Norton.

Fromm, E. (1941). *Escape from freedom.* New York: Rinehart.

Fromm, E. (1944). Individual and social origins of neurosis. *American Sociological Review, 9,* 380–434.

Fromm, E. (1950). *Psychoanalysis and religion.* New Haven, CT: Yale University Press.

Fromm, E. (1951). *The forgotten language.* New York: Rinehart.

Galanter, M. (1983). Charismatic religious sects and psychiatry: An overview. *Journal of Psychology and Theology, 11,* 143–146.

Galanter, M. (1985). Unification Church dropouts: Psychological readjustment after leaving a charismatic religious group. *American Journal of Psychiatry, 140,* 984–990.

Gardner, G. B. (1954). *Witchcraft today.* London, England: Rider.

Glueck, S., & Glueck, E. (1970). *Toward a typology of juvenile offenders.* New York, NY: Grune and Stratton.

Godwin, J. (1985). *The devil's disciples.* Chino, CA:

Goffman, E. (1961). *Asylums.* New York, NY: Anchor Books.

Goodman, F. D. (1975). The effect of trance on memory content. *Psychiatrica Clinica, 8,* 243–249.

Gore, T. (1987). *Raising PG kids in an X-rated society.* Nashville, TN: Abingdon Press.

Gould, C. (1988). *Symptoms characterizing Satanic cult abuse not usually seen in sexual abuse cases: Preschool age children.* Unpublished manuscript. Brentwood, CA: Author.

Halperin, D. (Ed.) (1986). *Psychodynamic perspectives on religion, sect, and cult.* Boston, MA: John Wright.

Harnischnacker, R., & Muther, J. (1987). The Stockholm syndrome. *Archive fur Kriminologie, 180,* 1–12.

Hassan, S. (1988). *Combatting cult mind control.* Rochester, VT: Park Street Press.

Heider, F. (1958). *The psychology of interpersonal relations.* New York, NY: Wiley.

Hines, T. (1988). *Pseudoscience and the paranormal: A critical examination of the evidence.* Buffalo, NY: Prometheus Books.

Hinsie, L. E., & Campbell, R. J. (1973). *Psychiatric dictionary.* Fourth edition. London, England: Oxford University Press.

Hoffer, E. (1951). *The true believer.* New York, NY: Harper.

Hoffer, E. (1955). *The passionate state of mind.* New York, NY: Harper and Row.

Hollingsworth, J. (1986). *Unspeakable acts.* New York, NY: Congdon & Weed.

Hopkins, E. (1988). Fathers on trial: Trumped-up charges of child abuse are divorce's ugly weapon. *New York,* January 11, 1988, 42–49.

Huxley, A. (1954). *The doors of perception.* London, England: Chatto & Windus.

Huxley, F. (1974). *The way of the sacred.* Garden City, NY: Doubleday.

James, W. (1902). *The varieties of religious experience.* New York, NY: Longmans Green & Co.

Jones, D. P. H., & McGraw, J. M. (1987). Reliable and fictitious accounts of sexual abuse of children. *Journal of Interpersonal Violence, 2,* 27–45.

Jung, C. G. (1958). *The undiscovered self.* New York, NY: Mentor.

Jung, C. G. (1966). *The relations between the ego and the unconscious.* Volume 7 of the Collected Works of Carl G. Jung. New York, NY: Pantheon.

Jung, C. G. (1968). *Part I. The archetypes and the collective unconscious.* Volume 9 of the Collected Works of Carl G. Jung. Princeton, NJ: Princeton University Press.

Jung, C. G. (1969). *The structure and dynamics of the psyche.* Volume 8 of the Collected Works of Carl G. Jung. Princeton, NJ: Princeton University Press.

Kahaner, L. (1988). *Cults that kill.* New York, NY: Warner Books.

Kahn, E. (1985). Heinz Kohut and Carl Rogers. *American Psychologist, 40,* 893–903.

Kaslow, F., & Sussman, M. B. (1982). *Cults and the family.* New York, NY: Haworth Press.

Kelley, D. M. (1946). Preliminary studies of the Rorschach records of the Nazi war criminals. *Rorschach Research Exchange, 10,* 45–48.

Kelley, H. H. (1967). The warm-cold variable in first impressions of persons. *Journal of Personality, 18,* 431–439.

Kimble, G. A. (1961). *Hilgard and Marquis' conditioning and learning.* New York, NY: Appleton-Century-Crofts.

Kluft, R. P. (Ed.) (1985). *Childhood antecedents of multiple personality.* Washington, DC: American Psychiatric Press.

Koestler, A. (1954). *The invisible writing.* New York, NY: Macmillan.

Kohut, H. (1971). *Analysis of the self.* New York, NY: International Universities Press.

Kohut, H. (1977). *The restoration of the self.* New York, NY: International Universities Press.

Kohut, H. (1978). The future of psychoanalysis. In P. Ornstein (Ed.), *The search for the self.* Volume 2. New York, NY: International Universities Press.

Kohut, H. (1984). *How does analysis cure?* Chicago, IL: University of Chicago Press.

Kriegman, D., & Solomon, L. (1985). Cult groups and the narcissistic personality: the offer to heal defects in the self. *International Journal of Group Psychotherapy, 35,* 239–261.

Laing, R. D. (1967). *The politics of experience.* Baltimore, MD: Penguin Books.

Langone, M. D. (1988). *Cults: Questions and answers.* Weston, MA: American Family Foundation.

Larson, B. (1982). *Larson's book of cults.* Wheaton, IL: Tyndale House.

LaVey, A. Z. (1969). *Satanic Bible.* New York, NY: Avon.

LaVey, A. Z. (1971). *The compleat witch.* New York, NY: Dodd Mead.

LaVey, A. Z. (1972). *The Satanic rituals.* New York, NY: Avon.

Lea, H. C. (1888). *History of the inquisition.*

Lefley, H. P. (1981). Psychotherapy and cultural adaptation in the Caribbean. *International Journal of Group Tensions, 11,* 3–16.

Levin, D. (1960). *What happened in Salem?* New York, NY: Harcourt Brace.

Lewin, K. (1951). *Field theory in social science.* New York, NY: Harper.

Lifton, R. J. (1963). *Thought reform and the psychology of totalism.* New York, NY: Norton.

Lifton, R. J. (1987). *The future of immortality and other essays for a nuclear age.* New York, NY: Basic Books.

Little Oxford Dictionary. Sixth edition. New York, NY: Oxford University Press.

Lockwood, G. (1981). Rational-emotive therapy and extremist religious cults. *Rational Living, 16,* 13–17.

Lyons, A. (1988). *Satan wants you: The cult of devil worship in America.* New York, NY: The Mysterious Press.

MacCollam, J. A. (1979). *Carnival of souls: Religious cults and young people.* New York: Seabury Press.

MacFarlane, K., & Waterman, J. (1986). *Sexual abuse of young children.* New York, NY: Guilford Press.

MacHovec, F. J. (1962). *Book of Tao.* White Plains, NY: Peter Pauper Press.

MacHovec, F. J. (1971). *I Ching.* White Plains, NY: Peter Pauper Press.

MacHovec, F. J. (1973). *Exorcism: A manual for casting out evil spirits.* White Plains NY: Peter Pauper Press.

MacHovec, F. J. (1975). Hypnosis before Mesmer. *American Journal of Clinical Hypnosis, 17,* 215–220.

MacHovec, F. J. (1976). The evil eye: Superstition or hypnotic phenomenon? *American Journal of Clinical Hypnosis, 19,* 74–79.

MacHovec, F. J. (1978). OK Zen. *Transactional Analysis Journal, 8,* 272.

MacHovec, F. J. (1980). The cult of Asklipios. *American Journal of Clinical Hypnosis, 22,* 85–90.

MacHovec, F. J. (1981). Hypnosis to facilitate recall in psychogenic amnesia and fugue states: treatment variables. *American Journal of Clinical Hypnosis, 24,* 7–13.

MacHovec, F. J. (1984a). The use of brief hypnosis for post-traumatic stress disorder. *Emotional First Aid, A Journal of Crisis Intervention, 1,* 14–22.

MacHovec, F. J. (1984b). Current therapies and the ancient East. *Journal of Contemporary Psychotherapy, 39,* 87–96.

MacHovec, F. J. (1985). Treatment variables in the use of hypnosis in the brief therapy of post-traumatic stress disorder. *International Journal of Clinical and Experimental Hypnosis, 33,* 6–12.

MacHovec, F. J. (1986a). The Tao of personality, therapy, and life. *Journal of Religion and Psychical Research, 9,* 75–80.

MacHovec, F. J. (1986b). *Hypnosis complications: Prevention and risk management.* Springfield, IL: Thomas.

MacHovec, F. J. (1988). *Humor: Theories, history, applications.* Springfield, IL: Thomas.

MacHovec, F. J. (1989a). *Interview and interrogation: A scientific approach.* Springfield, IL: Thomas.

MacHovec, F. J. (1989b). Minimizing hypnosis risk. *Psychotherapy in Private Practice, 6,* 59–68.

Maleson, F. G. (1981). Dilemmas in the evaluation and management of religious cults. *American Journal of Psychiatry, 138,* 925–929.

Malinowski, B. (1948). *Magic, science, and religion.* Glencoe, NY: Free Press.

Maple, E. (1966). *The complete book of witchcraft and demonology: Witches, devils, and ghosts in western civilization.* New York, NY: A. S. Barnes.

Martinez, R., & Wetli, C. V. (1982). Santeria: A magico-religious system of Afro-Cuban origin. *American Journal of Social Psychiatry, 2,* 32–38.

Maslow, A. H. (1970). *Motivation and personality.* Second edition. New York, NY: Harper and Row.

Maslow, A. H. (1971). *The farther reaches of human nature.* New York: Viking Press.

McKenzie, D. (1987). Teaching students who already know the truth. *Cultic Studies Journal, 4,* 61–72.

Meerloo, J. A. M. (1949). *Delusion and mass delusion.* New York, NY: Nervous and Mental Disease Monographs.

Meerloo, J. A. M. (1956). *The rape of the mind: The psychology of thought control, menticide, and brainwashing.* New York, NY: World Publishing.

Melton, J. G. (1986). *Encyclopedic handbook of cults in America.* New York, NY: Garland.

Melton, J. G., & Moore, R. L. (1982). *The cult experience.* New York, NY: Pilgrim Press.

Muggeridge, M. (1972). *The infernal grove.* New York, NY: William Collins.

Needleman, J. (1972). *The new religions.* Revised edition. Richmond Hill, Ontario: Pocket Books.

Norris, J., & Potter, J. (1985). The devil made me do it. *Penthouse,* December 1985, page 50.

Nugent, C. (1983). *Masks of Satan.* London, England: Sheed and Ward.

Omand, D. (1977). Exorcism: An adjunct to Christian counseling. *Counseling and Values, 21,* 84–88.

Orne, M. T. (1971). The simulation of hypnosis: why, how, and what it means. *International Journal of Clinical and Experimental Hypnosis, 19,* 183–210.

Patrick, T., & Dulack, T. (1979). *Let our children go.* New York, NY: Dutton.

Pattison, E. M., & Wintrob, R. M. (1981). Possession and exorcism in contemporary America. *Journal of Operational Psychiatry, 12,* 13–19.

Peck, M. S. (1983). *People of the lie: The hope for healing human evil.* New York: Simon & Schuster.

Perez y Mena, A. I. (1977). Spiritism as an adaptive mechanism among Puerto Ricans in the United States. *Cornell Journal of Social Relations, 12,* 125–136.

Prince, R. (1979–80). Religious experience and psychosis. *Journal of Altered States of Consciousness, 5,* 167–181.

Rabiner, C. J. (Ed.) (1988). Teenagers at risk: An adult perspective. *The Psychiatric Hospital, 19,* 151–154.

Rawcliffe, D. H. (1959). *Occult and supernatural phenomena.* New York, NY: Dover.

Rhodes, H. T. F. (1954). *The Satanic mass.* London, England: Rider.

Riesman, D. (1950). *The lonely crowd.* New Haven, CT: Yale University Press.

Ritzler, B. A. (1978). The Nuremberg mind revisited: A quantitative approach to to Nazi Rorschach. *Journal of Personality Assessment, 49,* 344–353.

Roberts, A. E. (1988). *Seekers of truth.* Highland Springs, VA: Anchor Communications.

Rocklin, R. & Lavett, D. K. (1987). Those who broke the cycle: Therapy with nonabusive adults who were physically abused as children. *Psychotherapy,* 24, 769–778.

Rogers, R. W., & Newborn, C. R. (1976). Fear appeals and attitude change: Effects of a threat's noxiousness, probability of occurrence and the efficacy of coping responses. *Journal of Personality and Social Psychology, 34,* 54–61.

Rosen, R. D. (1977). *Psychobabble.* New York, NY: Avon.

Ross, J. C., & Langone, M. D. (1988). *Cults: What parents should know.* Weston, MA: American Family Foundation.

Ross, C. A., & Norton, G. R. (1989). Differences between men and women with multiple personality disorder. *Hospital and Psychiatry, 40,* 186–188.

Rubinstein, I. H. (1981). *Law on cults.* Chicago, IL: Ordain Press.

Russell, J. B. (1986). *Mephistopheles: The devil in the modern world.* Ithaca, IL: Cornell University Press.

Sage, W. (1976). The war on cults. *Human Behavior, 5,* 40–49.

Saliba, J. A. (1983). *Religious cults today.* Liguori, MO: Liguori Publications.

Sandoval, M. C. (1977). Santeria: Afro-Cuban concepts of disease and its treatment ment in Miami. *Journal of Operational Psychiatry, 8,* 52–63.

Sandoval, M. C. (1979). Santeria as a mental health care system. *Social Science and Medicine, 13,* 137–151.

Sargant, W. (1957). *Battle for the mind: A physiology of conversion and brainwashing.* Garden City, NY: Doubleday.

Schwartz, L. L. (1978). A note on family rights, cults, and law. *Journal of Jewish Communal Service, 55,* 194–197.

Seligmann, K. (1948). *Magic, supernaturalism, and religion.* New York, NY: Pantheon.

Shapiro, E. (1977). Destructive cultism. *American Journal of Family, 15,* 80–83.

Shostrom, E. L. (1967). *Man, the manipulator.* New York, NY: Abingdon.

Shupe, A. D., Bromley, D. G., & Oliver, D. L. (1983). *The anti-cult movement in America.* New York, NY: Garland.

Silberer, H. (1971). *Hidden symbolism of alchemy and the occult arts.* New York, NY: Dover.

Silverman, S. M. (1975). The victimizer: Recognition and characteristics. *American Journal of Psychotherapy, 29,* 14–25.

Skinner, B. F. (1953). *Science and human behavior.* New York, NY: Macmillan.

Smith, M., & Pazdar, L. (1980). *Michelle remembers.* New York, NY: Pocket Books.

Spector, R. (1986). Case study 3: Strategic Tarot. *Family Therapy Networker, 10,* 36–37 and 68–69.

Springston, C. R. (1988). Ancient spirits, modern world. Three-part series. *Richmond News Leader,* August, 1988.

Stewart, I., & Joines, V. (1987). *TA Today: A new introduction to transactional analysis.* Chapel Hill, NC: Lifespace.

St. Clair, D. (1971). *Drum and candle.* New York, NY: Bell.

Streiker, L. D. (1984). *Mind bending.* Garden City, NY: Doubleday.

Summers, M. (1956). *History of witchcraft.* New York, NY: Citadel.

Summers, M. (Trans) (1971). *The malleus maleficarum of Heinrich Kramer and James Sprenger.* New York: Dover.

Summers, M. (1974). *Witchcraft and black magic.* New York, NY: Causeway Books.

Summit, R. (1983). The child sexual abuse accommodation syndrome. *Journal of Child Abuse and Neglect, 7,* 177–193.

Sutcliffe, J. P. (1960). "Credulous" and "skeptical" views of hypnotic phenomena: A review of certain evidence and methodology. *International Journal of Clinical and Experimental Hypnosis, 8,* 73–101.

Taylor, E. I. (1978). Psychology of religion and Asian studies: the William James legacy. *Journal of Transpersonal Psychology, 10,* 67–79.

Tavris, C. (1974). The force of authority. *Psychology Today,* June 1974, 76–78.

Terry, M. (1987). *The ultimate evil.* Garden City, NY: Doubleday.

Thomas, P. (1979). Targets of the cults. *Human behavior, 8,* 58–59.

Thorne, S. B., & Himelstein, P. (1984). The role of suggestion in the perception of Satanic messages in rock-and-roll recordings. *Journal of Psychology, 116,* 245–248.

Tivnan, L. (1979). The voodoo that New Yorkers do. *New York Times,* December 2, 1979.

Toffler, A. (1980). *The third wave.* New York: William Morrow.

Trevor-Roper, H. R. (1967). *The European witch-craze of the 16th and 17th centuries.* Baltimore, MD: Penguin.

Trostle, L. C. (1986). Nihilistic adolescents, heavy metal music, and paranormal beliefs. *Psychological Reports, 59,* 610.

Truzzi, M. (1972). The occult revival as popular culture. *Sociological Quarterly, 13,* 16–36.

Ungerleider, J., & Wellisch, D. K. (1978). *Coercive persuasion, cultism and deprogramming.* Continuing Medical Education Syllabus and Proceedings. Washington, DC: American Psychiatric Association.

Ungerleider, J., & Wellisch, D. K. (1979). Cultism, thought control and deprogramming: Observations on a phenomenon. *Psychiatric Opinion, 16,* 10–15.

Vanderkolk, B. (1987). *Psychological trauma.* Washington, DC: American Psychiatric Press.

Vermaseren, M. J. (1963). *Mithras, the secret god.* New York, NY: Barnes and Noble.

Wattenberg, B. J. (1974). *The real America.* New York: Doubleday.

Watts, A. (1963). *Two hands of God.* New York, NY: Collier.

Webster's ninth new collegiate dictionary (1983). Springfield, MA: Merriam-Webster.

Wetli, C. V., & Martinez, R. (1981). Forensic sciences aspects of Santeria, a religious cult of African origin. *Journal of Forensic Science, 26,* 506–514.

Wetli, C. V., & Martinez, R. (1983). Brujeria: Manifestations of Palo Mayombe in south Florida. *Journal of Florida Medical Association, 70,* 629–634.

Wolfe, B. (1974). *The devil's avenger.* New York, NY: Pyramid.

World almanac and book of facts 1988. New York, NY: Pharos Books.

Yalom, J. D., & Lieberman, M. A. (1971). A study of encounter group casualties. *Archives of General Psychiatry, 25,* 16–30.

Zillmer, E. A., Archer, R. P., & Castino, R. (1989). Rorschach records of Nazi war criminals: A reanalysis using current scoring and interpretation practices. *Journal of Personality Assessment, 53,* 85–99.

Zimbardo, P. G., & Hartley, C. F. (1985). Cults go to high school: A theoretical and empirical analysis of the initial stage in the recruitment process. *Cultic Studies Journal, 2,* 91–147.

INDEX

183